Readings in
LEARNING
DISABILITIES

Robert Piazza
Department of Special Education
Southern Connecticut State College,
New Haven, Connecticut.

Revised Edition

Special Learning Corporation

42 Boston Post Rd. Guilford, Connecticut 06437

Special Learning Corporation

Publisher's Message:

The Special Education Series is the first comprehensive series designed for special education courses of study. It is also the first series to offer such a wide variety of high quality books. In addition, the series will be expanded and up-dated each year. No other publications in the area of special education can equal this. We stress high quality content, a superb advisory and consulting group, and special features that help in understanding the course of study. In addition we believe we must also publish in very small enrollment areas in order to establish the credibility and strength of our series. We realize the enrollments in courses of study such as Autism, Visually Handicapped Education, or Diagnosis and Placement are not large. Nevertheless, we believe there is a need for course books in these areas and books that are kept up-to-date on an annual basis! Special Learning Corporation's goal is to publish the highest quality materials for the college and university courses of study. With your comments and support we will continue to do so.

John P. Quirk

2 3 4 5

ISBN 0-89568-119-6

SPECIAL EDUCATION SERIES

* ●Abnormal Psychology: The Problems of
    Disordered Emotional and Behavioral
    Development
  ●Administration of Special Education
  ●Autism
* ●Behavior Modification
  Biological Bases of Learning Disabilities
  Brain Impairments
  ●Career and Vocational Education for the
    Handicapped
  ●Child Abuse
* ●Child Psychology
  ●Classroom Teacher and the Special Child
* ●Counseling Parents of Exceptional Children
  Creative Arts
  ●Curriculum Development for the Gifted
  Curriculum and Materials
* ●Deaf Education
  Developmental Disabilities
* ●Developmental Psychology: The Problems of
    Disordered Mental Development
* ●Diagnosis and Placement
  ●Down's Syndrome
  ●Dyslexia
* ●Early Childhood Education
  ●Educable Mentally Handicapped
* ●Emotional and Behavioral Disorders
  Exceptional Parents
  ●Foundations of Gifted Education
* ●Gifted Education
* ●Human Growth and Development of the
    Exceptional Individual

  ●Hyperactivity
* ●Individualized Education Programs
  ●Instructional Media and Special Education
  ●Language and Writing Disorders
  ●Law and the Exceptional Child: Due Process
* ●Learning Disabilities
  ●Learning Theory
* ●Mainstreaming
* ●Mental Retardation
  ●Motor Disorders
  Multiple Handicapped Education
  Occupational Therapy
  ●Perception and Memory Disorders
* ●Physically Handicapped Education
* ●Pre-School Education for the Handicapped
* ●Psychology of Exceptional Children
  ●Reading Disorders
  Reading Skill Development
  Research and Development
* ●Severely and Profoundly Handicapped
    Social Learning
* ●Special Education
  ●Special Olympics
* ●Speech and Hearing
  Testing and Diagnosis
  ●Three Models of Learning Disabilities
  ●Trainable Mentally Handicapped
  ●Visually Handicapped Education
  ●Vocational Training for the Mentally Retarded

● Published Titles   *Major Course Areas

TOPIC MATRIX

COURSE OUTLINE:

Teaching the Learning Disabled Child

I. Overview
   A. Historical Influences
   B. Nature of Learning Disabilities
   C. Issues and Concerns

II. Diagnosis of Learning Problems
   A. Reading Disorders
   B. Language and Writing Disorders
   C. Perceptual Disorders
   D. Mathematical Disorders

III. Remediation of Learning Problems

IV. Educational Services

V. Professional's Roles

Readings in Learning Disabilities Revised Edition

I. Learning Disabilities-The Nature of the Problem, Issues and Concerns

II. Diagnosis of Learning Problems

III. Remediation of Learning Problems

IV. Educational Services

V. Future Trends

Readings in Learning Disabilities provides the college student in preparation for teaching exceptional children an insight into the field of learning disabilities. It is designed to correlate with an introductory course in learning disabilities.

Related Special Learning Corporation Readers

I. Readings in Dyslexia
II. Learning Disability Series
III. Readings in Hyperactivity
IV. Learning Disabilities: A Reference Book
V. The Classroom Teacher and the Special Child
VI. Readings in Special Education

CONTENTS

3. Remediation of Learning Problems

4. Educational Services

5. Future Trends

GLOSSARY OF TERMS

agnosia A loss of or an impairment of the ability to recognize objects or events when presented through various modalities.

alexia The loss of ability to read because of some brain damage.

anomia Difficulty in recalling or remembering words or names of objects.

apraxia Knowing what one wants to say, but being unable to evoke language on a voluntary basis.

auditory agnosia Inability to recognize sounds or combinations of sounds without regard to their meaning.

auditory discrimination The ability to differentiate speech sounds; their pitch and frequency characteristics.

auditory perception The ability to organize and interpret what is heard through the ear.

behavior modification A technique of altering undesirable behavior to a more appropriate state.

brain damage A structural injury to the brain which may occur before, during, or after birth and which impedes the normal learning process.

central nervous system (CNS) In humans, the brain and spinal cord to which sensory impulses are transmitted.

cognition Intellectual activities.

conceptualization The ability to formulate concepts by inferring from what is observed.

congenital Present in an individual at birth.

decoding The ability to understand what is expressed verbally or visually.

diagnostic testing A series of teaching or testing sessions in which teacher or therapist determines through observations, a child's specific learning strengths or weaknesses.

directionality Awareness of the verticle axis and the relative position of one side of the body versus the other.

discrimination The ability to perceive differences among stimuli presented visually or auditorily.

dissociation Inability to synthesize separate elements into integrated meaningful wholes.

distractibility Forced responsiveness to extraneous stimuli.

dysarthria Difficulty in the articulation of words due to involvement of the central nervous system.

dyscalculia Disturbances in arithmetic that result from disorders of quantitative thinking.

dysgraphia Extremely poor handwriting or the ability to perform the motor movements required for handwriting.

dyslexia Impairment in the ability to read, usually associated with some brain dysfunction.

encode The expression of meaning in symbols or code.

etiology The source or origin of a condition.

figure-ground perception The ability to attend to one aspect of the visual field while perceiving it in relation to the rest of the field.

formal diagnosis Evaluation by a team of professionals who determine a child's strengths, weaknesses and overall adjustment.

hyperactivity Excessive or constant movement.

hyperkinetic Disorganized, disruptive and unpredictable behavior; an over reaction to stimuli.

hypoactivity Extreme lack of movement or listlessness.

individualized education program (IEP) A formal written instructional program which tailors children's schooling to fit their individual needs. It is developed by school personnel and a child's parents in order to assess, place, set goals, and decide what special services a child will receive.

inversion Reading errors in which the directionality of letters is confused. Some examples are (u) for (n), (t) for (f), or (w) for (m).

laterality Ability of a person to differentiate between the two sides of his body; identify right from left.

learning disabilities A disorder in one or more of basic psychological processes involved in understanding or in using language, spoken or written, which many manifest itself in an imperfect ability to listen, think, speak, read, write, spell, to do mathematical calculations, or reason.

least restrictive envoronment (LRE) The "most normal education program" that a child can receive, including instructional services outside the classroom.

mainstreaming The placement of handicapped students into educational programs with normal functioning children.

memory The ability to store and retrieve upon demand previously experienced sensations and perception.

minimal brain dysfunction A mild neurological impairment that cause learning difficulties in the child with near-average intelligence.

modality A way of acquiring sensation-visual, auditory, kinesthetic, olfactory, and tactile are the most common.

multisensory Learning experiences in which several sensory modalities are used to reinforce one another.

neurological Dealing with the central nervous system.

neurological dysfunction When the something is "not working right" in the brain; this can cause a disturbance in the learning process.

perception The process of organizing or interpreting stimuli received through the senses.

perception of position The perception of the position of two or more objects in relation to the observer.

perception of spatial relationships The perception of the position of two or more objects in relation to each other.

perceptual disorders A disturbance in the awareness of objects, relations, or qualities, involving the interpretation of sensory stimuli.

perseveration Inability of a child to restructure his or her thinking quickly, either a verbal or a motor dysfunction.

phonetics The study of the production of vocal sounds.

psychological evaluation Diagnostic instruments that measure a child's native intelligence for learning, perceptual tests, and tests of emotional maturity.

psychomotor The motor effects of psychological processes and events.

reversal Reading errors in which the directionality of the word letter is perceived in "reversed" or "backwards" order. For example, "was" is read for "saw", "b" is read for "d".

sensory motor The combined functioning of sense modalities and motor mechanics.

sequentialization The ability to order and structure events in a predesignated sequence.

soft neurological signs The behavioral symptoms that suggest possible minimal brain injury in the absence of hard neurological signs.

stimulus An external event which causes physiological change in the sense organ.

syndrome A cluster or pattern of symptoms which characterizes a specific disorder.

syntax The way in which words are ordered, relative to one another, to form phrases, clauses, or sentences.

tactile agnosia Inability to recognize objects by sight.

tactile perception The ability to interpret and give meaning to sensory stimuli that are experienced through the sense of touch.

vestibular Pertaining to the sensory mechanism for the perception of the organism's relation to gravity.

visual motor The ability to coordinate visual stimuli with the movements of the body or its parts.

visual perception The ability to identify, organize, and interpret what is received by the eye.

photo: Office of Human Development Services,
Department of Health, Education and Welfare

PREFACE

Children with learning disabilities constitute a fairly recent addition to the field of special education. Because research, diagnostic techniques, and new programs have developed so rapidly over the past decade, this emerging exceptionality has been receiving increased services in our public schools. Many youngsters who historically would have failed and become frustrated in regular classes are presently being placed in resource rooms and self-contained classes at both the elementary and secondary levels. Efforts are now being made to provide inservice assistance to regular classroom teachers so that the disabled learners in their classes can remain in the least restrictive educational environment.

Readings in Learning Disabilities will provide the learning disabilities specialist, the regular educator, and the teacher in training with an overview to the area. The first section of this book will look at various problems, issues and concerns the learning disabilities field still faces. The next two sections focus on diagnostic and remedial processes that may be helpful when implementing educational programs. The last two sections will familiarize the reader with current educational services and future concerns of the field. Issue oriented articles, research reports, and practical suggestions that can be used when providing direct services to the learning disabled youngster will hopefully give the reader a balanced view of the field.

photo: David Carofano

LEARNING DISABILITIES THE NATURE OF THE PROBLEM, ISSUES AND CONCERNS

Recent studies indicate that approximately 10 million youngsters demonstrate some type of learning disability. This evidence also shows that undiagnosed learning disabilities may be the basic problem with large numbers of children who do not do well in school - the under-achievers, the disciplinary problems, the dropouts.

Defining the learning disability population has not been an easy task. One reason for this is that each child exhibits a different combination and severity of problems. Leaders in the field with diametrically opposed viewpoints as to the diagnosis and remediation of learning problems have also led to difficulties with the stating of a totally accepted definition.

The most widely accepted definition is one formulated in 1968 by the National Advisory Committee on Handicapped Children. This definition is stated as follows:

"Children with specific learning disabilities" means those children who have a disorder in one or more of the basic psychological processes involved in understanding or in using language, spoken or written, which disorder may manifest itself in imperfect ability to listen, think, speak, read, write, spell, or do mathematic calculations. Such disorders include conditions as perceptual handicaps, brain injury, minimal brain dysfunction, dyslexia, and developmental aphasia. The term does not include children who have learning problems which are primarily the result of visual, hearing, or motor handicaps, of mental retardation, of emotional disturbance, or of environmental disadvantage.

Learning disability regulations that appear in the Federal Register in the later part of 1977 have helped delineate this population even more, however. These guidelines have indicated for a child to be counted as learning disabled he/she must demonstrate a significant discrepancy between intellectual potential and *academic* achievement. The discrete academic areas to be considered are oral expression/language, listening comprehension, written expression, basic reading skills, reading comprehension, math reasoning, and math calculation skills.

This section presents information that will enable the reader to grasp a clearer understanding of specific characteristics demonstrated by learning disabled youngsters. Intellectual qualities, perceptual disturbances, academic deficiencies, and attitudinal concerns will be addressed.

Why Johnny Can't Learn —A Surprising Answer

Lawrence Galton

In the United States today, there are 6 to 10 million children more or less like Joan and John—or, more accurately, like Joan and John as they were until recently.

At 9, Joan had serious learning difficulties. She had seemed unusually clumsy much of her life. She fell frequently. She could print but not write cursively. She had difficulty with reading, frequently lost her place, left out words. Her attention span was short. Special tutoring didn't help.

John, at 15, was failing in school despite an IQ of 138. His reading was three years below grade level. He was disruptive in class, could not sit still. He was unable to cope with everyday home responsibilities, pick up after himself, clean his room. He neglected homework, left his books in school, got assignments wrong. When his parents made him do homework, it took him three times as long as other children.

In just six months, the lives and outlook of both youngsters changed dramatically. They are now moving up to grade level, no longer find schoolwork difficult, enjoy it. John's disruptiveness is gone; so are Joan's short attention span and clumsiness.

In both cases, the changes were achieved through a whole new approach to the problems of learning-disabled children. It's based on the belief that many, even most, of those problems are not the result of laziness, intellectual inadequacy, willfulness, or personality or emotional disorders but rather of physical imbalances—imbalances that are not always obvious but can be found and corrected, often with remarkable speed.

The approach has been developing for many years as investigators have sought better answers to a huge problem. A leader in its development and application is the New York Institute for Child Development, where Joan and John were helped.

Created in 1968, the Institute is a national, nonprofit facility that has treated more than 3000 learning-disabled or hyperactive youngsters and currently works with more than 300 a year from all over the U.S. and Canada. It reports an 87 percent success rate in helping children, often achieving two- to four-year growth rates in reading comprehension in six months. Along with scholastic achievement often go striking changes in personality and behavior, all as a result of correction of physical imbalances.

When a parent brings a child to the Institute, there is a preliminary interview that may last three hours, covering the child's life, medical and school history, and particular problems. The parent takes home a seven-day diet record on which everything the child eats over the next week is to be noted, and also a list of tests—blood and urine, thyroid, glucose tolerance and others —to be performed by a laboratory.

Two days of evaluation and consultation follow. The child is put through tests for vision, hearing, coordination, and more. Consultation involves a physician, nutritionist, physical therapist, developmental optometrist, educational specialist. At the end, both parent and child receive a thorough explanation of what has been found—at which point there is often a long sigh of relief from the child.

Says Dr. Alan C. Levin, pediatrician and medical director of the Institute: "When findings are explained, most kids feel as if the weight of the world has been taken off them. They realize they are not lazy, not stupid, but have physical problems they can do something about.

The common underlying problems that the Institute finds are often overlooked because they may not even be considered.

Vision problems: These are common— but rarely problems of acuity. Most youngsters have 20/20 vision. Troubles often lie with difficulties in using both eyes together for extended periods. Some children have difficulty copying from the blackboard and get assignments wrong because it takes them longer to change focus from near to far. Some work so hard to focus while reading that they become fatigued and words blur; they may even see double. They spend so much energy trying to maintain focus and a single image, they can't concentrate on what they are reading. To some children, "se espo trun" is what "see spot run" looks like; they have spatial relationship and letter inversion problems.

Auditory problems: These, sometimes due simply to allergies, may account for difficulties in mastering sounds needed for phonetic skills, for poorly modulated voice, and for articulation problems.

Gross and fine motor ability problems: Symptoms of gross motor difficulties can include poor body balance and generalized awkwardness, with an impact on visual performance skills. Impaired fine motor ability, which involves efficient coordination of small muscle groups in manual skill activities, may account for poor pencil grasp, awkwardness in tying and buttoning.

Darral Chapman, chief of therapy at the Institute for Child Development, guides patient in an eye-coordination exercise that helps overcome learning disability.

Eye-hand coordination problems: Writing and other fine motor tasks can be accomplished quickly and easily only when eyes work well with hands. Coordination difficulties can account for poor handwriting, neat but slow writing, poor performance in ball sports involving ability to catch and hit.

Ocular-motor function problems: Inability to control eye movements adequately can be manifested by turning the head instead of moving eyes, omission of words, skipping of lines, repetition in reading, using fingers to guide reading.

Diet problems: These are very common. Time after time, the seven-day diet records show very high intakes of sugars, starches and junk foods. In one Institute study of 265 children proven to be hyperkinetic, 74 percent showed abnormalities in glucose-tolerance testing. Their high sugar and refined carbohydrate intake stimulated insulin production, which led to low blood sugar—

Therapist watches child catch ball while bouncing on trampoline. This exercise is designed to improve balance and eye-hand coordination.

and the low sugar activated the adrenal glands to pour out hormones that in excess may cause the type of behavior seen in hyperkinetic children.

Treatment is multi-faceted. A basic part is a nutritional plan. Generally, it cuts down on sweets and refined carbohydrates, and removes artificial colors and flavors as much as possible. Six high-protein feedings a day may be prescribed.

A home exercise program is designed to correct perception, motor and coordination problems. It requires 20 to 30 minutes daily. One exercise for jerky reading has the child lie on the floor and follow with his eyes the movement of a ball suspended from the ceiling. As the child does this, eye motion smoothes out.

Another exercise, useful for some vision and balance problems, uses a simple, homemade balance beam: a 2 by 4-inch board supported on a few bricks so it is about 6 inches off the floor. The child walks back and forth, balancing and at the same time pointing a finger at his toes, lining up vision

with fingers and toes. If there are major balance difficulties—which can affect vision as well—exercises may include somersaults and hanging upside down by the knees to stimulate the balance mechanism.

Many other exercises are used for specific purposes. Progress is monitored during visits to the Institute—weekly, biweekly or monthly, depending how far the child must come—and, as progress is made, the program is altered to help further progression. Some improvement in ball sports is often noted within a month. This commonly comes first. Within two to three months, most youngsters begin to find school and homework becoming easier. Usually, it takes six months before reading and other school work begin to approach grade level.

The objective is to enable a child to come to learning in a new way, with physiological functions intact. Once a child can see well, hear well, speak and write well, and sit still, he becomes capable of learning.

That striking changes in behavior and personality can occur is understandable. Says Dawn Burness of the Institute staff: "I think we adults may not realize what these kids go through in school: stress and failure every day. No adult would put up with it. He would either get fired for incompetence or choose to leave the job and find something more appropriate. Children have no alternative to school. They try to make alternatives. Some daydream, look out the window, retreat into a world of their own. Others skip classes or make nuisances of themselves in school and at home. Actually, they are eager for a better alternative—and when they get it, especially because they can help themselves, they seize it and they change."

Says Darral Chapman, chief of therapy: "A great many behavior problems are frustration reactions. A lot of the time these kids are biochemically mad before they are overtly mad. Because of the stress they are under and the pouring out of adrenalin, they are angry inside and look for an excuse to take out the anger—so a lot of unexplained temper tantrums and outbursts are explained by what perceptual and vision and other problems do biochemically."

What's needed to help learning-disabled or hyperkinetic youngsters is a total, multi-faceted approach. Hopefully, there will be more facilities such as the Institute that can provide it all under one roof.

Short of that, what can you do for a child who is doing poorly in school and who may be a behavior problem as well?

First, don't assume the child is stupid, lazy or willful, or it's all because of some deep-seated emotional upset. Start with the assumption that there is probably a physiological reason or set of reasons. You may have good grounds for the latter assumption if you answer yes to three or more questions in the accompanying list.

Once you suspect your child has a physiological problem, trust your instincts, follow through, don't be easily put off by well-meant assurances from others—possibly even from a physician who has not looked thoroughly into the matter—that the child "will outgrow it."

Insist on a thorough physical examination. If your physician will not oblige, find one who will do a complete workup—blood, urine, other testing—and who will then correct any abnormalities, however slight. Such a physician may be a pediatrician actively interested in learning disabilities. It may be necessary to seek one with the help of the nearest medical school's pediatrics department.

You may need an eye doctor—possibly a developmental optometrist—who will test thoroughly not just for acuity but for focus, movement, coordination and other problems, and work out a program for their correction. A state or city optometric association may be able to provide names of developmental optometrists nearby.

If the child is generally clumsy, a physical therapist may be needed, and the pediatrician may be able to recommend an experienced one.

Easy? No, decidedly not. Perhaps pressure by informed parents may eventually lead to the establishment of state or regional diagnostic and treatment centers for the learning-disabled. Meanwhile, the individual parent may have to hunt for those who can help and even act to coordinate their efforts —a tough task but rewarding for what it can mean to a child's development and whole life.

No Easy Answers
The Learning Disabled Child

SALLY L. SMITH

Associate Professor, American University,
in charge of the Learning Disabilities Program

Founder and Director,
The Lab School of The Kingsbury Center,
Washington, D.C.

Why?

It is not because the parents haven't tried.

It is not because the parents don't care.

It is not because the child is stubborn.

It is not because the child is dull.

It is not because the child is lazy.

It is not because the child is spoiled.

Why does a child have learning disabilities?

They do not occur for these reasons. There is no known simple explanation.

. . . there is no one cause

. . . there seem to be many that are held responsible for learning disabilities

BEFORE BIRTH

maternal malnutrition

bleeding in pregnancy

poor placental attachment to the uterus

toxemia in pregnancy

infectious disease of pregnant mother—German measles, a virus disease, influenza or a chronic disease

alcoholism during pregnancy

the taking of certain drugs during pregnancy

RH incompatibility

8

"Why?" Sally L. Smith, *No Easy Answers--The Learning Disabled Child*, Department of Health, Education and Welfare Publication, 1978.

DURING BIRTH

long or difficult delivery producing anoxia (not enough oxygen in the brain)

prematurity

cord around neck or breech delivery

poor position in the uterus

dry birth where the water broke prematurely

intracranial pressure at the time of birth due to forceps delivery or a narrow pelvic arch in the mother

rapid delivery exposing the infant too quickly to a new air pressure

AFTER BIRTH

length of time to produce breathing after birth (often with prematurity, difficult delivery or twins)

high fever at an early age

sharp blow to head from fall or accident

meningitis or encephalitis

lead poisoning

drug intoxication

oxygen deprivation due to suffocation, respiratory distress, breath holding

severe nutritional deficiencies

HEREDITY

There are many families in which reading disabilities can be traced through several generations. Usually the father, an uncle or other relatives had the problem.

It is not worth agonizing over which of these factors produced the problems of a particular child. It might be something else not even mentioned here, not known yet! Placing blame, pointing an accusing finger, feeling overwhelmed with guilt, giving way to fear that some thoughtless action produced a child's learning problems have never been found to help parents help children with the problem. Sometimes it temporarily helps teachers (who feel totally frustrated by the learning disabled child) to blame parents but that doesn't help the children either. Teachers, like parents, usually wish to do the best they can for each child and often seek an easy cause that can be remedied fast. The causes of learning disability are beyond teacher control as they are beyond parental control.

All races, religions, economic classes . . . . fat, thin, tall, small . . . . youthful parents, older parents . . . . have produced children with learning disorders.

In proportionately very few cases have doctors found evidence of actual brain damage. In fact there are many brain-damaged children who do not have learning disabilities. There are scientists who are working in the area of medical computer science to detect signs of brain damage or dysfunction which previously could not be monitored; these clinicians hope that, by locating exact areas and types of dysfunction in the brain, more precise treatments will be possible. The Quantitative Electro-physiological Battery (QB), currently being used at the Brain Research Laboratory of New York Medical College, holds out many interesting possibilities, but it does not yet provide any total answers. Some neurologists point out that stroke victims, adults who have suffered damage to their brains, those with cerebral palsy, show many impairments of language and thought similar to those of children with learning disorders. There is a theory that learning disability is simply "an extremely mild and narrowly selective form of cerebral palsy." In a special school educating only intelligent children with learning disabilities, there were 56 children. Four of them had known brain damage. But there were 36 who acted just like them; the other 20 simply seemed immature and needed more time to grow up.

We don't know much except that there is a lag in the development of learning disabled children, that their central nervous systems are delayed in maturing. Neurological examinations most often fail to reveal any medical evidence that would support a diagnosis of brain injury. The absence of "hard signs" of brain injury led the medical world to believe that the constellation of "soft neurological signs" had to be noted. This is what led up to such medical terms as "minimal cerebral dysfunction," "minimal brain injury," "minimal brain dysfunction," (MBD).

The soft signs are such conditions as:

persistence of some primitive reflexes of central nervous system which should no longer be present after certain ages

distractibility (lack of concentration)

hyperactivity

impulsivity

perseveration
inconsistency

left-right confusion

irritability

talkativeness

awkwardness

poor speech

social immaturity

Scientists, neurologists, neurophysiologists are right now seeking answers to the causes of neurological immaturity, what's responsible for this maturational lag that we currently call "learning disabilities."

There are those specialists who say that the cause doesn't matter; we must focus on educating the child. True, we must reach the child early and give him readiness. We must find ways to teach him to do the things he cannot do. There are those specialists who say that the cause *does* matter for then we will be able to treat the child faster and more efficiently. It is possible within the next 5 to 10 years that advances in neurochemistry and neurophysiology will pinpoint the dysfunctioning parts of the brain. When more precise localization of brain anatomy is correlated with various thinking processes, masses of research will have to be done to determine which part of the brain responds best to what type of education. At this point, there are no sudden cures, no easy answers.

The learning disabled child needs more time to grow, more time to do his work, more time to learn. He must work hard. His parents and teachers must work hard with him and provide him with the supports he needs in order to learn properly and to behave appropriately. Those are the only reliable cures at this point.

The field of learning disabilities, which did not become a recognized field that received Government grants until the late nineteen sixties and early seventies, faces many unanswered questions about causes.

Why is there so much learning disability today when there was not 10, 20, 30, 50 years ago? Part of the explanation may lie in the fact that these children were dumped into already established categories of "mentally retarded" or "emotionally disturbed." Many learning disabled children are still being written off as "culturally deprived." Disadvantaged conditions and poor schooling are cited as the causes of learning disabilities in inner-city children. Sometimes they are. However, insufficient account has been taken of the effect of high fevers, malnutrition, lead poisoning, maternal malnutrition, lack of proper prenatal care, and similar factors which may contribute to learning disabilities, causing poor performance at school.

In fact, there may not be more cases today, but more recognition of the problem. There are some specialists who claim that, until the advent of miracle drugs and the widespread use of antibiotics, many learning disabled youngsters died of respiratory ailments before they ever reached school age.

It is also possible that the one-room schoolhouse of yesteryear allowed for slow maturing. There were heterogeneous groupings which allowed a child to proceed at his own pace. In the early years of this century, as the frontier disappeared and Americans moved toward the cities, mass education took on a vast, new importance. Public school systems burgeoned, paralleled by the growth of public libraries, and standardization of education at all levels became the new order. No longer could parents direct their children's education as they saw fit. The rise of modern industry required standardized human components in its management, and our upwardly mobile society came to see education as a measurable step to individual success and to a prosperous, enlightened Nation. Only in a culture obsessed with education would the failures at school be considered as disabled people.

Our national panic when Russia launched "Sputnik" in 1957 was merely the latest phenomenon in the trend to standardization, now seen on a worldwide scale. The American public, worried that the Russians were smarter, more educated, more efficient than we, exerted pressure on the educators to hurry up. Out went a lot of the "play" in nursery schools and kindergartens; letters and numbers replaced motor activities in many preschools. It is possible that the child who needed more time, more sensory-motor activities, was deprived of them, and his development lagged further. As our population becomes more concentrated in cities and suburbs, our schoolrooms have become more crowded. We are surrounded by BIGNESS—the bigness of Government, of cities, of buildings, of business, of supermarkets, of jumbo eggs and giant-size aspirin. The standardization of quantity rather than quality often determines our values: how much we own, how many high grades we have, how many correct answers.

A child cannot always conform within the given time period and, too often, is then classed as a failure. Perhaps because of the uncertainty of our times, the rapid changes in lifestyles, the vanquishing of accepted traditions, we have become more dependent on "the right answer" than before and less tolerant of individual differences. The child with a learning disability, under this pressure, may become so burdened with defeat and failure that he doesn't even learn at his own pace and thus widens the gap.

There are those who subscribe to the theory that our polluted air and rivers—noise—our unclean environment—have contributed to the increase in delayed development in our children. Some believe that insecticides and pesticides pollute our children's brains.

Are there more children with immature brains today? We don't know. If so, there is no easy answer as to why.

Why are boys affected so much more frequently than girls? The ratio is seven to one nationally, and some believe that it is ten to one. There are theories that the male organism is more vulnerable at birth, more prone to injury since the infant mortality rate is much higher among boys than girls. Some theorists claim that the male fetus is somewhat larger than the female and thus is more susceptible to injury at birth. One researcher claims that male heads are larger and so have more trouble exiting at the time of birth. We don't really know.

Why is the learning disabled child much harder to manage and teach in hot, humid weather, before storms, on very hazy days and, some say, when there is a full moon? Educators have noted that weather and seasons affect their performance, but nobody yet knows why.

Is there a connection between hypoglycemia (low blood sugar) and learning disabilities? So far, no substantive connection has been proven.

Doctors have noticed a significant relationship among allergic reactions and hyperactivity and learning disabilities. Some of them have treated the children with antihistamines, corticosteroids, and megavitamins, and some of the children experienced relief from allergies which decreased hyperactivity and improved learning; some did not. This did not provide any general answer.

A few years ago, there were doctors who felt that these children had a vitamin B deficiency or some other kind of vitamin deficiency, and many of the children were pumped full of vitamins with no significant success. There are always a few children who improve dramatically, but, for any cure to be more than a panacea, it has to cure many. So far, it hasn't.

There are a few specialists, convinced that the learning disabled children are lacking in protein, who recommend a high protein diet (much red meat, eggs, soybeans, etc.) Although some youngsters have demonstrated more energy to learn as a result of this, no known instant school successes have resulted from this treatment. Some doctors state that high protein diets are dangerous and can cause metabolic imbalance.

A current theory is that food additives cause hyperactivity and therefore many cases of learning disability. The child is put on a special diet, monitored constantly, and, in a number of cases, has improved. Still, there is no definite proof of this connection and no clear evidence that food additives cause learning disabilities.

There are some educators who believe that learning disabilities do not exist, that there are simply unmotivated children. Others believe there are merely undisciplined students. Their remedies follow their interpretation of the causes. Every once in a while a child improves under their care, but these "hard-liners" do not have the answer for children with learning disabilities in general.

Today, big money can be made by taking advantage of the prevalence and seriousness of learning disabilities. Along with excellent schools and treatment centers, a number of "instant remediation" parlors have opened. From pinching ears, to systematic yelling, to acupuncture, to transcendental meditation, to tactile treatments, to patterning of one sort or another, to helium experiences, parents are being promised substantive help by fly-by-night groups. All kinds of causes are enumerated, and these entrepreneurs usually make parents feel responsible for the problem as well as for the success of the treatment.

In our culture, where speed is a supreme value and where we prize the frozen dinners, the freeze-dried coffee, the soup can, we grab for the instant answer. Unfortunately there is no one way. There is no easy answer.

TWISTED WORDS:
The Torment of Dyslexia
by Eileen Simpson

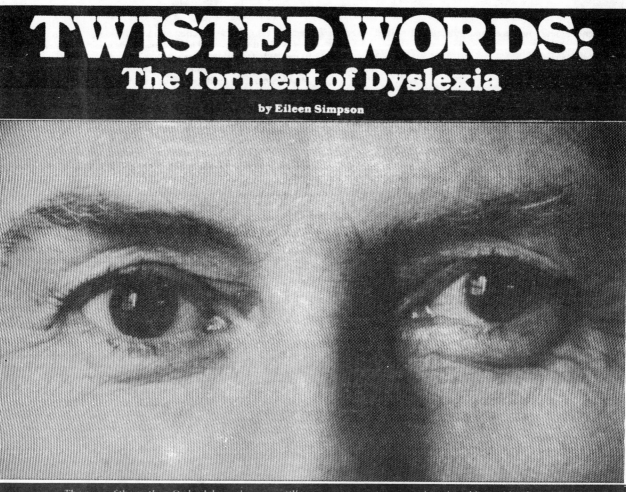

The eyes of the author: On bad days, they can still turn a sentence into an indecipherable jumble of words.

There are an estimated 23 million people in the United States of normal or high intelligence who, because of a flaw in their brains' ability to process language, have great difficulty reading. The name of their disorder is dyslexia. To dyslexics, written words appear reversed or hopelessly scrambled. In fact, in testing dyslexic children it is often found that the child reads no worse—sometimes even a little better—if the book is held upside down.

Dyslexia occurs in every country and seems to have little to do with cultural, emotional or family circumstances. Even the great and the celebrated are not immune. Gustave Flaubert, W. B. Yeats, Hans Christian Andersen, Thomas Edison, Woodrow Wilson, General George Patton and Nelson Rockefeller were all so afflicted as children that their parents feared they would never learn to read. (Rockefeller says that even today when he reads a speech aloud he has to have long words in his text broken into syllables and sentences broken into segments. Then he rehearses it up to six times.)

I am dyslexic. I learned to read years after my classmates, and I was an adult before I could write with any fluency. Throughout my childhood I believed something was wrong with my brain. Today, though I am by no means completely "cured," I lead a normal life. Were it not for the fear that haunts all dyslexics of revealing intellectual failures and limitations, I would almost have forgotten what it was like to be unable to read and write. But in order to write the book on which this article is based, I had to fight the old shame of ridicule and the new fear of being patronized: I suffered a relapse. My symptoms returned full blown, sharply reminding me of what life had been like in the limbo of illiteracy.

The fall term was already under way when my sister and I were reg-

The author is a psychotherapist and writer. Adapted from Reversals: A Personal Account of Victory over Dyslexia. *Copyright © 1979 by Eileen Simpson, to be published in February by Houghton Mifflin.*

istered at P.S. 52, an elementary school in Inwood at the upper tip of Manhattan Island. We were separated in the principal's office, and a messenger led me through a dank tunnel, up a flight of stairs, through a maze of corridors and down a hall. She knocked on the door of a fourth-grade classroom.

A geography lesson was in progress. An elderly spinsterish-looking woman, who had been holding a pointer to a map, took the note the messenger handed her. It was a brief account of my previous education: kindergarten through second grade at a boarding school run by nuns in Dobbs Ferry, N.Y.; third grade at a nonsectarian school in Farmingdale, N.J. While the teacher read it, I stood with my hands linked behind my back; 80 eyes focused on me. Slim and tall for my age, I felt very much the new girl and wished I could take cover.

After assigning the class busywork, the teacher handed me a paper covered with arithmetic problems and told me to go to work. Bewildered by my new surroundings, by the circuitous route I had traveled to 4A-2, by the size of the class and, above all, by the curtness of the instructions, I tried to make out what I was supposed to do. Was it a test? Addition, subtraction and multiplication problems were jumbled together. Subtractions were easy to recognize; they were always just two stories high. Divisions were under those little shelters. What about the others? The sign in front of this one meant (didn't it?) to multiply. Yet if it was multiplication, why were there so many numbers? It must be a problem meant for a higher grade.

The teacher said time was up. She frowned at my paper, slashing it with giant X marks made with a red pencil. Didn't I know my multiplication tables?

I wondered at her question. Of course I knew them. What must have happened was that I'd mixed up the signs and had added where I should have multiplied. The $\times$ and $+$ signs had a way of spinning around— $\times + \times + \times + \times + \times +$ —faster and faster, like the spokes of a bicycle wheel, so that I couldn't tell one from another. Would I now be permitted to melt into the class?

1. NATURE

The teacher handed me a book and, indicating the place, asked me to read.

"Aloud," she barked.

Aloud? Bewilderment gave way to alarm. I hadn't been asked to read aloud since second grade.

"Speak up! I haven't got all day."

The text became a gray blur, a screen on which I projected wavy lines. By the chalky odor her clothes gave off, I could tell the teacher was leaning closer to me. I kept my eyes riveted to the page.

"What's this word?" She hit the first word with her pencil.

I flinched as if she'd hit me.

"You don't know? What's this one? This one?"

I was not looking at the words. All my attention was concentrated on my throat and teeth. Swallowing hard and clamping my jaws together as tightly as I could, I had but one thought: I must not let a roomful of strangers see me cry.

School had never been like this before. At the Catholic school in Dobbs Ferry, we'd read the same stories over and over. Memory took me a long way. Called on to begin a story, I was at a loss until I learned to associate the look of the page with the title. The first page of the Wedding Feast of Cana had a molelike imperfection in the paper, say. Or the corner of the Jonah story was dog-eared. Or the beginning of the Loaves and Fishes hung loose from the binding.

If I was called on in the middle of a story, I "read" (really, recited from memory) as well as or better than my classmates. I hesitated just the right amount of time between words. From time to time, mimicking the other children, I appealed to the teacher for help on a word that was "too hard." In order to know when to turn the page, I watched my neighbors covertly.

The author at nine (left) with sister Marie

At Farmingdale the class had read in unison. I chanted along as loudly and as happily as the others. Before long I had the illusion that I read as well as my classmates.

But at P.S. 52 there was no way to fool either myself or the teacher, whose name was Miss Henderson. "Speak up! *Speak up!*" she'd shout, giving up all pretense of controlling her temper as weeks of failure repeated themselves. "If you continue to defy me, you'll get a failure in conduct as well as in reading."

The threat of a double failure, together with the habit of wishing to please, forced me to "speak up," although I knew it would get me into deeper trouble. The words that I knew, I said. Others I guessed at. More often than not I guessed wrong. Whereupon Miss Henderson would shout, "Wrong! Wrong!" Then with a "Class?" she'd invite my classmates to correct me. They did so with gusto. Their roar often frightened me so that I didn't catch what they said. Which meant that if the word was repeated in the next sentence, I would be stuck again. What could I do then but be silent?

Mutism, temper, humiliation, tears. Mutism, temper, humiliation, tears. So went the inescapable and inexorable round of my days.

My nights were troubled by dreams in which Miss Henderson and the mocking chorus figured prominently. I awakened feeling dull and achy, as if I were coming down with the flu. I ate breakfast without appetite, dragged myself to school, and waited through the other lessons in a state of apprehension for the oral reading period.

I said nothing at home about my daily agony in 4A-2. My sister, Marie, and I had recently come to live with our Aunt Agnes, who asked us to call her Auntie to mark her role as guardian and distinguish her from our other aunts (for although we had neither parent, our mother having died when I was two months old and our father when I was five, we had a large family of close relations).

When our report cards came, Auntie congratulated Marie on her string of A's, signed her card and dismissed her. Then she took up my card. The report was blunt: failure in reading. She blew a hissing noise against its edge. This meant that she was dangerously vexed but uncertain what course of action to take. "Tssssss." It was the sound of steam about to blow the lid off a pot. "Tsssssss." She waved the card at me. "What is the meaning of this?"

What could I say? When she pressed me, I offered the excuse that Miss Henderson's reader was "too hard."

Auntie took out her glasses and pinched them onto her nose. "Bring it to me. Read."

So I read. That is to say I repeated my daily performance. I clutched at recognizable words, guessed at others and invented what I thought would make suitable connectives.

A clap of thunder brought my improvisation to an end. "What is this gibberish? I can't believe my ears." She pointed: "What's this word? And this one? *How is it possible? You seem to know nothing. Do you even know the alphabet?*"

Auntie sounded scared. The terror in her voice frightened me.

"Stop crying. Now listen to me. And listen carefully. From now on you're to bring me your book every evening after dinner, do you hear? *I* will see to it that you learn to read."

My evenings with Auntie were no better than my days with Miss Henderson. Under her harsh scrutiny, I got worse instead of better. *Saw* looked like *was* to me, *of* looked like *off*. And reading was not my only problem. One day Auntie sent me on an errand to a new grocery store four blocks from home. I was so long in returning, she demanded an explanation: Where had I been?

I had been lost.

Lost? How could I have been when the store was on Academy Street, the street we lived on? I did not realize until later that in a row of identical buildings, I had looked for number 431 instead of our number, 341. My incoherent explanation troubled rather than angered Auntie. Was a nine-year-old girl who had no sense of direction "all there"?

Auntie decided to take me to see the family doctor. She gave him a brief version of what had been happening in the past few months. Was there something the matter with the b-r-a-i-n? She spelled the word, thinking I was as poor at guessing as I was at spelling.

Dr. Hess made light of her concern. Why worry about a little trouble in school? I'd outgrow it, probably. A slow developer. That was all.

On the long subway ride home Auntie whistled her dry whistle. Tsssssssssss. At P.S. 10, the school where she herself was a teacher, "slow developer" was a euphemism for retardation. There were special classes, "ungraded" classes, for such children. She was angry with Dr. Hess for suggesting that I was one of them (even though the thought had crossed her mind more than once) and was irritated with him for speaking as he had in front of me. It was all very well for him to talk about patience, she said aloud, but if I didn't learn to read now, it would ruin my *whole life.*

The process was already well under way. I had always been considered a model of good conduct, as bright and lively as any nine-year-old. Now I behaved as though I were dull witted. The expression on my face, even my posture, had changed. I was always tired. My legs buckled under me. I fell constantly, ripping my stockings and scraping my knees. I walked into objects as though they weren't there. The cord I pulled to turn on a light came off in my hand. When I prepared vegetables, I cut my finger. When I dried dishes, they broke. I lost my lunch box, my mittens, my hat and my coat. More than once I hid my hated reader in the broom closet. For a while, in a gesture of rebellion, I stopped bathing. I even began to pilfer small change from Auntie.

I knew there was something wrong with my brain. The "something" felt, when I was calm enough to analyze it, like a mechanical failure: a switchboard with lines that had become scrambled. In moments of panic—during oral reading lessons—the mechanism broke down completely: messages were neither sent nor delivered. Now the "something" had become so general that I was convinced I was defective both intellectually and morally. I was stupid. I was a liar. I was a petty thief. I was an awkward, accident-prone, slovenly, stooped, stuttering, dirty crybaby. And my whole life was going to be ruined.

Reading is the most complex skill a child entering school is asked to develop. What makes it complex, in part, is that letters are less constant than objects. A car seen from a distance, close up, from above or below, or in a mirror still looks like a car even though the optical image changes. The letters of the alphabet are more whimsical. Take the letter *b*. Turned upside down it becomes a *p*. Looked at in a mirror, it becomes a *d*. Capitalized, it becomes something quite different, a *B*. The *M* upside down is a *W*. The *E* flipped over becomes ∃. This reversed *E* is familiar to mothers of normal children who have just begun to go to school. The earliest examples of artwork they bring home often have I LOV∃ YOU written on them.

Dyslexics read, spell and write letters upside down and turned around far more frequently and for a much longer time. In what seems like a capricious manner, they also add letters, syllables and words or, just as capriciously, delete them.

The inability to recognize that g, *g* and G are the same letter, the inability to maintain the orientation of the letters, to retain the order in which they appear and to follow a line of text without jumping above or below it—all the results of the neurological flaw—can transform a page of words into a dish of alphabet soup.

Also essential for reading is the ability to store words in memory and to retrieve them. Dyslexics lack this kind of memory. So, too, do they lack the ability to hear what the eye sees, and to see what they hear. If the eye sees *off*, the ear must hear *off*, not *of* or *for*. If the ear hears *saw*, the eye must see that it looks like *saw* on the page and not *was*. For the dyslexic lacking these skills, a sentence or paragraph becomes a kind of coded message to which he can't find the key.

Dyslexia is probably inherited, although some experts are reluctant to say this because they fear people will equate "inherited" with "untreatable." Treatable it certainly is: not a disease to be cured, but a malfunction that requires retraining.

The first full-scale study of dyslexic children and their educational needs was made in the mid-1920s by Samuel T. Orton, an American neurologist and psychiatrist. In the course of studying mental health problems in Iowa, Orton discovered that among the children reported by their teachers as dull and failing in school, there was a fairly high proportion whose errors in reading and spelling did not seem to be related to low intelligence. In his first article, published in 1925, he used the word *strephosymbolia*—twisted symbols—to describe the phenomenon. These children twisted what they heard, what they wrote and what they said. Orton recognized that dyslexia, as it was later named, is not a single symptom; rather, it is a syndrome (a cluster of symptoms), which may include physical awkwardness, poor penmanship, hyperactivity, stuttering, directional disorientation, a weakness in visual memory, as well as the more familiar difficulties with spelling, writing, arithmetic and, of course, reading. He suggested that dyslexia is caused by a lack of synchronization between the left and right hemispheres of the brain.

Today, with the invention of new equipment to analyze brain waves and observe cortical activity, and with the research now being conducted on patients who have undergone split-brain operations, it is possible that the mystery of what causes dyslexia will soon be solved.

But the situation is paradoxical. In some schools children are tested in kindergarten to screen those who are likely to develop reading disabilities. A vigorous remedial program may follow. Just as frequently, what follows is an indifferent program or no program at all. In schools where the principal denies the existence of the syndrome and the teachers have come from schools where they have not been taught to recognize the symptoms, dyslexics have as little chance of being recognized as they had in the 19th century.

The gravest maladjustments occur among those in large classes in low-income neighborhoods who drift to high school with no real academic testing. These adolescents find their way not to reading clinics but to correctional institutions. A study of one such institution found that 31 percent of its teenage nonreaders were not retarded or functionally illiterate. They were dyslexic. While in upper-class families untreated dyslexics often become ne'er-do-wells and black sheep, among the disadvantaged they frequently become criminals. The most

chilling example of a man with above-average intelligence and a reading disability that went untreated is Lee Harvey Oswald.

One way or another, intelligent dyslexics do learn to read—inefficiently, painfully, slowly. What proper teaching spares those who receive it is the inefficiency, a good deal of the pain and the terrible waste of years.

Despite my aunt's prediction, my life was not ruined. I even learned to read, after a fashion. But it was a long and painful process. In the beginning I cried with frustration because I couldn't understand billboards and movie marquees, couldn't write notes to my friends, couldn't even read a valentine sent to me by a boy I was fond of. I felt horribly left out when my sister and the other girls at school gossiped about their favorite books.

If I had had remedial training, I would have learned to read more systematically. As it was, I learned over years of trial and error to recognize certain combinations of letters and string them together into words and sentences. But since I hated books, I had a hard time paying attention to what I read.

The breakthrough came on an overnight train ride shortly after my 12th birthday, when I picked up a book called *The Outdoor Girls at Deepdale*. The dust jacket showed two girls, about 17 years old, dressed in white blouses and long skirts. I looked to see how many pages there were. A third as many as in *Little Women*, which I had given up on in despair. I could tell that this was not the kind of *real* book my teacher would have approved of. But the print was large; that meant it would go fast. It opened with a sprightly dialogue. The girls were excited about having lost something. What could it be?

I read until I knew—not the whole book, but enough to be able to tell my sister the plot. It took considerable restraint to control my euphoria, to keep from crying out, "Wheeeeeeee!"

After I stopped hating reading, my academic performance went from terrible to mediocre. I managed to struggle through high school with erratic grades, my reading slowly, slowly improving. Later on at Hunter College, I even became a book lover, although my written work remained so poor that I was assigned to a special course we called Idiot English. But it was not until I was 22 that the nature of my disorder was diagnosed—and then not by a psychologist, but by a poet.

I met him at a party in Greenwich Village. He walked into the crowded room—a black-and-yellow muffler, as long as he was tall, wrapped around his throat, eyeglasses, high cheekbones, the slim build of a runner—obviously ill at ease among strangers. In the few minutes we had together I tried to make conversation. The muffler?

From Clare College, Cambridge. He had been there on a fellowship. Now he was an instructor at Harvard. There was nothing literary about our brief exchange (how to distinguish the two Cambridges was our subject), but I knew that John Berryman wrote verse and was poetry editor of *The Nation*.

Six months later, when he was back in New York for the summer, he asked me to go dancing. At the hotel where Tommy Dorsey was playing, John crooned his French translation of *Night and Day* into my ear and led me through set after set with demon dips and dervish whirls.

My life rapidly became complicated. How could I let a man as passionate about the written word as was John fall in love with me without telling him about my early difficulties, my patchy education, my continuing struggle? When I first tried to tell him these things, he wouldn't listen. He, too, was badly educated, he said. He hadn't studied Greek; his knowledge of German was rudimentary.

I shook my head to show he didn't understand.

He might have remained in ignorance for some time longer had I not gone to Long Island for a week to visit my sister and her family. Yes, yes, yes, I would write, I promised as I boarded the train.

The train hadn't picked up speed before I regretted my promise. I hated writing letters. I never could think of anything to put down on paper. And even if I could, would I want to risk addressing it to one who taught English A at Harvard? Might he not correct it in red pencil and return it the way Auntie had done with my thank-you notes? Each day, seeing John more and more as an English instructor and less and less as the man I was falling in love with, I found reasons for procrastinating. I delayed and delayed. I agonized throughout the week. At the eleventh hour, I scribbled a note and put it in the mail.

In Penn Station, where John met me on my return, he led me over to a bench in the waiting room, looking as grave as a doctor who has read the X rays and must confront the patient with the bad news. "You thought you'd scare me off with this, did you?" He took the note from his pocket. "I must admit that at first it took my breath away. Then I saw it for what it was, not a love letter but a test of affection. Tell me about it."

He held the letter for me to see. It looked something like this:

Deare
Time for olny a hurried note. M. and children well. Swimming every day despite gary skies. Tomorrow we calabrent M's birthday. See you Thursday.
In haste.
Love
E.

Eileen Simpson today: more good days than bad

Ashamed and repelled, for one wild moment I thought of denying that I had written it. I snatched the note from John's hand and tore it up. I knew how to spell "celebrate." And as for "deare"! I told John again what I had tried to tell him before. It was an abridged version of my academic history, but all the facts were there—the failure to learn to read in elementary school, the difficulty with keeping letters and digits in their proper order, the inability to read aloud. This time he listened.

"It's as I suspected," he said. "Yours is not the functional illiteracy of the night school students I had when I taught at Wayne University. Your errors are not ordinary spelling errors. Hasn't anyone told you you have dyslexia?"

Braced for ridicule, it was a moment before I felt the welling up of pure joy. My affliction had a *name!* To get hold of the word, I repeated it: "Lysdexia."

John laughed. "There it is. A perfect example. You've scrambled the letters."

John and I were married a year later. If I say that John was my teacher, the most important I would ever have, I am likely to be misunderstood. The pedagogic role he played with me was a subtle one. Had he been aggressively didactic, I would have rebelled against his tutelage. Instead, he allowed me to learn in the way I was most capable of learning, osmotically. The only direct recommendation he ever made was about what I should read.

"You hate Hardy, do you? I suppose they ruined him for you in high school. Try *Jude.* You'll see."

I saw.

"*Crime and Punishment* should be read in one sitting."

In an all-night, eye-aching session I read it.

"You don't know Trollope? I envy you beginning him. Here. Read *The Eustace Diamonds.* I warn you, you'll become addicted."

(Never: "What? You *don't know* so and so?")

"Read this." "Read this." "Read this," he said, reaching down volume after volume from the shelves of our book-lined apartment.

Having found the perfect library and an unshockable librarian, I read and read, gulping down one novel after another.

By the end of the year not only John, but I, too, had forgotten that I was dyslexic. With the enormous gain in self-confidence that came from finding I could use my brain in a way that one had to use it in John's company, the painful memories that had been revived by my "deare-olny-calabrent" note also faded. I now was ready to pass in academia.

And so I did. I took an advanced degree in psychology at NYU. The next year I became an intern at the Rutgers Psychological Clinic under the formidable Dr. Anna Starr. Ironically, my first assignment was to test the boys and girls who came to the clinic because they could not learn to read. It was up to me to discover whether their failure

was the result of limited intelligence, emotional problems or dyslexia.

One might have thought that a history such as mine would have been ideal preparation for helping those similarly afflicted. It is true that I was quick to diagnose dyslexics and enjoyed testing them. But I had to leave their training to others, for merely to enter the room where they were struggling over their workbooks or chanting their exercises made me feel low spirited, even oppressed. (Other dyslexics, who don't feel as I did, often make gifted remedial teachers.)

When Dr. Starr pressed me to stay on at the end of my appointment in order to supervise the reading center, I confessed my feelings to her and offered my case history. She was incredulous. What nonsense! I could never have been like the children at the center. To pretend that I had been was "self-dramatization." Perhaps I had been a little slower in reading than in other subjects . . . but dyslexic? Impossible!

I have my own psychotherapy practice now, and I also spend much of my time writing. I have published scholarly articles, short stories and a novel. Sometimes I even think of myself as "cured." Since there is no cure for dyslexia, what I mean is not that I am or ever will be symptom free, but that my symptoms are manageable—on good days.

On good days I spell reasonably well. Words I'm uncertain about I can find in the dictionary without difficulty. But I have not advanced so far that I would ever think of playing a word game for pleasure.

In my speech there is no trace of the early confusion I once sought to cover up by clowning. What I say is precisely what I mean to say.

My sense of direction is adequate for everyday use if I depend on feel rather than left/right, east/west. In a strange city, especially a complex European one, I get lost probably twice as often as other tourists.

My memory, which has always been excellent in some areas, serves me well even where it is weakest: in the recall of proper names.

Employing digits, whether in conversation, dialing telephone numbers or doing accounts, I make errors caused by transpositions less than a quarter of the time.

On bad days, which are brought on by fatigue, strong preoccupations or illness, I have little confidence in my ability to spell. The dictionary proves useless because I can't think of the opening letter or syllable that will help me find the word I want.

In conversation I say one thing when I mean to say another—"The car they sold him was a melon," "You can't pull the wool over my ears" —and am usually unaware of having done so.

On bad days my directional guide is so completely out of order that I walk blocks out of my way. I am capable of overshooting the entrance to my apartment building, or even the door of my office.

My memory for proper names is so treacherous I have an acute awareness of what it must be like, at least in this regard, to be senile.

Numbers become scrambled so that I misdial, misaddress and miscalculate three quarters of the time. In conversation, I might say that Columbus discovered America in 1942, and wonder why people are amused.

On bad days I stay away from the library. Even on good days I can't read and eat at the same time (as during a solitary meal I've wished I could do), nor can I attend to two competing sounds—a voice and a radio, or two people talking to me simultaneously.

Yet the proportion of good to bad days has increased steadily and is now so high that I am less and less troubled by these vexing remnants of my disorder. As for reading, it remains one of my greatest pleasures, a pleasure blunted only by a feeling that I must hurry to make up for lost time. Even today I occasionally look up from a page, suffused with joy and wonderment. I think of an old movie in which James Cagney says euphorically, "Look at me, I'm dancin'! I'm dancin'!" and want to shout, "Look at me, I'm reading! I'm reading!"

FOCUS...

Behavioral Characteristics of Children with Learning Disabilities

Disorders of Motor Activity

Hyperactivity

The child who is frequently restless, engaged in random activity, and erratic in behavior; the child who cannot sit still.

Perserveration

The child who is unable to shift from one topic to the next; in oral reading. This child may repeat a phrase several times before he can continue.

Hypoactivity

The child who is very quiet, lethargic, and causes no disturbance in class; very difficult to get this child to work in class.

Incoordination

The child who is physically awkward, this child may frequently fall, stumble or appear to have clumsy behavior in general.

Disorders of Emotionality

Social Maladjustment

The child who is unable to make successful contact with the world around him; the child cannot get along with other students.

Lack of self control

The child who is constantly disturbing the class; the child who may be very disruptive on the playground; picks on other students.

Temper Outbursts

The child who when the "breaking point" is reached, he/she may yell, scream or cry, and sometimes it is for no apparent reason.

Quick shifts in emotional state

The child who gets frustrated easily; most tasks he/she starts, ends in a disaster.

17

Disorders
of
Perception

Poor Visual Memory

The child who reverses letters in reading; the child who inadequately reproduces geometric forms and experiences figure-ground confusions.

Poor Auditory Decoding

The child who is unable to differentiate between sounds (phonetics) or inability to recognize tunes.

Poor Kinesthetic Decoding

The child who may have problems in directionality and in space orientation. The child may have difficulty determining right from left.

Disorders
of
Symbolism

Expressive Vocal

The child who when asked to tell of a certain experience he/she is unable to express his/her thoughts verbally; lack of ideas for expression.

Expressive Motor

The child who has difficulty with the forulation of thought for writing. Spelling errors are a common sign of this difficulty.

Receptive Auditory

The child who has difficulty understanding spoken symbols. The child frequently asks to repeat and can be confused with directions or commands.

Receptive Visual

The child who subvocalizes when reading to his or herself. As a result, this strongly effects their comprehension and distorts their response.

Disorders
of
Attention

Short Attention
Span
(Distractibility)

The child who is attracted to every available stimulus regardless of its pertinence to the task at hand. The child can be distracted by people walking by the room, the buzzing of the room's neon lights, or just by the quiet person next to him.

Excessive
Attention

The child who displays abnormal fixations of attention on unimportant details, while disregarding the essentials. The child may give all of his/her attention to the page number instead of looking at the printed material on the page.

Disorders
of
Memory

Poor Visual
Memory

The child who is unable to revisualize letters, words, or forms. This also may result in poor spelling habits.

Poor Auditory
Memory

The child who is unable to reproduce rhythm patterns or sequences of digits, words, or phrases.

Poor Short-
term Memory

The child who is unable to remember what was told to him/her within a short period of time.

Poor Long-
term Memory

The child who is unable to remember what was told (or learned by him/her after a long period of time.)

Focus prepared by David Carofano
Consultant: Dr. John Sullivan

Nutrition and learning

CHRISTINE M. OLSON

Dr. Christine M. Olson is a Professor in the Division of Nutritional Sciences at Cornell University.

Most of us are aware of the devastating impact that severe malnutrition can have on a child's mental performance. But a child does not have to suffer severe malnutrition in order for his or her behavior to be affected by nutritional status. Less severe types of malnutrition, by far more prevalent in this country than the severe types, may also affect mental performance.

Iron deficiency anemia is certainly the most prevalent nutritional deficiency problem in the United States today. Scientific evidence indicates that severe anemia has behavioral manifestations which may interfere with learning. Dr. Doris A. Howell studied the learning ability of 89 mildly to moderately anemic preschool children and compared their results with those of 89 nonanemic preschool children. Stanford-Binet, Goodenough, and Gestalt tests demonstrated that the intelligence quotients (IQ's) of children in the two groups were similar. However, tests of attentiveness and ability to focus on, orient to, and sustain interest in a learning task revealed significant differences between children with iron deficiency anemia and those who were not anemic (1).

The results of Dr. Howell's studies are in agreement with those of Dr. Jefferson L. Sulzer and his associates. In a study of first and second grade children, Sulzer found that attentiveness was significantly lower in anemic children. A check of the school records indicated that the anemic children were described as inattentive, easily distracted, lacking persistence, and having less sense of competence. If the anemic children were also short for their age, the differences were even greater. This suggests that chronic undernutrition, indicated by shortness in stature, interacts with current anemia to affect even further their school performance (2).

In the only study of adolescent children, Drs. Thomas E. Webb and Frank A. Oski found that iron deficiency manifested itself as restlessness, irritability, and disruptive behavior. The scientists state that these behaviors had reached such levels of severity as to impair ability to learn in a regular classroom setting (3).

In spite of numerous investigations, scientists are unable satisfactorily to explain the biochemical and physiological basis for the behavioral changes seen in anemic children. Whatever the explanation, the potential psychological impact of the reported behavioral changes is of considerable concern. A child who withdraws from or is inattentive to the environment is one who fails to learn. By missing one step in the learning process, (s)he is less equipped to learn the next, and falls further behind as learning proceeds. Thus this interruption of the learning pattern may permanently impair intellectual development, even though the neurological structures are intact.

Dr. Stanley Gershoff of Harvard University and Dr. Michael Latham of Cornell University have suggested that repetitive periods of prolonged hunger are more common

---

"Tests of attentiveness and ability to focus on, orient to, and sustain interest in a learning task revealed significant differences between children with iron deficiency anemia and those who were not anemic."

---

than nutrient deficiency diseases as major nutrition problems in the United States today. Hunger is a common occurrence just before payday when some families have no money to buy food. Hunger is also found among school children who miss breakfast and possibly lunch because they have no money or because they do not have the time to eat.

The hungry child is disadvantaged in the school setting in many ways. Hunger is a decidedly uncomfortable feeling. Thus the hungry child wants to get rid of this feeling and spends precious learning time worrying about when (s)he will eat next. His or her attention is diverted from the learning situation and performance falls. A group of experiments, popularly called the Iowa Breakfast Studies, has shown that merely skipping breakfast, to say nothing of more extreme hunger, has an effect on school performance. Skipping breakfast had a detrimental effect on the work output and work rate of 12- to 14-year-old boys. In addition, the boys' scholastic attitudes and attainments, as rated by teachers, improved when they ate breakfast (4).

In a society where "The Hungry" are often "The Poor," and where mass media constantly bombard us with images of what life should be like, a hungry child cannot help but think that (s)he is relatively deprived. Youngsters struggle for an answer to the question "Why?" Some answer with society's answer: "I am unworthy." As a consequence, the child's self-image plummets. Unfortunately, the child who is distracted from learning because of hunger is apt to get feedback from teachers and peers which reinforces this already low self-image. The result is a decrease in the child's aspirations and motivations.

The public recognition of a child as poor or unworthy and the stigma attached to this label may affect teachers' expectancies. It has been shown by Rosenthal and Jacobsen that teachers' expectancies have a definite impact on the child's performance. When the child is defined as one to be stigmatized, it seems probable that teachers' responses to him or her will not be such as to encourage performance. Experiencing the presence of this negatively self-fulfilling prophecy, the child does not achieve (5).

The solutions to both of these nutrition problems are within the reach of this society. What's more, the means for solving them are available. By consuming iron-rich foods, most people can avoid anemia. Those without the means to afford these

> "By missing one step in the learning process,
> (s)he is less equipped to learn the next, and falls
> further behind as learning proceeds."

foods can obtain them through the Special Supplemental Food Program for Women, Infants and Children (WIC), Head Start, or the Food Stamp Program. Iron supplements, both dietary and medicinal, are available to those with special needs. Schools have available the option of participating in the School Lunch and Breakfast Programs. What remains is the need for a strong commitment by both individuals and institutions to make use of available aids, to encourage awareness of their existence, and to solve these nutritional problems.

NOTES

1. Howell, D.A. "Consequences of Mild Deficiency in Children. In *Workshop on Extent and Meaning of Iron Deficiency in the U.S.,* Food and Nutrition Board (NAS-NRC): Washington, D.C., 1971.
2. Sulzer, J. L., Hansche, W. J., and Koenig, F. "Nutrition and Behavior in Head Start Children: Results from the Tulane Study." In *Nutrition, Development and Social Behavior.* DHEW Pub. No. (NIH) 73-242: Washington, D.C., 1973.
3. Webb, T. E. and Oski, F. A. "Behavioral Status of Young Adolescents with Iron Deficiency Anemia." *Journal of Special Education* 8(1974):153.
4. *A Complete Summary of the Iowa Breakfast Studies.* Cereal Institute: Chicago, Ill., 1976.
5. Kallen, D. "Malnutrition, Learning and Behavior." *Ecology of Food and Nutrition* 2(1973):133.

Classroom Behavioral Styles of Learning Disabled Boys

David D. Richey, PhD, and James D. McKinney, PhD

Observational studies have uniformly failed to find the cluster of symptoms associated with LD. Instead, one or another seems to typify most of the LD children in any context — in this case classroom distractibility. As the authors note, other behavior often associated with LD was found among some of the children — though not enough to distinguish them from normal learners. Such documentation of the heterogeneity of the LD group logically questions the relevance of comparing LD and normal children, and suggests the need for subtypes of LD to be identified, at least for research purposes. — G.M.S.

The classroom behavior of 15 learning disabled boys was compared to that of 15 matched normal boys in order to determine differences in behavioral style and to examine the learning disabled children's behavior in different classroom environments. Results indicated that of 12 discrete kinds of classroom behavior only one, distractibility, differentiated the two groups. There was very limited support for the stereotyped cluster of negative behavior often associated with learning disabilities. The study also supports the position that characteristics of the classroom environment may exert much influence in fostering or minimizing specific behavior related to academic achievement and competence.

In recent years evidence has accumulated which indicates that specific kinds of task-oriented, social, and affective behavior are highly predictive of academic performance (Cobb 1972, Samuels & Turnure 1974). For example, McKinney, Mason, Perkerson, and Clifford (1975) found that the frequencies of 12 categories of classroom behavior compared favorably to IQ in predicting second-grade achievement. Moreover, the general portrait of the competent child provided by these studies was one of an attentive, independent learner who interacted with his peers in a task-oriented fashion. On the other hand, children who were distractible, dependent, and passive in peer-group activities were less likely to succeed academically.

To the extent that these negative styles of responding are characteristic of learning disabled children, one might expect individual differences in classroom behavior to contribute to their academic difficulties and potential for progress. Although past literature has cataloged the various deficits displayed by learning disabled children (Bryan 1974a, Bryan & Wheeler 1972), few studies have compared the classroom behavior patterns of learning disabled and normal children as measured by observational techniques.

Our present knowledge about classroom behavior patterns of learning disabled children has been obtained primarily from screening instruments that rely on teacher ratings at the time of referral to special educational services (Bryan 1974b; Foreman & McKinney 1975; Keogh, Tchir, and Windeguth-Behn 1974; McCarthy & Paraskevopoulos 1969). In general, comparative studies with these instruments support a widely accepted stereotype of learning disabilities that includes descriptions of inappropriate classroom behavior as well as cognitive and psycholinguistic deficits. Some frequently cited characteristics of learning disabled children include hyperactivity, emotional lability, distractibility, impulsivity, social immaturity, and aggressiveness (Bryan 1974a).

Studies that have compared the overt classroom behavior of learning disabled and normal children have yielded equivocal results. Bryan and Wheeler (1972) examined the ratings of observers who were unaware of the child's

Reprinted by special permission of Professional Press, Inc. from the *Journal of Learning Disabilities*, 1978, Vol. 11, No. 5, pp 38-43. ©1978 Professional Press, Inc.

classification on four categories of Bales' (1971) Interaction Process Analysis scale. Results of this study indicate that learning disabled children were less task-oriented but did not differ in other categories of behavior. A follow-up study by Bryan (1974b) using the same instrument determined that learning disabled children spend significantly less time attending and more time waiting than their normal classmates. There also was evidence that, while the learning disabled children did not differ in the quantity of their social interaction with peers and teachers, their patterns of interaction were different. The teacher was less responsive to learning disabled children. Barr and McDowell (1972) found that emotionally disturbed children displayed higher frequencies of negative physical contact and vocalization compared to learning disabled children, but did not differ in out-of-seat behavior. Finally, Forness and Esveldt (1975) reported significant differences in on-task behavior and teacher responses to behavior displayed by students with learning problems and normal children in regular classrooms.

The primary goals of this study are to compare the classroom behavior of third- and fourth-grade learning disabled boys to those of their normal classmates as displayed in the same regular classroom activities and to examine the relationship between aspects of classroom environment and behavior patterns of learning disabled children.

SETTINGS

Two elementary schools in the Durham County, North Carolina, public school system were used, from each of which were selected three third-grade and two fourth-grade rooms. The third-grade classrooms at both schools were operated on an open classroom, learning center model, while fourth-grade classrooms were more traditional. Since both schools were participating in a demonstration program (McKinney & Kreuger 1973), previously classified subjects were available. The two schools used a service model within the demonstration project in which children identified as learning disabled spent approximately 30 to 40 minutes a day for three to four months with a learning disabilities specialist. LD children retained an ongoing involvement with their regular classrooms and typically returned to them full-time after intervention was

completed. There was little or no remediation by the regular teachers in their classroom.

SUBJECTS

Two groups of third- and fourth-grade male students, 15 per group, were subjects. The learning disabled group represented all of the available third- and fourth-grade males so identified at the schools. The normal children were selected from the same classroom and were matched on IQ,* age, race, and socioeconomic status, derived from Hollingshead's *Two Factor Index of Social Position*. The average IQ was 104.4 (SD = 12.6). Two of the children were black, 28 white; 23% were upper class, 40% middle class, and 36% lower class.

OBSERVATIONAL TECHNIQUE

The Schedule for Classroom Activity Norms (SCAN) is a time-sampling system for coding a variety of classroom behavior related to academic achievement and adjustment (McKinney, Gallagher, & McKinney 1974, McKinney et al. 1975). This procedure codes classroom behavior every 10 seconds into one of 27 discrete categories. The frequencies of discrete behavior are then combined in a mutually exclusive fashion to form 12 general categories of task-oriented, social, and affective behavior. The final 12-category system was based on a factor-analytic study of 90 second graders (McKinney et al. 1975), which describes the development of this instrument and the data reduction procedure.

In addition to child behavior, SCAN codes four aspects of the classroom environment. Coding the freedom-of-task choice distinguishes among: (1) teacher present working with child or group on specified task, (2) teacher not present, but a specified task has been assigned, and (3) free-choice activities. Coding the type of activity distinguishes between: (1) curricular with specific teacher expectations for performance, and (2) extracurricular with no specific teacher expected performance. Coding the size of the group distinguishes among: (1) an individual, (2) a small group with two to six children, and (3) a large group with more than six children. Teacher-specified content is coded according to language, math, social studies, etc.

---

*IQ data were taken from school records and in no instance were more than 18 months old. IQ tests providing data include the *Lorge-Thorndike Intelligence Test*, *Cognitive Abilities Test*, and the *Slosson Intelligence Test*.

PROCEDURE

Two observers collected data over a period of three weeks. All observations were in the morning and during the same period for each of the three days of observation on a particular subject pair. The observers placed themselves in the classroom where they were least obtrusive. One observer coded the behavior of the learning disabled child at the end of each 10-second interval for five minutes, while the second observer coded that of the matched peer. The two observers switched subjects during the second five-minute period, thereby counter-balancing observer effects over each 10-minute session. Data were collected on each pair of children on each of three days and were summed to provide a total frequency of occurrence for each category. Thus, for each subject, a total of 180 moments of behavior were recorded.

The first step at the beginning of each three-day period of observation was the completion of an interobserver reliability check. Subjects were selected at random in each classroom and observed by both observers for five minutes. The average reliability based on six five-minute periods during the study was 91%, ranging from 90% to 93%. Before initiating the study, each observer achieved, with an experienced observer, an average reliability of 95%, with a range of 90% to 100%.

RESULTS

In the preliminary analyses it was discovered that six of the 12 SCAN categories were observed too infrequently to permit meaningful comparisons and accounted for only 17% of the behavior, so they were eliminated from further examination.

Group Comparisons

Means and standard deviations, in proportions, for the six remaining SCAN categories are presented in Table I. In order to determine the significance of differences among the schools, grade levels, and groups with respect to the six SCAN behavior categories, a 2×2×2 multivariate analysis of variance was performed. The two schools were included as a factor in the analysis, but results are not discussed as they have no interpretive significance. The overall test of the grade-level effect by Wilks lambda criterion (Cooley & Lohnes 1962) indicated that the six SCAN categories reliably discriminated third and fourth graders: F (6/17) = 2.71, $p < .05$.

TABLE I. Means and standard deviations for six selected behavior categories for group, grade level, and school.

| Variable | Learning Disabled | | | | Normal | | | |
| | School 1 | | School 2 | | School 1 | | School 2 | |
	Gr.3	Gr.4	Gr.3	Gr.4	Gr.3	Gr.4	Gr.3	Gr.4
SDA								
X	.34	.18	.32	.13	.38	.14	.44	.17
SD	.16	.12	.14	.09	.17	.04	.29	.16
ATT								
X	.15	.11	.16	.28	.22	.25	.13	.26
SD	.11	.05	.18	.19	.19	.15	.14	.19
DST								
X	.15	.14	.16	.13	.08	.05	.08	.13
SD	.08	.07	.10	.08	.04	.04	.09	.06
PR								
X	.04	.08	.06	.21	.08	.07	.06	.14
SD	.04	.05	.04	.05	.04	.07	.06	.09
GM								
X	.11	.13	.15	.05	.09	.13	.13	.08
SD	.06	.04	.08	.02	.04	.04	.05	.03
SI								
X	.03	.15	.05	.06	.05	.13	.05	.03
SD	.03	.09	.05	.04	.08	.11	.05	.04

Note: SDA = Self-directed activity; ATT = Attending; DST = Distractibility; PR = Passive responding; GM = Gross-motor activity; and SI = Social interaction

The univariate comparisons for each of the six behavior variables between third and fourth graders support the conclusion that the overall differences in behavior could be attributed to differences in self-directed activity and passive responding. Third graders exhibited a significantly higher proportion of self-directed activity than fourth graders: $F(1/22) = 13.55$, $p < .001$. Fourth graders exhibited a significantly higher proportion of passive responding: $F(1/22) = 11.17$, $p < .001$.

While the overall test for group effects failed to reach the required significance level, learning disabled children could be differentiated from normal children on differences in the frequency of distractibility. Subjects in the learning disabled group exhibited a significantly higher proportion of distractibility than the normal subjects: $F(1/22) = 4.88$, $p < .03$.

Analysis of Classroom Environment

To explain further the findings regarding main and interaction effects the data on environmental setting were examined. Only freedom of task choice and size of group environmental factors were considered, as the other two areas, type of activity and teacher specified content, are curricular and were not varied in this study.

There were two levels of freedom of task choice: teacher present (TP) working with a child or group on specified task and teacher not present (TNP), but a specified task had been assigned. There were three levels of size of group: individual (I), small group (SG), or large group (LG). Table II presents the mean proportion of total behavior under different environmental settings for groups and grade levels.

No behavior occurred during either a TP-I setting or a TNP-LG setting for any of the subject

groupings. Learning disabled and normal children were observed in highly similar settings. Both groups spent approximately three-fourths of their time in either TNP-I work or TP-LG situations. The most notable difference between grades was that third-grade behavior tended to occur in TNP-I settings while approximately one-half of the fourth-grade subject behaviors occurred during TP-LG conditions.

DISCUSSION

The present study yielded only one dimension of classroom behavior which differentiated the two groups. Learning disabled children exhibited a significantly higher frequency of distractibility. This finding tends to confirm the results of previous studies using both a teacher rating approach (Foreman & McKinney 1975) and a direct observation technique (Bryan 1974b). There was no indication that learning disabled children as a group possess a negative behavioral style including conduct problem behavior, hyperactivity, passivity, and dependency. Therefore, very limited support was found for the stereotyped cluster of behavior that is frequently attributed to LD children.

At the same time learning disabled children were consistently more distractible than normal children regardless of the regular classroom setting. However, Bryan (1974b) provided evidence that learning disabled children engaged in significantly more task-oriented behavior and less nontask-oriented behavior in special education rooms as compared to regular classrooms. Therefore, since distractibility has been shown repeatedly to be negatively associated with achievement, it certainly is a behavior which should be dealt with in the regular classroom in

TABLE II. *Mean proportions of total behavior: Subject groupings by environmental setting.*

Subject Grouping	TP			TNP		
	I	SG	LG	I	SG	LG
Learning disabled	.00	.18	.31	.40	.11	.00
Normal	.00	.11	.34	.42	.13	.00
Gr3	.00	.07	.14	.62	.17	.00
Gr4	.00	.21	.48	.23	.08	.00

Note: TP = Teacher present; TNP = Teacher not present; I = Individual; SG = Small group; and LG = Large group.

conjunction with special education programming. The learning disabilities specialist should have the skills necessary to assess the child behavior in the classroom and to assist the regular classroom teacher in developing skills for the management of attentional problems.

As previously indicated, all of the learning disabled children in the present study had been involved in remediation. While the possible confounding effects on the results of this study are acknowledged, evaluations of the learning disability program have suggested that regular classroom teachers' ratings indicate that they perceived minimal progress in task orientation and social and affective behavior for children in the deficit-model remediation.

One important reason for the finding that third graders exhibited more self-directed activity than fourth graders might be that the classrooms at the schools were organized differently. The third-grade classrooms at both schools were set up and operated on the open-classroom, learning center model. Fourth-grade classrooms tended to be more traditional with desks in rows and more time spent in making presentations to the total class or otherwise requiring their attention.

While the present investigation did not find evidence for a losing behavioral style associated with mildly to moderately learning disabled children, it does suggest that behavior that is inconsistent with achievement may be partially eliminated by particular regular classroom arrangements and teacher approaches. With the exception of distractibility, the social, affective, and, to some extent, task-orientation behavior patterns of learning disabled children were affected in the same way as those of their normal peers. Perhaps classroom settings that foster behavior inconsistent with achievement and competence are especially damaging to learning disabled children, since their experience of the classroom is typically compounded by substantial academic problems and a history of failure.

ACKNOWLEDGMENTS
The authors acknowledge the cooperation of the Durham County school system, Ms. Marion Krueger, Project MELD, and the principals and teachers involved with the study at the two schools.

ABOUT THE AUTHORS
David D. Richey took his degree in 1975 from the University of North Carolina at Chapel Hill. At present he is an assistant professor of special education at Tennessee Technological University, where he teaches both graduate and undergraduate courses and is engaged in community service. James D. McKinney received his degree in school psychology from North Carolina State University. He is an associate professor of education at the University of North Carolina, Chapel Hill. Requests for reprints should be sent to Dr. Richey, Department of Educational Psychology and Counselor Education, Tennessee Technological University, Cookeville, Tenn. 38501.

REFERENCES
Bales, R.F.: Interaction process analysis. In E. Hollander and R. Hunt (Eds.): Current Perspectives in Social Psychology. New York: Oxford University Press, 1971.
Barr, K.L., McDowell, R.L.: Comparison of learning disabled and emotionally disturbed children on three deviant classroom behaviors. Exceptional Children, 1972, 39(1), 60-62.
Bryan, T.: Learning disabilities: A new stereotype. Journal of Learning Disabilities, 1974, 1, 304-310.
Bryan, T.: An observational analysis of classroom behavior of children with learning disabilities. Journal of Learning Disabilities, 1974, 7, 35-43.
Bryan, T., Wheeler, R.: Perception of learning disabled children: The eye of the observer. Journal of Learning Disabilities, 1972, 5, 484-498.
Cobb, J.A.: Relationship of discrete classroom behavior to fourth-grade academic achievement. Journal of Educational Psychology, 1972, 63, 74-80.
Cooley, W.W., Lohnes, P.R.: Multivariate Procedures of the Behavioral Sciences. New York: Wiley, 1962.
Foreman, B.D., McKinney, J.P.: A comparison of classroom behavior ratings of learning disabled and non-learning disabled children. Paper presented at the annual meeting of the Southeastern Psychological Association. Hollywood, Florida, May, 1974.
Forness, S.R., Esveldt, K.C.: Classroom observation of children with learning and behavior problems. Journal of Learning Disabilities, 1975, 8, 382-385.
Keogh, B.K., Tchir, C., Windeguth-Behn, A.: Teacher's perceptions of educationally high-risk children. Journal of Learning Disabilities, 1974, 7, 367-374.
McCarthy, J.M., Paraskevopoulos, J. Behavior patterns of learning disabled, emotionally disturbed, and average children. Exceptional Children, 1969, 36, 69-74.
McKinney, J.D., Kreuger, M.: Models for Educating Learning Disabled Children: Final Report. Raleigh, N.C.: North Carolina State Department of Public Instruction, Division of Development, June, 1973.
McKinney, J.D., Gallagher, J.J., McKinney, M.C.: Relationship between learning styles and academic achievement. In Developmental Research on the Improvement of Kindergarten in North Carolina. Chapel Hill, N.C. Frank Porter Graham Child Development Center, University of North Carolina, July, 1974.
McKinney, J.D., Mason, J., Perkerson, K., Clifford, M.: Relationship between classroom behavior and academic achievement. Journal of Educational Psychology, 1975, 67, 198-203.
Samuels, S.J., Turnure, J.E.: Attention and reading achievement in first-grade boys and girls. Journal of Educational Psychology, 1974, 66, 29-32.

READING FAILURE AND THE LEARNING-DYSLABELED CHILD

MELVIN D. LEVINE, M.D.

Division of Ambulatory Pediatrics,
Children's Hospital Medical Center

It is easier to be an adult than a child. In middle life, there are multiple options for the consummation of strengths; vocational and avocational niches offer refuge to the most divergent of functional profiles. During childhood, academic and social demands are rigid, allowing for little or no eccentricity, and sometimes alienating those youth who are destined to become better adults than children. A child may be made to feel guilty if he or she does not demonstrate high levels of attainment or working capacity in language arts, quantitative thinking, motor activities, and social adaptability. There is the expectation that a young brain can be a "perfect machine."

Expectations are conditioned by cultural and economic exigencies. A high level of talent with bow and arrow (largely a visual-motor activity) will not reap the rewards brought by rapid word finding and verbal comprehension. Those with the latter are likely to become bosses. In other cultures, the opposite might be true. Dr. Snyder's special article in this issue of *Pediatrics* (page 791) suggests strongly that certain children have "the right not to read." A more general statement might be that they have the right to be authentic, to allow their uniquely wired neural circuits to operate at their own pace, and to accomplish the tasks for which their systems were designed. This is a most defensible stance. It forces us to question assumptions underlying the adult's incessant efforts to change children. It encourages us to recognize, respect, and preserve individual varia-

tion. The position is weakened seriously by limitations in our knowledge of child development. We cannot differentiate style from handicap clearly. The young brain does not come with an owner's manual! We have no way of ascertaining whether a particular central nervous system is being misused or whether it is in need of repair. If an individualized style is extremely discrepant from societal expectations, the resultant unhappiness and human tragedy may indeed constitute a "handicap."

The term *dyslexia* connotes a miswired system. Most educators and physicians have inferred from this diagnosis that work needs to be done to repair specific defects in information processing. As Dr. Snyder notes, most clinicians and investigators are recognizing the misapplication of such terminology. Children who fail to read "at grade level" reflect a heterogenous group of disorders, maladaptive styles, variations on normalcy, and specific teaching disabilities. It is clear that this label, like so many others, is potentially dangerous and offers little relevance with regard to etiology, prognosis, or therapeutic direction.

Individual children with reading failure may fall into one or more subgroups, each of which contains subcategories. Among these one might include the following:

1. Children with specific *"handicaps"* of information *processing*. This might include youngsters with visual-spatial disorientation; language disabilities; significant short- or long-term memory problems; deficits of temporal-sequential organization; and difficulties with higher order conceptual functions such as rule application, abstraction, and inferential reasoning. Weaknesses in one or more of these areas may range from subtle to incapacitating. Individual children

"Reading Failure and the Learning-Dyslabeled Child," M.D. Levine, *Pediatrics*, Vol. 63, No. 5, May 1979. ©1979
Arthur Retlaw and Associates.

may show one or more of these deficits in a substrate of unique strengths and preferences.

2. Some children with reading problems may have *maladaptive patterns of selective attention*. Difficulties with concentration or focus may impede the acquisition of reading skills. In some cases, this may be accompanied by other impairments, such as impulsivity, task impersistence, easy fatigability, distractibility, and poorly modulated activity.

3. Some youngsters may have difficulty reading because of particularly *strong learning styles or orientations*. For example, such specialization might facilitate quantitative thinking.

4. There may be a group of children who acquire academic skills but only at their own *pace*. Dr. Snyder points out that these youngsters will learn to read (ultimately) with or without specialized intervention.

5. Some children have difficulty learning because of *disruptive home and school experiences*. Those who are depressed or preoccupied with emotional turmoil and chronic feelings of inadequacy may be distracted from learning.

6. *Socioeconomic and cultural factors* may be associated with reading failure. In some cases, a lack of academic motivation and learning incentive decelerates the acquisition of reading skills.

7. Inevitably, some children must occupy the *bottom of every curve*. But, then, why have curves?

Dr. Snyder's admonitions may be relevant only for certain subgroups. The problem is that the diagnostic process is not well enough developed to make such determinations unequivocally. Moreover, the technology is not in place to answer certain fundamental questions: Which children will improve spontaneously? Who is actually underachieving? Who is most likely to benefit from intervention? Who is handicapped and who is stylistically specialized? Who is somehow destined to be at the lower end of the reading curve? Who will develop a severe learning inhibition while struggling to learn? Studies of the natural history of reading failure have suffered from the lack of a taxonomy or system of classification. This makes the rigorous study of specific intervention difficult to replicate. Dr. Snyder has selected reports that suggest the futility of intervention. However, one can also cite investigations demonstrating the efficacy of cognitive interventions.[1,2] The final verdict is not yet in.

One needs to weigh the advantages and liabilities of reading intervention programs. As Dr. Snyder notes, when they take a toll on the child emotionally, they are undesirable. On the other hand, some investigators have commented on the psychotherapeutic benefits of individualized educational support.[3] One also needs to consider carefully the "ripple effects" of delayed skill acquisition. Low self-esteem, depression, social failure, somatic symptoms, and withdrawal are all complications of mastery deprivation. Academic lags have been associated with major psychopathology, including delinquent antisocial behavior[4,5]

The child who becomes a nonreader may have seriously limited options in our culture. Do we have the "right" to impose early constriction of opportunity?

Concerted investigation is needed to refine the clinical phenomenology of reading failure, and then to evaluate specific interventions. While awaiting technological strides, the only morally justifiable stance is one of moderation: We need to teach to strengths. We must recognize and nurture individual styles. We need to give serious consideration to the right not to read (or at least the right not to read *yet*). We also need to recognize rights in other academic areas, especially the *right not to write*. For the school-age child, a central mission is the avoidance of humiliation. Our programs must help children to save face, to sustain a respectable level of self-esteem, and at the same time to develop optimally and with authenticity. We must strike a balance between strengthening weaknesses and developing existing assets. Parents, educators, and pediatricians all need to work in concert to help children thrive functionally. The challenge is to accept and foster cognitive heterogeneity in a culture whose childhood standards, and the educational institutions they spawn, are ironically uniform.

REFERENCES

1. Arnold L, Barnehey N, McManus J, et al: Prevention by specific perceptual remediation for vulnerable first graders. *Arch Gen Psychiatry* 34:1279, 1977.
2. Wilson S, Harris C, Harris M: Effects of an auditory perceptual program on reading performance. *J Learn Disabil* 9:670, 1976.
3. de Hirsch K: Interactions between educational therapist and child. *Bull Orton Soc* 27:88, 1977.
4. Hogenson D: Reading failure and juvenile delinquency. *Bull Orton Soc* 24:164, 1974.
5. Mauser A: Learning disabilities and delinquent youths. *Acad Ther* 9:389, 1974.

LABELING OF LD CHILDREN AND TEACHER PECEPTION

Hubert R. Vance
Fred Wallbrown

Hubert R. Vance, PhD, is director of the Child Study Center at James Madison University, Harrisonburg, Virginia 22801. Fred Wallbrown is a member of personnel services in the College of Education, Wichita State Unviersity, Witchita, Kansas.

Within the past decade great interest has emerged regarding the term "learning disabilities." Difficulty is frequently encountered in making generalizations about the various behavior patterns of children with learning problems. In this broadening field, little research has been directed to the different behavioral and social patterns of boys and girls who have been labeled learning disabled.

In addition to the obvious biological difference between boys and girls, roles and stereotypes have been constructed and psychological notions of masculinity and feminity pervade our thinking about how boys and girls should act. In this society, a "real" boy plays baseball or football, climbs trees, hates school, and likes blue as his favorite color. A "real" girl plays with dolls, jumps rope, is polite to adults, and likes pink dresses. Children who do not conform to these stereotypes are "sissies" or "tomboys." Our society finds it easier to understand the girl who acts like a boy, however, than we do the boy who acts like a girl. The girl's behavior may be attributed to her desire to improve her status; the sissy on the other hand, is to be ostracized because some feel he is imitating a group that ranks below him. There is little in our value system that makes his behavior acceptable.

Somehow all of these attitudes and stereotypes are conveyed to children. Indeed, it is clear that the concepts of masculinity and femininity are learned quite early in childhood (Mischel 1970). Even preschoolers indicate considerable knowledge of which activities are appropriate for girls and which are appropriate for boys (Mussen 1969). Education continues the process of socializing children into sex roles that was begun by parents. In this article the significance of sex-role stereotypes as they relate to the behaviors and social interaction patterns for learning-disabled girls and boys are explored. This basic review is the first in a series of articles investigating the classroom behavior of girls and boys who have been labeled "learning disabled." In many instances there is a dichotomy of roles in regard to expectations for boys and girls in school. If children are generally vulnerable to such controls, how much worse must be the plight of learning-disabled children.

The behavioral characteristics associated with learning disabilities have been amply documented. The characteristics observed in children with specific learning disorders are: hyperactivity, incoordination, problems with perception, symbolization, and inattention (Myers and Hammill 1969, Bryan 1974). Although there is an apparent consensus among professionals in the field that such behaviors are observed in these children, very little research has been completed concerning the frequency, duration, intensity, or conditions under which a behavior must be demonstrated by a child in order for him to be characterized by that behavior. R. C. Towne and J. M. Joiner (1968), and Bryan (1974) contend it is important to determine whether the behavior associated with the term "learning disabilities" is based on fact or fiction. They point out that, whatever the label means to others, and regardless of its accuracy or connection with the child's immediate behavior, each person's expectations and interpretations of the child's behavior will be affected by his definition of what this "kind" of person is supposed to be like (Towne and Joiner 1968).

The works of R. Rosenthal and L. Jacobson (1966) as well as W. B. Brookover (1959) indicate how the expectations of others have an affect upon how one behaves. Three hypotheses form the basic substance of W. B. Brookover's (1959) conception of the relationship between school learning and one's behavior. They are: (1) people learn to behave in ways that each considers appropriate to himself; (2) appropriateness of behavior is defined by each person through the internalization of the expectation of their "significant others"; and (3) the individual learns what he believes the "significant others" expect him to learn in the classroom and other situations.

Bryan (1974) conducted observational studies on task-oriented and social behavior of learning-disabled and normal children in the classroom. Ten children classified as learning disabled by the special education staff were matched by sex, age, and grade with an average achiever. These pairs were observed for alternating five-minute periods and their behavior recorded at ten-second intervals. The observations extended for five school days over a period of five months. Results of the studies indicate that children who were labeled learning disabled spent significantly less ($p = .01$) time engaging in task-oriented behavior and significantly more ($p = .01$) time in non-task-oriented behaviors than did their peers. Analysis of Bryan's observational data, by subject area, indicated that the learning-disabled children spent significantly less time engaged in attending behaviors to arithmetic, language arts, and teacher instructions than did the comparison group of children. When compared to their peers, learning-disabled children did not exhibit any difference in the amount of time engaged in attending behavior to the subjects of social studies, writing, and library. These results seem to indicate that children with learning problems learn: (1) to look reasonably busy; (2) not to be disruptive; (3) not to get into trouble; and (4) not to work in school (Bryan 1972).

Bryan (1974) concluded that in the research setting, the learning-disabled child engaged in more attending and task-oriented behavior (paying attention, attending to teaching, etc.) than when placed in the regular classroom setting. Further results of Bryan's research indicated that the regular classroom teacher

1. NATURE

was three times more likely to respond to verbal elicitations (interaction) of the regular student than she was to the learning-disabled child. Also, the learning-disabled child in the regular classroom received more negative reinforcement ("Stay in your seat," "Don't talk out of turn") than did the regular child. Bryan's data indicated that a different pattern occurs when the child with learning problems is with a learning disability teacher in a resource setting. In general, these studies seem to indicate that the learning-disabled child experiences a somewhat unusual relationship with his teachers and peers.

N. A. Vacc's (1968) study on the behavior of the emotionally disturbed child in the regular classroom versus a resource setting was in agreement with the findings of Bryan (1972). Analysis of the Vacc data indicates that children who had been labeled emotionally disturbed and placed in a regular classroom exhibited overt changes in behavior in a negative direction, were less accepted, and were rejected more often than their class peers.

The importance of these studies is very relevant and apparent when a teacher is expected to work with a learning-disabled child with emotional problems or a child with emotional problems who also has a learning problem. When both disorders are present, the child's social and academic problems increase geometrically. A. O. Ross (1967) points out that it is difficult to make a distinction between a child who is primarily learning disabled who has acquired emotional problems due to the lack of educational achievement, as opposed to an emotionally disturbed child who has developed the significant educational discrepancy as a result of a specific emotional problem. The difference in labels elicits different sets of behaviors from those interacting with the child. The findings of J. M. McCarthy and J. Parashevopovlos (1969) indicate that teachers of the emotionally disturbed and learning-disabled children perceive the problem behaviors of the pupils to vary within each label of exceptionality with some overlap between these two groups. Teachers of the emotionally disturbed children perceive their pupils to have more behavior problems of greater severity than did the teachers of the learning-disabled or average child.

One can quickly perceive the differences in the perceptions of teachers and other significant people who interact with the learning-disabled child and the actual behavior patterns indicated by the studies of McCarthy and Parashevopovlos (1969), Vacc (1968), and Bryan (1974). Instead of depicting a disruptive, attention-seeking child, these studies indicate that the learning-disabled child tries to look reasonably busy, to not be disruptive, to not get into trouble, and that he engages in social interactions in about the same proportion of time as do those in a peer comparison group. One might question how much the label affected the teachers' expectations and influenced their interpretation of the actual behavior of various examples of exceptionality in their classrooms.

An interesting study by P. J. Caplan and M. Kinsbourne (1974) adds another perspective to the behavioral characteristics of the learning-disabled child. These authors hypothesized that the sex of a child would affect that child's response to school failure and the behavior exhibited because there are different compensating roles available to males and females. For the female "being well behaved" is an alternative way of winning social approval, whereas most boys who are failing have to resort to excellence in either sports or leadership (qualities which are less valued in the classroom and which are much more difficult to attain). Almost all girls can be nice, and can be nice in any situation; but only a few boys can excel in sports or leadership. In addition, boys who are good athletes are often good leaders and are achieving rather than failing in their school work. For these reasons, a boy who is failing usually has a much more difficult time coping in the classroom than does the failing girl. The work of Caplan and Kinsbourne suggests that there is an attitudinal change on the part of teachers toward boys and girls who experience failure in the classroom. For instance, each sex considered being "smart" more important than being nice, which was contradictory to the attitudes which the teachers suspected that they would have. The failing boys, however, tended to adopt more hostile, antisocial, and unrealistic attitudes than did failing girls. These differences in behavior and attitude suggest that boys who fail tend to adopt a form of defense which leads them to be dealt with more harshly in school; and this, in turn, significantly affects the teachers' expectations and attitudes toward them. Failing girls, on the other hand, tend to adopt a form of behavior which supports the standard that the teacher has set and thus bring about social approval (Caplan and Kinsbourne 1974). This research raises the question whether attitudinal changes experienced by teachers who don't work with exceptional children, especially learning-disabled children, are the same for those teachers who have learning-disabled children in their classrooms. Perhaps there are other explanations why learning-disabled boys significantly outnumber the girls not only in self-contained special classrooms but in the mainstream of education.

These findings place added emphasis on the teacher's task of accurately recognizing the scope and depth of the learning problems of children. The inconsistency of behavior, expected or overt, often determines whether or not a child is referred for a psychological assessment. Once labeled, the process of labeling in itself may evoke unique reactions on the part of the child (Kavaraceus 1967). The labeling process might take the form of resistance on the part of the professional, who might maintain a distance, either psychologically or concretely. Thus, whatever the label means to others, and regardless of its accuracy in connection with the child's immediate behavior, each person's expectation and interpretation of the child's behavior will be affected by his definition of what this kind of person is supposed to be like (Towne and Joiner 1968).

In our review of the literature on learning disabilities, most research focuses primarily upon refining diagnostic tools and devising remediation procedures. Although there is little research to date focusing on the social aspect, the following findings have definite implications for professionals and paraprofessionals.

1. There are indications that the actual behavior of the learning-disabled child in the classroom does not correspond with either the teacher's expectation for the learning-disabled child or to the actual behavior perceived by the teachers within the classroom. Those directly involved in the education of children should attempt to avoid associating unsub-

stantiated notions with the label of learning disabilities. With the wide variation of behaviors grouped under the heading of learning disabilities, educators should resist any preconceived notion concerning the behavior of any individual child so labeled.

2. Classroom tasks ordinarily thought to be more pleasurable or easier for the average child (e.g., games, painting, remembering words to say, etc.) may be as laborious as reading for learning-disabled children. Thus, planning of classroom learning activities by the regular teacher when confronted with a mixed classroom becomes of paramount importance. Teachers should be aware in planning educational activities that learning-disabled children attend more efficiently in an educational setting characterized by more teacher attention, immediate feedback, and greater proportion of positive reinforcement.

3. Both learning-disabled children and those who experience classroom failures tend to have an unusual interpersonal relationship with peers and with teachers. Contingencies must be planned which will increase learning and which will affect the nature and frequencies of desirable behavior. An attempt must also be made to understand what these children are communicating about their feelings and emotions through their behavior. The affective sources of behaviors must not be forgotten and the child must be helped to find more acceptable methods of communicating his feelings or protecting himself from psychological stress (Long et al. 1971).

4. Teachers should be on the alert to the possibility that a child in the classroom may be giving a pretense of working and being busy in order to gain social approval for being well behaved or in an attempt to avoid punishment. They must provide alternative ways for children to gain success other than the ones traditionally associated with schooling (e.g., achieving good grades, being a nice person or leader, and being good in athletics). Students who are failing need to be provided a way to express their frustration; for even if the child does find an alternate role (like being well behaved), this role will never completely compensate for the frustration and resignation the child often feels as a result of failing.

5. A label is merely a brief descriptive, organizational device, and should not be used as an explanation. If it is, the explanation becomes myth, fiction, and usually functions to the detriment of the labeled individual (Whelan 1972).

Many of the implications and suggestions listed here can be implemented in teacher preservice training programs. For those already in the field, professional staff development should be offered centering around the stigma of labeling; and an attempt should be made to make professionals more sensitive to the problems associated with being an exceptional child. Implicit in these suggestions is the need for the development of quality training programs which adequately prepare teachers for special classes. There is also a need to prepare supervisory personnel who are carefully trained to work in consultative capacities within the public school, and who would be in a position to focus on important research needs and who could encourage creative program planning.

In conclusion it is hoped that these suggestions will provide a point of departure for those involved with the welfare of children with special problems. Perhaps it would be well, however, if this article were viewed as a challenge to all concerned professionals to come forth with constructive ideas which would help us to categorize and deal more humanely and effectively with children who are in some ways different. At the same time, graduate and undergraduate training programs must develop programs that are both effective and efficient to help all educators, but especially special educators, to become more effective in their role as agents of change.

The March 1972 issue of *Exceptional Children* indicates that the aim of special education is "to emphasize the education of the special *child* rather than his identification or classification" (p. 575). This aim was formulated in 1923; and even though fifty years have passed, special educators are just now beginning to realize that labels—particularly those that denote defective or negative personal attributes—may not be necessary to achieve this old, but relevant and very current aim. Perhaps if this aim were prominently displayed each day for all professionals interested in special education to observe, the energies devoted to devising and using labels could be added to those energies expended on the continuous quest for improved instructional practices.

References

Bryan, T. S. 1974. An observational analysis of classroom behaviors of children with learning disabilities. *Journal of Learning Disabilities* 7:1 pp. 92-98.

Caplan, P. J., and Kinsbourne, M. 1974. Sex differences in response to school failure. *Journal of Learning Disabilities* 7:248-256.

Kavaraceus, W. C. 1962. Helping the socially inadapted pupils in the large city schools. *Exceptional Children* 28:399-408.

Long, N. J.; Alper, R.; and Butl, F. 1971. Helping children cope with feelings. In *Conflict in the classroom*, eds. N. J. Long et al. Belmont, California: Wadsworth.

McCarthy, J. M., and Parashevopovlos, J. 1971. Behavior patterns of learning disabled, emotionally disturbed, and average children. In *Conflict in the classroom*, eds. N. J. Long et al. Belmont, California: Wadsworth.

Ross, A. O. 1971. Learning difficulties of children: dysfunction, disorders, disabilities. *Journal of School Psychology* 5:2 pp. 82-92.

Towne, R. C., and Joiner, J. M. 1968. Some negative implications of special placement for children with learning disabilities. *Journal of Special Education* 2:217-222.

Vacc, N. A. 1968. The study of emotionally disturbed children in regular and special classes. *Journal of Special Education* 5:419-426.

Whelan, R. J. 1972. What's in a label? A hell of a lot. Proceedings, the Missouri Conference, *Legal and educational consequences of the intelligence testing movement; handicapped and minority group children*. 34-59.

photo: David Carofano

DIAGNOSIS OF LEARNING PROBLEMS

Diagnosis is one of the most crucial aspects of providing educational services for the learning disabled child. It involves the asking of educationally relevant questions about a child's learning behavior for the purpose of instruction. It is intended to produce useful instructional objectives that will lead to appropriate educational methods.

Diagnosis and assessment may take a variety of forms. Formal standardized tests are the most frequently used of these, due to the ease of administration and the availability of comparative information. Criterion - referenced tests, which are informal tests that establish an expected level of achievement on an individual basis, are often preferred by educators. This is due to the fact that they specify criteria for performance on an individual basis. Other forms include observational and interview techniques, informal probes, and task analysis, which focuses on specific tasks of broader academic areas.

Testing involves four major purposes. First, it provides documentation that enables a child to become eligible for learning disability services. It does this by showing significant differences between potential and academic achievement.

Secondly, diagnosis helps the program for a child in a general manner. It does this by indicating which specific areas need remediation. By looking at the severity of deficits one can also make decisions about the amount of time special services may be needed.

A third major reason for testing assists the learning disabilities teacher in writing goals and objectives for the child's individualized instructional program. Criterion referenced tests are useful for this purpose.

Lastly, testing may be done for evaluative indications. A learning disabilities specialist must know whether progress is being made with students in his/her class. Appropriate evaluation often helps to restructure or modify a child's educational plan so that optional success is attained.

The following section provides articles that look at the role of diagnosis and evaluation in the educational environment. Ways to improve this process are offered. Also, informal procedures that will enable the educator to properly plan for learning disabled children are discussed.

Learning Disabilities:

Diagnosis and Management

Marcel Kinsbourne, M.D., Ph.D.

It is important for both parents and teachers to understand the differences between "learning disabilities" and other more general labels. If distinctions are blurred between learning-disabled children and the larger group of children who have various other kinds of trouble in school, then programs cannot be planned for an individual child. Using a term in too general a way is confusing for people who wish to fit the remedy to the child, because children differ with respect to their learning requirements.

In order to learn anything an individual needs both ability and motivation. Motivational problems are not learning disabilities, strictly speaking. The majority of illiterate people, who are not motivated to learn because of their family background, social circumstances or emotional state, are not considered to be learning disabled.

If a child is not motivated, then the logical remedy is to find something that does motivate him. This course is invaluable for individuals who have the ability necessary for learning, but it is of no use for those people who lack that ability — who, in other words, have a learning disability. Of course a young child whose ability is inadequate and who consequently fails for several years will acquire a low self-image and expect to continue to fail. Later, even though the child's abilities may have matured enough for him to learn successfully, he may lack the motivation to use them. In that special circumstance particular rewards are initially useful, but the most consistent motivator is success in the learning situation.

Two types of ability are important for learning. One is attention, or concentration — what one might call "task orientation." The other is processing or mental capacity — the ability to solve the problem once the individual is trying to do so and is concentrating on it.

If a person has the necessary mental power but does not focus it on the task, his processing power is not being used. It might as well not be there. That is the case with "hyperactive" children, who have a deficit of attention. Conversely even a person who concentrates very hard may fail if he lacks the mental processes needed to perform tasks. Such people have a deficit of processing, such as selective reading unreadiness. So on the one hand some people cannot focus their attention; on the other hand some are unready for a particular level of instruction. Some unfortunate children have both problems, which must be sorted out because the steps to take toward solving them are quite different. Terms such as "dyslexia" should not be used to include both problems of attention and problems of processing. Labeling both with a single word implies that two quite different entities are either the same or always linked. This confusion obstructs the helper's own mental processes as he tries to figure out how to help the child. Of the misleading general terms, only one — "minimal brain dysfunction" — is even less productive than "dyslexia," but others, like "selective language disorder," "selective reading disorder" and so forth are also harmful. It is important to keep in mind that children who have trouble learning differ from one another. Even two children who have reading problems differ in the exact nature of the disability.

Definition of Learning Disabilities

Children with learning problems are not those who score low on tests of most cognitive abilities. Rather, children who are slow in all mental processes and in their ability to focus on a task are more appropriately considered mentally retarded. Sometimes they are called "slow learners." Mental

"Learning Disabilities: Diagnosis and Management, Part One." Marcel Kinsbourne, M.D., Ph.D., *Exceptional Parent*, Vol. 7, No. 5, October 1977. ©1977 Psy-Ed Corporation.

retardation is very different from learning disability.

Children with learning disabilities have selective difficulties. They are neither bright nor dull; in fact they are both bright and dull, in different respects. But not all learning difficulties qualify as learning disabilities.

"Learning disability" implies a selective weakness that impinges on academic performance. The inability to carry a tune is a clear-cut selective deficit. It does not differ in principle from a selective deficit in reading or arithmetic. The only differences are practical ones; no one cares greatly about humming tunes, there are meager social and financial rewards for the ability, and one cannot be admitted to college on that basis. So adult anxiety does not focus on that particular selective deficit.

But the learning-disabled child is unfortunate enough to do a poor job at school, one of the few areas where society insists that children do well. One cannot overestimate the impact of societal expectations on the child or the ways that they distort our efforts and theories. One disturbing consequence of social pressure is that children with school-related learning difficulties are constantly stuck with labels like "brain damage" or "minimal cerebral dysfunction," whereas tone-deaf children are not. Although the reading-disabled probably have a dysfunction in one brain area, the "amusicals" certainly have a similar dysfunction in another. Learning-disabled children, as I have said, are only those whose deficits obstruct traditional school learning.

Reading is the topic most often discussed under the heading of "learning disabilities." Some children are selectively immature in abilities relevant to reading. In order to understand them it is useful to think first about how individuals differ from one another and then about the ingredients of reading readiness.

Individual Differences

Adults differ from each other with respect to many physical and mental attributes, but children differ from each other much more, because they differ in an additional way. Adults are static at the level of full development; their differences will probably be about the same five years from now.

Children also vary in their patterns of development. At any given time normal children have different patterns of ability. These patterns themselves change within a child over time. Mental development is not linear; children do not grow at a steady rate but rather in fits and starts, just as their physical height increases unevenly. A child's current abilities do not reliably predict future abilities, particularly in the first three years of life.

The age at which a child first learns to walk, for instance, is a topic of great concern. Parents whose

children walk at nine months are proud, and parents whose children walk at 18 months are ashamed. But at five years all these children are walking, and it makes no difference at what age they first learned. Nor does it predict anything. else. The early walker is not necessarily going to be the person who walks through examinations with no trouble in high school. This pattern is almost equally true for language development. Among thousands of children, some of whom develop language early and some late, there will be group differences 20 years later, but for the individual child the timing of language development predicts very little. This is something to keep in mind when one talks about early identification and early action.

The typical feeling reported by parents of a learning-disabled child is surprise: their child seemed normal during the first five years of life, so why isn't he learning now? This reaction distinguishes learning disability from mental retardation, where it is usually clear from the beginning that the child is slow. That feeling of surprise (if he has been so smart all along, why is he dumb now?) is really based on an unjustified expectation — that human beings will be uniform in their development. They are not.

Many children who, on entering first grade, have unexpected difficulty in mastering the material, are experiencing a temporary lag in mental development. That initial difficulty does not necessarily predict an enduring disability, but it can be made permanent if the child becomes so discouraged that an ongoing problem develops. This crystallization of problems occurs increasingly because parents and other helpers are excessively anxious.

What Is Involved in Reading Readiness?

When we ask children to learn to read, we are asking them to do quite new things, which are not required in the everyday preschool environment. So the way they handle mental challenges in preschool situations may not indicate how they will do when they have to perform the tasks required to learn to read. One word describes what it takes to read, though there are many subsidiary tasks: in order to learn to read, the child has to be analytic. Language learning involves learning both spoken language and written language. Superficially, the only difference is that the first is based only on sound and the second also involves sight. The difference is an important one. An infant learning a spoken language is surrounded by it, almost cannot stop hearing it. The sentences at first sound to him like gobbledygook; but because no one has told him that he has to study those sentences, the baby is not anxious about it. Then he begins to notice recurrent words or phrases, and they begin to make sense. Not much selective attention is needed to pick up individual words when the child keeps hearing them. So in a natural environment the beginnings of oral language come easily.

But with vision an incredible amount of richness competes for notice; moreover, letters and words are not as eye-catching as colors, bold shapes and movement. The ability to focus selective attention on one or two letter shapes, or even one or two attributes of these shapes, does not come naturally to the young child. It is something that he has to develop over the years.

Selective looking, looking at the important attributes of the written code, is hard for young children. They are not necessarily very efficient lookers. They see normally, their eyes are perfectly in order and the world looks to them as it looks to us. But they are not good at looking actively. They do not know, for instance, how to scan a page efficiently in order to pick up the information they need and reject the rest. They generally stop too soon, before they have seen all that is relevant. They look redundantly, going over one part twice rather than proceeding efficiently over the whole page. They look unsystematically, scanning in one direction one time and another direction the next. Without systematic strategy it is hard to pick up the distinctive features of letters, which have to be noticed in order to learn what goes with what.

Quite a few children entering first grade are still not very analytical either in listening or in looking. It is much easier to hear and reproduce a total word than to identify the sounds that make it up. The ability to say "hat" comes very early, but saying "h-a-t" is hard and unnatural. Children need specific teaching to learn to do that; they will not do it spontaneously. They will learn whole words spontaneously, but to break words up they need an analytical listening attitude.

Thus reading readiness necessitates selective and analytical looking and listening. Teaching strategies should be based on knowing what the child is looking at and listening to and then on adapting the child's style of paying attention to the specific task at hand. This statement generally applies to the slow reading learners in the early grades. If they use better looking and listening strategies, they learn to read more easily. It is less true of older children who are behind in reading but are still achieving above second- or third-grade level in other subjects. Children like this need different teaching strategies, which parents should understand in order to make sense of what is going on with their child.

Problems in Reading

In order to achieve at a third-grade level, for instance, a child needs to be a reasonably good looker and listener. To read beyond that level he needs additional language skills. Even a child who has learned to break words down and put them together again can have very poor paragraph comprehension. Such a child may not understand the paragraph's content, even though he can decode each individual word.

We have developed listening comprehension paragraphs, comparable to reading comprehension paragraphs. Each child reads such paragraphs and also listens to them read aloud. Then the comprehension level for those paragraphs the children read and those they heard are compared. We find that some older children comprehend no better when listening to text than when reading it. In a natural environment this problem is easily overlooked. It is less obvious when a child is not listening well to complex material than when he is not reading it well; we have more control over determining what a child is getting out of a paragraph he reads than one he hears.

This evidence suggests that the remedial work children need for reading falls into one or both of two separate categories. One is decoding work, which is focused on calling the words, saying them right and spelling them right; it requires practice in looking, listening and remembering and is highly structured. The other category, language performance, is less well understood. It has something to do with flexibility in combining phrases and grammatical forms.

Verbal memory is built on an implicit knowledge of language structure. For example, the more a child knows about how a language is structured, the more easily and efficiently he can remember the material, because some of the groupings are so familiar that they can be coded as a unit rather than element by element. I also suspect that an older, selectively backward reader who managed to get beyond the decoding stage usually has a language performance problem that interferes with his remembering material.

Dr. Kinsbourne is a pediatric neurologist and child psychologist. He is currently Professor of Pediatrics at the University of Toronto Medical School and Professor of Psychology at the University of Toronto. He heads the hospital's Learning Clinic and Neuropsychology Research Unit. Dr. Kinsbourne's research deals with brain-behavior relationships in adults and children, with heavy emphasis on learning disability and hyperactivity both from the point of view of the basic mechanisms involved in these disorders and common sense ways of helping the children overcome them.

The Assessment of Children with Learning Problems: A Planning Process Involving the Teacher

Mark N. Ozer, MD

Mark N. Ozer, M.D., is in full-time practice with children with developmental problems as well as a range of neurological diseases. He is also associate professor of child health and development at George Washington School of Medicine and associate professor of neurology at Howard University School of Medicine. Since 1965 he has been involved in the development of procedures for assessment and treatment of children with learning and behavioral problems. He serves as consultant for public school and health systems in training of staff and planning and evaluating programs for delivery of coordinated services for handicapped children.

Planning and evaluating the success of short-term objectives can too easily be overlooked due to the demands that surround IEP construction. Rather than increase teacher dependence on evaluation teams and their diagnostic findings, the author proposes a planning process designed to enhance individual problem-solving. — G.M.S.

The role of the special resource teacher is redefined as that of a consultant to the classroom teacher in increasing the teacher's awareness of his or her own problem-solving experiences with the referred child. A specified planning process emphasizing what has been accomplished and what has been effective is carried out. The product of this ongoing staff development program is greater participation by the classroom teacher in writing plans and greater awareness of the process of problem solving itself. This process of independent problem solving may then be transferred to the child.

The "product" of the assessment of children with learning problems must reflect a change in needs. The product has traditionally been data leading to a decision as to diagnostic category and then appropriate administrative placement of the child. There has been particular difficulty in the application of the approach to the child with learning disabilities. Administrative decisions have been more difficult with varying criteria for this category among different states (Gillespie, Miller, & Fiedler 1975). It has also appeared obvious that the large number of children with learning problems could not and perhaps should not be dealt with in the self-contained special education classroom. It was for class placement that the categorization process was originally carried out. The needs have changed. There is a need for greater latitude in the degree and type of "intervention" in the usual educational programming for the individual child. Intervention appropriately might be simply the development of data for use by regular classroom teachers (Deno 1968). In recognition of this change in need, the product of assessment may now be seen as data leading to specific edueational plans for implementation by the regular classroom teacher.

The process by which such data are generated must also change from the traditional testing model. It has been suggested in the past that the diagnostician be concerned with sampling the conditions under which the child may succeed (Ozer & Richardson 1974). In this more functional analysis, variation may be made in both the stimulus conditions as well as the feedback contingencies (Bijou & Baer 1963, Bijou & Peterson 1971). The data provided to the teacher would therefore reflect the actual teaching of school material rather than a static measure of present function.

INVOLVEMENT OF THE TEACHER

The remaining problem, however, is the ability and commitment of the teacher in carrying out whatever plans are generated. The teacher must be an active participant in writing plans. In an earlier paper, the role for the special education teacher was redefined as that of a "teacher consultant." The goal of the consultant is to increase the competence and confidence of the regular teacher in dealing with the variety of needs in the classroom via an ongoing program of staff development (Ozer & Dworkin 1974). Referring the individual child with learning difficulties becomes the context for exploring "what works" rather than merely a confirmation via tests of the child's problems. Moreover, the specific concerns with the referred child provide the context for exploring how to solve problems not only for this child but for others as well. The teacher is therefore an increasingly active and independent participant in the development of educational plans and is then encouraged to carry out a similar procedure with students, helping them to become increasingly responsible for their own planning and problem solving.

It is suggested that data about a child no longer be derived by the consultant in a testing situation but rather focus on increasing the awareness and changing the perceptions of teachers' own experiences with the child. It is the clarification of these experiences in an interview with the consultant that becomes the source of diagnostic data. The type of questions asked of, and increasingly by, the teacher is crucial to this new approach. The questions are designed to introduce the teacher to a way of thinking that is problem solving in orientation. The teacher is to participate in the development not only of educational plans but also of the planning process. The product of the diagnostic assessment has now changed to that of an increased awareness by teachers of how they have solved problems and how they may do so in the future.

A teacher consultant provides initial guidance to the teacher in carrying out the planning process described here. The specific procedures for this staff development program are described elsewhere (Ozer 1975b). In general, the interview is budgeted at 30 minutes initially and 15 minutes for subsequent follow-up interviews. The objectives of any specific staff development program will vary with the needs and resources of the school system. The staff serving as teacher consultants, after training, will also vary. Examples have included special education resource teachers, reading teachers, and speech therapists.

THE PLANNING PROCESS

The steps in the planning process include (1) clarification of the ends (objectives), (2) clarification of the means (resources), (3) synthesis of these ends and means into a plan including time for implementation, and (4) evaluation of follow-up.

This last step is an integral part of the planning process since the activity is viewed as ongoing. At this time the degree of accomplishment of the initial plan and of what worked is evaluated. Revision will be made of the plan in light of experience, and steps 1 to 3 will be repeated.

Each of these steps has a similar process: exploration, selection, and specification. At each interaction with the consultant, the ends and means may be somewhat different, but the structure of the planning process remains the same. The awareness with which the individuals define their ends and means in terms of their own experience and the awareness of the planning process itself may be expected to increase. Ownership of both the specific plans and the process by which they are developed may therefore be increased.

A prototype "Teacher Planning Form" used by the Program for Learning Studies in Washington, D.C., for regular classroom teachers includes the following questions:

1. Definition of concerns—What are your concerns about the child's progress at this time?

2. Awareness of positive accomplishments—In the area of your greatest concern, what has he/she been able to do successfully this past week?

3. What worked—What do you think made it possible for the child to be able to accomplish what you mentioned in question 2?

4. Setting goals—What would you like the child to be able to do by the end of the next period of time?

5. Plan—Incorporate the ideas that you consider most useful and the priority goal in a plan for the future.

The clarification of ends requires an exploration of concerns, as illustrated by question 1. Emphasis is on current concerns. The objective is that at least three areas be explored in conjunction with the teacher. General curriculum areas such as language arts, number work, or behavior have served at the time of the initial interaction. At the end of discussion of this question, the teacher needs to select an area of priority.

In question 2 the selected area of concern is transformed into a specified description of what the child has done successfully. Again the objective is to generate at least three such occurrences. The measure of specificity is that the description include what was accomplished, with a modifying adjective as to number and time when accomplished. Here is an example:

A 9-year-old boy in a special education program is reviewed with his teacher. The concerns explored were speech clarity and language, including writing as well as reading and numbers. The teacher selects number work as her area of priority. She states that he was able to learn to add one digit numbers on the worksheet she had prepared on Tuesday and did three correctly. He was able to count by 1's up to 20 last week without error and to learn to count by 1's backward from 10 today without error.

It is in the context of these relatively specified occurrences during the recent past that exploration now continues in question 3 with the means by which these were accomplished. The objective is for the teacher to explore at least three ideas that may have been useful. In the example being used, the teacher considered that what worked for the student included his use of fingers when counting, his need for an opportunity to be shown visually, and his need for repetition with frequent positive recognition. The teacher selected as most useful his ability to use a concrete object such as his fingers in counting. A more specific description of the means by which he accomplished the task would include not only what worked but also who was involved and the amount of time spent. As a more highly specified example, counting with his fingers worked when the teacher spent 15 minutes a day for two days in a group with three others. Resource allocation for planning would require specification of the costs involved, including the number of people, their level of training, and the amount of time needed.

The attempt has been made to help raise the teacher's awareness of what had been accomplished and how it was done in the recent past. The synthesis of these experiences might now continue in the writing of a plan for the future. In question 4 exploration continues with the objective to elicit at least three possible goals. The frequency with which plans are made and revised would vary with the child's rate of progress and the availability of time for such planning. Emphasis is on making goals relatively short-term since results may then be seen more clearly. In the example, the teacher considers having the student learn to add two-digit numbers, subtract one-digit numbers, or add one-digit numbers more accurately.

In question 5 the plan is actually written. It becomes necessary to select the highest-priority goal. In the example, the teacher selected that the student learn to add one-digit numbers more accurately. Specifically, he would do so to 90% accuracy on the worksheets by the following Friday, and he would be encouraged to use his fingers. The teacher would be available to work with him at least twice in the learning center for 15 minutes on Tuesday and Friday of the following week.

2. DIAGNOSIS

The final step in the planning process is evaluation at the time of follow-up. In the example, the interval for implementation of the plan was one week, and the degree of accomplishment of the previous goal (90% accuracy) in adding one-digit numbers was evaluated. One measure of the success of the consultant in transmitting a planning process is that realizable goals be set. The criterion generally used is the accomplishment of 75% of the goals. If teachers are realizing 100% of their goals, they are likely setting goals too low. If they are realizing considerably less than 75%, they are setting their goals too high. They may then become discouraged and transmit such discouragement to the child. The particular level of goal attainment being sought should, of course, vary with the individual situation and may change over time.

At this evaluation step, there is an opportunity to review not only what was accomplished but, even more important, what worked in making such accomplishment possible. The emphasis is on increasing the teacher's awareness of his own competence by encouraging verbalization of both the products and the process of achievement. The use of written records is another technique to help raise this awareness; awareness of the process may have greater general applicability to solving problems in the future.

When the process of planning has been completed for the first time, it may be carried out again. Exploration of new concerns goes on before selection and specification. The objective for the consultant at this second stage may be for the teacher to carry out the process more independently or with an additional child. Objectives would obviously differ depending on the skill of the individual teachers in any specific staff development program.

DISCUSSION

The procedures outlined in this prototype planning process have been carried out in many different settings. In some, where staff has been available, the major emphasis has been on training teacher consultants, who then carry the responsibility for staff development. In others the training has gone on directly with teachers.

The principles of such a planning process may also be applied to a variety of different problems and clients, including family therapy (Ozer 1975a) and students (Gawlick, McAleer, & Ozer 1976). It has been described as a continuum of such consultation in reference to meeting the needs of large populations (Ozer 1976). The format used for the interview may be made more explicit for different ages and types of handicap. The degree and type of skill of the consultant affect the emphasis of the interview.

It is suggested that the proper role of diagnostic personnel in short supply is to increase the competence and confidence of teachers to deal with the variety of needs of their students. The product of the assessment of children with learning problems must be data that may be used for educational planning. The very process of such assessment must be such that the teacher not only participates in the planning but also begins to own the technology of planning itself. The role of the special educator may be redefined as well as specified as a teacher consultant.

REFERENCES

Bijou, S.W., Baer, D.M.: Contributions from a functional analysis. In L.P. Lipsett, C.C. Spiker (Eds.): Advances in Child Development, Vol. 1. New York: Academic Press, 1963, pp. 197-231.

Bijou, S.W., Peterson, R.F.: Psychological assessment in children: A functional analysis. In P. McReynolds (Ed.): Advances in Psychological Assessment, Vol. 2. Palo Alto, Calif.: Science and Behavior Books, 1971.

Deno, E.: Educational aspects of minimal brain dysfunction. In Proceedings of the 6th Delaware Conference on the Handicapped Child. Wilmington, De.: Alfred I. Dupont Institute, 1968.

Gawlick, R., McAleer, M., Ozer, M.N.: Language for adaptive interaction. American Annals of the Deaf, 1976, 121, 556-559.

Gillespie, P.H., Miller, T.C., Fielder, V.D.: Legislative definitions of learning disabilities: A roadblock to effective service. Journal of Learning Disabilities, 1975, 8, 660-666.

Ozer, M.N.: Enhancing the family as a planning unit. Cybernetics Forum, 1975, 7, 17-19. (a)

Ozer, M.N.: Introduction to the Collaborative Service System. Washington, D.C.: Program for Learning Studies, 1975. (b)

Ozer, M.N.: Health Concerns: Diagnostic Issues. White House Conference on Handicapped Individuals. U.S. Department of Health, Education, and Welfare, Office of Human Development, 1976, 35-43.

Ozer, M.N., Dworkin, N.E.: The assessment of children with learning problems: An inservice teacher training program. Journal of Learning Disabilities, 1974, 7, 539-544.

Ozer, M.N., Richardson, H.B.: The diagnostic evaluation of children with learning problems: A "process" approach. Journal of Learning Disabilities, 1974, 7, 88-92.

Diagnosing Difficulties in Learning Basic Math Facts

William P. Dunlap, PhD, and Charles S. Thompson, PhD

Though most learning disabilities appear to concern reading, many children possess difficulties in mastering the basic math facts. The authors describe a specific procedure which they have found useful in teaching children with arithmetic disabilities. While no supporting data regarding the effectiveness of this procedure are available, the method is described in sufficient detail so that interested practitioners can experiment with it. Comments from our readers on the utility of the procedure and on this type of article in general would be appreciated by the editorial staff of the Journal. — G.M.S.

A procedure, employing a tachistoscope, is presented to enable teachers to identify the nature of arithmetic difficulties. Record-keeping procedures are detailed which allow teachers to measure a child's understanding and ability to compute basic facts. Computational methods used by the child are readily revealed, suggesting means of remediative activities.

Mastering the basic facts is a major goal of both modern and traditional arithmetic curricula. When children have memorized the facts, they possess the prerequisite skills to master the multi-digit computational algorithms. In designing and using activities which will facilitate the understanding and memorization of basic facts, teachers face several questions.

(1) When do I change Johnny from instructional activities to activities which emphasize the memorization of basic facts?

(2) Does Johnny know a method(s) for determining answers to basic facts?

(3) If he does, what method does he prefer to use for computing answers to basic facts?

Reprinted by special permission of Professional Press, Inc. from the *Journal of Learning Disabilities*, 1977, Vol. 10, No. 9, pp. 585-589. ©1977, Professional Press, Inc.

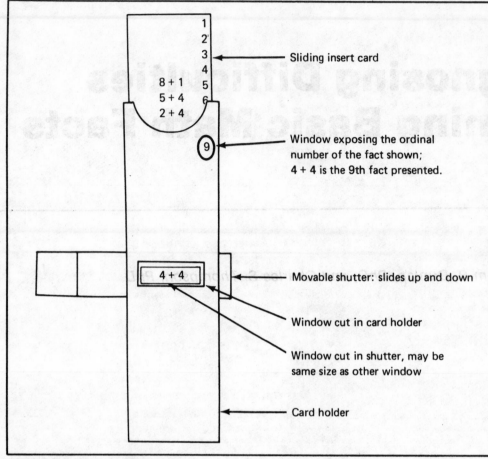

1
2
3 ← Sliding insert card
4
5
6

8 + 1
5 + 4
2 + 4

9 ← Window exposing the ordinal number of the fact shown; 4 + 4 is the 9th fact presented.

4 + 4 ← Movable shutter: slides up and down

← Window cut in card holder

← Window cut in shutter, may be same size as other window

← Card holder

FIGURE 1. Tachistoscope.

(4) Does Johnny still need to use manipulative aids, pictures, or symbols to compute the basic facts?

(5) Does Johnny have immediate recall of the basic facts? If not, which ones does he need to memorize?

DESCRIPTION OF THE TEST

While working with children who have been referred to the Learning Improvement Center, School of Education, University of Louisville, we have developed a procedure which enables us to answer these questions and to obtain other important information regarding a child's knowledge of the basic facts. The basic idea for this procedure has been used by teachers and diagnosticians in reading for several years, and we have modified and adapted it for use in teaching arithmetic.

A tachistoscope (see Fig. 1) is used to present the basic facts. It is easily constructed from a manila folder or other semi-rigid paper. The tachistoscope flashes each basic fact for ½ second, and the child must respond within 5 seconds. The child's response to the basic fact is recorded on paper containing two columns and a space for observations. One column is labeled "flash" and the other "analysis." If the response is correct, a plus sign is recorded in the flash column beside the basic fact and the next basic fact is flashed.

When the answer is incorrect, a minus sign is recorded in the flash column beside the basic fact. Then the shutter is opened and left open to expose the basic fact for "analysis;" during this time the child may resort to any method he knows to determine an answer to the basic fact. For example, he may choose to use manipulative aids (poker chips, tongue depressors, blocks), pictures (3 + 4 might be illustrated as III and IIII, or XXX and XXXX) or symbols (3 × 4 = 4 + 4 + 4) to obtain an answer. For this portion of the test the examiner completes two tasks. One task is to record in the analysis column whether the answer is correct or not. The second task is to record the methods and materials which the child used to compute the answer. This information becomes valuable later for diagnosing the child's learning difficulties.

When a basic fact is flashed via the tachistoscope, the child does not have time to apply analytical skills or methods. He must be able to recognize the basic fact and automatically and immediately give the correct response. The basic fact must be committed to memory so thoroughly that only a brief exposure evokes the correct response. In effect, the test measures the child's memory of the basic facts.

The second portion of the procedure, in which the shutter is left open, gives a measure of the child's understanding of the operation, of the basic fact, and of his ability to apply analytical skills to obtain an answer. It, moreover, indicates the representational or abstraction level at which the child is operating. A child using manipulative

---

TABLE I. Comparison of performance on the flash and analysis sections for four children.

Child	Performance Level	
	Flash	Analysis
Ann	High	High
Bill	High	Low
Chuck	Low	High
Diane	Low	Low

---

aids to solve basic facts problems is operating on a different level from the child who uses pictures or symbols to solve them.

ANALYSIS OF TEST RESULTS

A comparison of results of the two sections of the test gives some valuable and helpful hypotheses in formulating instructional activities for children. For example, consider the comparisons of the performances on the flash and analysis sections for four children (see Table I).

The most desirable situation is shown for Ann. Ann has not only memorized the basic facts but also possesses the analytical skills necessary to determine answers to any basic facts when she forgets them. This child does not need any particular instructional activities other than ones to reinforce the skills she possesses already.

Bill has a good memory of the basic facts, but he does not possess the analytical skills which are necessary when he forgets answers to basic facts. This situation is indicative of a child who has memorized the basic facts without understanding the operation. Children who exhibit this performance need instructional activities involving manipulative aids and pictures to develop understanding, skills, and methods for computing answers to basic facts.

Chuck seems to have developed the analytical skills but has not memorized the basic facts. He may be relying on manipulative aids or pictures instead of making the transition to symbolic processes and the memorization of basic facts. In this situation, the child needs to participate in instructional activities which emphasize the memorization of basic facts or the rate of response, such as timed tests, flash cards, and games.

Diane's responses represent the least desirable situation and the most difficult to correct, since she needs both developmental and drill activities. First, manipulative aids and pictures should be utilized to develop understanding and analysis skills for computing answers to the basic facts. After successfully completing this instructional phase, the child should engage in drill activities to facilitate

2. DIAGNOSIS

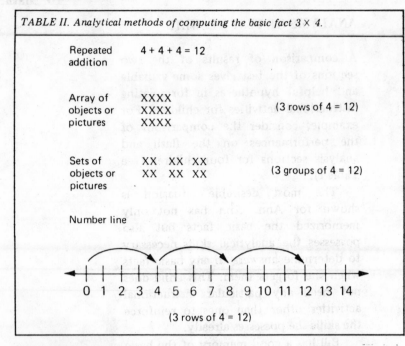

TABLE II. Analytical methods of computing the basic fact 3 × 4.

Repeated addition	4 + 4 + 4 = 12
Array of objects or pictures	XXXX XXXX XXXX (3 rows of 4 = 12)
Sets of objects or pictures	XX XX XX XX XX XX (3 groups of 4 = 12)
Number line	(3 rows of 4 = 12)

memorization and also to increase the rate of response.

In addition to comparing overall results from the flash and analysis sections, an examiner can gain valuable information from the observations he recorded during the analysis portion of the test. For instance, to compute the answer to the basic fact, 3 × 4, a child may use any one of several methods or analytical skills (see Table II).

Since the child will choose the method he feels more secure with, it is reasonable to use this method to teach this fact as well as other multiplication facts. This method could also be used to teach other multiplication facts and other aspects of multiplication, such as commutative, associative, or distributive properties.

Afterwards, the test administrator can examine the basic facts which were answered incorrectly on each of the sections — flash and analysis. A child may not know certain groups of facts such as addition facts whose sums are greater than nine, subtraction facts whose minuends are greater than nine, multiplication facts for zero, and division facts of a number divided by itself. With this information, instructional activities can be devised that will emphasize a particular group of facts which has not been memorized, instead

of studying all of the facts in order to learn just a few.

In other situations, the facts which were missed may be indicative of the child's difficulties with another mathematical skills. For instance, if a child constantly misses exercises similar to 6 × 9 and 9 × 6, then this may indicate that he does not know the commutative property of multiplication. By learning the cummutative property, the child could simplify the mastery of these facts. The inability to compute subtraction facts whose minuends are greater than nine may indicate that the child does not know the concept of place value or regrouping. If the child were to study and master these skills, then the process of mastering the subtraction facts could be simplified and shortened.

CONCLUSION

This simple, short diagnostic procedure on the basic facts can yield valuable information. The teacher does not need sophisticated equipment or diagnostic training. The equipment can readily be constructed and implemented. Yet with this procedure, the teacher can discover the extent of a child's memorization of the basic facts as well as specific information about the child's understanding.— *School of Education, University of Louisville, Louisville, Kentucky 40208.*

REVIEW: CHILDREN WITH READING DIFFICULTIES

GERTRUDE H. KEIR Department of Psychology, University College, Gower Street, London WCIE 6BT

Reading is an important skill. It enters into the learning of most subjects in school: it is a leisure time occupation and it frequently determines the kinds of jobs open to the school leaver. Moreover, failure to acquire good reading attainment is often associated with emotional disturbances and social maladjustment. It is not an accident that many children referred for child guidance treatment are poor achievers, notably in reading, while the adult illiterate, though often lacking other academic skills, is usually acutely sensitive over his failure to learn to read.

For these, and other reasons, both teachers and parents experience anxiety when a child falls behind the reading standards of children of his own chronological age and is therefore a backward reader. Teachers may feel that they have failed to teach one of the most important skills in the curriculum, while parents often feel it to be, in some vague and ill-defined way, a reflection on themselves. It is then no wonder that problems connected with failure in learning to read have generated an enormous interest, not only in teachers and parents but in educationists, social workers and doctors, whose advice may have been sought, as well as in the public at large. This interest has been reinforced by continual exposure to the problem through the mass media, the press, television and radio.

Parents of that class of poor reader described as having dyslexia have formed themselves into the British Dyslexia Association consisting of more than twenty contributing societies.* We have seen the publication of Government documents, for instance the Tizard Report (1972) on children with specific reading difficulties, as well as reports on research carried out in educational and other institutions on a wide variety of subjects in the general field of reading. A very recent example of this

2. DIAGNOSIS

is the Schools Council Research Project—Children's Reading Interests (1974) undertaken at the University of Sheffield Institute of Education. The literature devoted to reading development and failure has been almost overwhelming in quantity. As far back as 1935 a bibliography of well over a thousand titles appeared in the United States. The survey of Gray (1956) into literacy skills in a world context instigated research in many countries. Associations connected with reading, such as The International Reading Association and the United Kingdom Reading Association publish their own journals. In-service training courses for teachers, workshops and conferences have been run for many years by Local Education Authorities, the Department of Education and Science and similar bodies.

It will be clear, then, that reading is not a newly discovered area of failure, either in the identification of the main problems, in the assessment of poor readers or in attempts to find methods of successful treatment. Most Local Education Authorities have remedial reading services, whether in ordinary schools or in special classes or centres, while most child guidance clinics offer some form of remedial therapy, carried out for the most part by educational psychologists. Indeed, the study of reading forms parts of the syllabus, both theoretical and practical, in most training courses for educational psychologists. It is nearly thirty years since the writer, appointed to the training course set up at University College, took such students into schools where the work was weighted towards the diagnosis and treatment of reading failure of children of all ages and types.

In all this activity certain questions continually call for answers derived from accumulating knowledge and expertise. What do we mean by difficulty in reading? What do we know about conditions in the home or school environment which contribute to it? What characteristics of the child lead to failure in learning? What can be done about this? What methods of teaching are most suitable for remedial work? These questions are simple to put, but difficult to answer. This is partly because knowledge about reading and its difficulties comes from the study of children in many different settings: for instance, in primary and secondary schools, both for normal and for educationally subnormal children, in groups already singled out for special treatment e.g. tutorial and remedial groups, reading clinics, child guidance clinics, departments of psychology in hospitals—to mention the most common. The selection of children for such treatment in all of these may vary considerably and the study of their attainments, their personal characteristics and learning capacities may yield differing results. There are many other reasons for discrepancies in research results. The general design of the research may contribute. For instance, one can select for study children already ascertained as differing in reading attainment and compare them in respect of home environment, school placement and experience, and personal characteristics such as attitudes to reading, to school and teachers, to peers, their level of intelligence, reasoning, verbal ability, memory, sensory and perceptual functioning, general emotional and social adjustment and so on. The aim is then to compare groups, readers of different levels—good, average, poor— in order to find out what other variables are most significantly related with their reading progress. Or we can start from another angle: children from defined kinds of home or school environments, children of good *vs* poor intelligence, the socially adjusted *vs* the maladjusted and so on, and compare the types of reading progress made by these groups. So the research design itself creates problems. These have been well discussed by Applebee (1971).

Conflicting results also bedevil the issues connected with the most effective methods of teaching reading, whether this is to normal readers or failures. Those who seek a detailed study of this area will find it in Chall (1967) or in the International Reading Association Report, in which the efficacy of nine modern approaches to the teaching of reading was discussed (Vilschek 1968). A brief appraisal of the problem will be found in Keir (1974). In view of these comments, then, we should not expect to find unanimity in results or in their interpretation and therefore no unequivocal answers can yet be given to the questions posed above. In returning to them only a selection of facts and the issues raised can be given here.

What do we mean by difficulty in learning to read? Reading is a developmental skill, it improves with the age and increasing maturation of the child, as well as with training and experience, that is, reading sophistication. There are also degrees of reading failure, differing in severity in terms of comparison between the chronological age of the child and the age at which he functions in reading—whether he is reading at the level of children younger than himself and how much younger these are. A child of six may have hardly made a beginning in reading, but this is quite a different matter from a child of, for example, nine or ten who is reading at the level of a very beginner. This is fairly self-evident. A comparison can also be made between the general intellectual level of the child and his reading level. We know that intelligence counts towards success in most learning and we tend to expect good performance in most areas from bright children. Such a child may be only average or below in reading, while excelling in other subjects. We can then say that his standard is somewhat below what we could expect from him, that is, he is retarded, though not backward for his chronological age.

A more usual example would be the child within the average range of intelligence whose reading age is below the average for the class (that is, he is backward) and who is also reading well below that expected for someone of his intellectual capacity (i.e. he is retarded). The same distinction can be made with children of limited ability: some learn slowly but surely, while others lag behind what they are capable of achieving. Of course intelligence is by no means the only thing that enters into learning, and the distinction between retardation and backwardness is not always a useful one to make. Sometimes these terms are used interchangeably, which adds to the confusion. However, it is always important in the case of a poor reader to assess his intelligence along with other characteristics. The rate of learning and the kind of reading goals he might achieve are related to his intelligence and reasoning as well as to his attitudes and interest.

The kinds of reading skill we have in mind when judging the progress of a child alter with his level of maturation and length of training. At the beginning children learn simple skills of recognizing letters, single and digraphs, and their place in words: the function of words in sentences, the association between words seen, heard and spoken. This is true no matter the method or the order in which these are

2. DIAGNOSIS

taught. Failure at this stage may simply mean that the child does not understand the nature of the task, as Reid (1966) pointed out in her study of young learners. Many children having difficulty at this stage make progress once they do get the hang of the thing. During the primary school period some of the psychological processes on which the development of reading skill depends continue to mature. For instance memory and attention span increase, so the child is able to take in and retain longer sequences of printed material. The development of intelligence and capacity to reason and solve problems, the ability to classify and so recognize exceptions to rules increases his skills of recognition and comprehension. Longer practice increases speed, which in turn also helps comprehension, for a slow reader may have forgotten the beginning of a sequence of thought by the time he has struggled through to the end. So the criteria for competent reading now include speed or fluency of reading, power of recognition or attack on unfamiliar words at a more difficult level, and increasing understanding of sentences and paragraphs graded in length and difficulty.

The usual way of judging progress is by comparing a child's progress through a set of basal readers with that of the other children in the class. However, teachers' standards of acceptable reading do differ, so this easy method does raise problems. Some teachers like to use an inventory, either in published form or one of their own devising, which will indicate the child's errors, his level of phonic skills, his word attack, power of punctuation, level of independent reading, his enjoyment and interest in the task and so on.

But the most usual practice is the use of standardized tests of reading, individual or group. Such tests assess skills such as word recognition, word attack, understanding of sentences and paragraphs. The most usual scores are on accuracy, rate of reading and some form of comprehension skills. For the seriously backward who need a remedial programme, further diagnostic tests will provide more detailed information than the standard attainment test is able to do. These will pinpoint in detail weaknesses in phonic knowledge, types of common errors made in the reading of words—omission of letters, substitution of letters and so on.

Even with skilled remedial help in schools, however, some children still fail to make progress, and we have to ask the question—what is holding them back? Why did they not learn in the first place, and why can they now not use the special help given them? It is here that we have to take a second look at the child, a close and detailed look. It is no use devising a remedial programme to deal with errors and fill in gaps if to this the learner brings faulty habits of attention, poor attitudes to reading, to the school and to the teacher and inadequate feelings—lack of self-confidence, fear of failure and the like. It is time, then, that we turned to the child, and asked the question, what sort of children fail in reading?

We can expect to find at least three boys for every girl. Various reasons have been put forward to account for this, some rather doubtful, others more firmly supported by evidence. Those interested in these, and other, gender differences will find a useful summary in Hutt (1972), a full treatment is contained in Ounsted & Taylor (1972).* If

* Recent important articles are Fairweather (1976) and Thompson (1975).

we consider differences which could be connected with early learning we can select three which seem to be relevant. It has been suggested that girls (a) develop verbal skills earlier than boys; (b) prefer the more sedentary types of activity; and (c) are more adaptable, conforming and socially minded.

a Girls use speech earlier than boys and both their vocabulary and sentence structure develop sooner. Thus, the Reynell Developmental Language Scales (1969) give separate scores for girls on both verbal comprehension and expressive scales up to the age of four years, girls being about a month ahead, quite a big difference in early development. Verbal fluency in later childhood continues to be superior, according to Garai & Scheinfeld (1968). The differences in these verbal skills may be due to differences in early handling by the mother, a study by Moss (1967) indicating that mothers tend to imitate the vocalizations of their daughters more than those of their sons. Attention to auditory stimuli seems to occur oftener in girls than boys. These facts, if valid, may have relevance for the early teaching of reading, linked as it is by the teacher with speech and conversation.

b There is no doubt that boys prefer physically active pursuits, while girls go for quieter, more sedentary ones, of which reading could be one. The Sheffield Study (1974) shows that girls not only read better but read more, whatever the level of attainment.

c The identification of the girl with the mother and the feminine role may well lead to the conforming behaviour which marks girls in school and may contribute to easier acceptance of teaching by women teachers in infant schools.

A second thing we notice about backward readers, whether in the ordinary school, or in special classes and so on is the large number of summer-born children. This means or has meant a shorter time in the infant school, since entry is later in the year. A review of the facts and issues raised will be found in Choppin (1969). The effects of this on attainment in the infant school are discussed by Barker Lunn (1972) while Thompson (1971) notes that the effects are still present during the secondary stage of education, taking the view that these may be due not only to the length of schooling but also the effects of school organization.

There are many other features connected with the child's schooling which are of importance. For instance the nature of his first school experience, where he first learns simple skills with other children, all sharing the attentions of only one or two adults and experiencing what may be the first separation from the mother. The child's reactions to this may well be forerunners of later school failure. Absence from school, frequent change of schools or of teachers may lead to gaps in his education or to confusion brought about by different methods of teaching. While these are important in a number of children they diminish in importance when we consider the relation of learning competence to the interest, motivation and the learning attitudes of the child, in turn related to the value placed on reading in the school.

It is obviously impossible to consider all the attributes of the child which may be closely linked to the kind of home atmosphere in which he is brought up, and which are of importance in learning.

Important contributions on many of these will be found in the publication edited by Reid (1972) which consists of reprints, edited

2. DIAGNOSIS

versions of already published work, as well as some new contributions.

Vernon (1971) is worth consulting over details of studies carried out in a wide range of topics. In addition to material presented by Vernon (1957) it contains a critical exposition of research results published since that time.

In what follows, we can consider only three selected issues relevant to the question--what sort of children have difficulty in reading, and what features in their environment relate to this: the cultural/educational background, the interest taken by the parents in the child's progress at school, and the general nature of family interactions.

1 Interest in the first of these has been stimulated by work on disadvantaged families and the language problems of immigrants. The latter has led to language development programmes, special courses of training for teachers, and special classes in schools with high immigrant populations. This kind of study has merged with work being carried out on social class, language and reading. It is generally agreed that lack of communicative opportunities in the home, such as type of parent–child verbal interaction, books and so on, lead to inadequate development of the child's vocabulary and syntactical skill. A recent study by Francis (1974) on the language skills of children from different social backgrounds and their relevance to reading in its early stages has shown that differences exist between differing social groups both in vocabulary scores and levels of speech skills.

There were, however, wide differences within each group. Francis concluded that the vocabulary of school entrants from disadvantaged homes was adequate to start reading. During the second year of schooling, however, the advantaged children forged ahead. She considered this to relate in part to the amount of reading children did at home, and the lack of reading material in disadvantaged homes, while pointing out that many of the latter children were making very good progress in reading.

2 Interest taken by parents, particularly the mother, in school and in school progress, has been repeatedly shown to contribute to the achievement of the child. However, there are problems here connected with the assessment of interest. External criteria such as number of visits to the school, hearing the child read at home, both involving direct parental contact with teacher and child, may indicate anxiety rather than affectionate attachment and interest. The parent who does neither can be accused of neglect, but this is not necessarily so. There are neglectful parents who take no interest in school or the child's progress, who provide no backing in the home for the development of education through leisure pursuits, who may even have a hostility to schooling. These attitudes are soon reflected in the child's lack of concern about reading or hostility to schools. On the other hand, there are the over-anxious parents who start to worry if their child cannot read at 5 or 6 years and will start asking what is wrong. They are likely to predominate in problems of slow learning in middle class children whose parents, often professional, have academic expectations. Such anxiety may be firmly resisted by the child, whose best weapon is refusal to learn to read. The writer has met this situation fairly frequently, in the small informal clinic for learning difficulties in children and adults which operates at University College, a legacy from the late Sir Cyril Burt. Parental expectations and attitudes to academic success need

not be expressed verbally for the child to recognize them and react in some way.

3 The above comments could be equally well included in family interactions, which covers very many other situations: the dependent child whose parents may continue the practice of reading aloud at bed-time without encouraging some active participation from the child: the child threatened by the presence of a younger sibling and clinging to the rewards of babyhood. The rewards of poor reading can be important and should always be kept in mind when assessing the extent and duration of the problem.

For instance, one adult (diagnosed as dyslexic before referral to University College) disclosed the fact that the only one of her family who cared about her had been her grandfather and he always read to her at night. She was nearly nine before she began to read. This item of information was not revealed until remedial work was well under way. Aspects of the home situation, such as inconsistent discipline, marital discord, separation and like have long been recognized as leading to maladjustment in the children. This may result in poor attention and affect level of concentration, degree of day-dreaming, persistence, motivation and the like, so that learning may be severely handicapped. The relation between maladjustment and reading has long claimed attention. It is discussed in Reid (1972) and a useful summary of the main facts will be found in Sampson (1966). It is difficult to estimate the precise effects of the home, for the poor reader who is maladjusted will almost certainly have this reinforced by the experiences of failure. Indeed, failure in reading arising from different causes, such as absence, unsuitable teaching, early entry to school, poor intelligence will almost certainly set up some mild degree of maladjustment. Such cases have been well documented in studies which extend back thirty years or more; Keir (1959) using case studies, has described such family inter-actions, while Caspari (1974) presents the main features of a method of treatment derived from Freudian principles of development and behaviour. It is time to enquire whether there exists a group of back-ward readers who can be described as having dyslexia. Those inter-ested in this issue should consult a recent review and discussion by Reid (1969) reprinted in Reid (1972) while Vernon (1971) also devotes a section to it. It is a matter on which opinions are sharply divided, con-victions strong and tempers often irascible. The term was first used by members of the medical profession to whom were referred from time to time children whose reading performance was low or lower than expected in view of their intelligence and achievement in other subjects. Such consultants may have had experience of adults with pathological disturbances of some aspect of language. Those who had were not slow in pointing out similarities in types of errors made in reading in certain cases of these adults and children whose reading performance was poor. For instance, it was in connection with children sent to him for ophthalmological examination as part of an investigation into reading backwardness that Hinshelwood, in his publications of 1902 and 1917 developed the notion that reading disability in children was due to a localized defect in that area of the cortex commonly associated with speech. Sir Henry Head also discussed dyslexia in connection with his work on aphasia and kindred disorders. To this day most of the pro-tagonists of the theory that specific reading disability is connected with

2. DIAGNOSIS

some kind of physical nexus are medically oriented in their approach to the problem. Keeney (1968) suggested five basic forms: (1) specific developmental; (2) secondary as a result of organic pathology, slow maturation, emotional disturbances, uncontrolled seizure states or environmental disturbances; (3) slow readers (bradylexia) as a result of sensory and other handicaps without symbolic confusion; (4) acquired as a result of brain lesions, and (5) mixed forms. It is this ragbag which Spreen (1970) appears to accept in his contribution to Bakker's recent publication. At any rate it is printed without comment.

Developmental dyslexia is the type to which the book is devoted and the hypotheses for which are discussed in the second chapter by Satz and Sparrow. The focus is on 'those children who fail to acquire normal reading proficiency, despite conventional instruction, sociocultural opportunity, average intelligence, and freedom from gross sensory, emotional or neurological handicap'. This is definition by exclusion. It is also a definition not accepted by certain workers in the field, for instance Geschwind (1962) who has advanced the theory that a bilateral maldevelopment of their angular gyrus region might be a plausible explanation of maturational lag leading to reading failure. Other workers would include emotional disturbance of some description. At first great attention was paid to the kinds of errors made in reading (or spelling or writing, for some definitions included these in different combinations) reversals of letters and transpositions of letters in words being singled out for special attention. Increasing knowledge has brought realization that errors may not present any consistent pattern; and that they occur so frequently among young children learning to read, that it is impossible to use them to identify the presence of dyslexia.

Opportunity of instruction of the conventional type still finds favour, but suitable opportunity must be matched by a suitable will to learn, and learning attitudes are barely considered. Neither is the notion that what is suitable for one child may not be suitable for another. For instance a child with poor auditory memory will find it hard to profit by phonic teaching.

Hostility to teaching, present in many seriously backward readers may have to be reckoned with (Keir 1964) but it is seldom mentioned in discussing 'conventional type of instruction'.

However, there are a number of people who need this notion of specific dyslexia, with or without interest in any special etiology, and who would not agree that its acceptance can do no harm to parents, teachers and the child (e.g. the latter can be burdened by a sense of suffering from something strange, a life long condition, for which little can be done).

Finally, if dyslexia is associated with a developmental lag the latter should surely mature as the child makes progress in reading. That dyslexics do make good progress is indisputable. That there are differences in the speed with which they make it is also indisputable. But what about maturational lag? There must be degrees of this—a complicated thing.

We are now face to face with treatment. It is not only in the most serious cases—the writer would suggest that these can be assessed in terms of generalization of behavioural disturbances to reading, and vice versa—that the investigation should be linked with the treatment.

The weaknesses and strengths in psychological processes of learning, once discovered, should be closely woven into the projected pattern of remediation. This latter may take the form of play therapy in some cases, with or without instruction in reading techniques. Of the processes, intelligence, memory, perception, attention, persistence and the like none is more important than attitude and motivation. Anxieties and conflicts can impede learning, even in school children whose behaviour does not give rise to outward behavioural signs. Assessment in such cases ought to include a projective type test, the Make a Picture Story being favoured by the writer. This will often reveal what ordinary conversation will not, for the child may not be conscious of his attitudes, or be unwilling to reveal them. Results of these and other tests can enable the examiner to map the inner self of the child so that obstacles to the learning attitude may be dealt with. Reading skills must be taught, techniques for teaching must be adapted to cognitive and other processes; but providing practice in participating in active learning because he wants to and ensuring the rewards of success through a programme of help, tailored to suit his needs, will ensure that even the most backward learner will progress. If he does not, the remedial teacher and the psychologist must look to their own skills and understanding.

REFERENCES

Applebee A.N. (1971) Research in reading retardation: two critical problems. *Journal of Child Psychology and Psychiatry* **12**, 91–113

Barker Lunn J. (1972) Length of infant schooling and academic performance. *Educational Research* **14**, 120–127

Caspari I. (1974) Educational therapy. In *Psychotherapy Today*, ed. Ved Varma, pp. 215–232. Constable, London

Chall J. (1967) *Learning to Read: the Great Debate* McGraw Hill, New York

Choppin B.H. (1969) The relationship between achievement and age. *Educational Research* **12**, 22–29

Fairweather H.(1976) Sex difference in cognition. *Cognition* **4**, 231–280

Francis H. (1974) Social background, speech and learning to read. *British Journal of Educational Psychology* **44**, 290–299

Garai J.E. & Scheinfeld A. (1968) Sex differences in mental and behavioural traits. *Genetic Psychology Monograph* **77**, 169–299

Geschwind N. (1962) The anatomy of acquired disorders of reading. In *Reading Disability: Progress and Research Needs in Dyslexia*. ed. J. Money and J. Maltimore, pp. 115–129. Johns Hopkins Press.

Gray W.S. (1956) *The Teaching of Reading and Writing–an International Survey*, UNESCO, Evans, London

Hutt C. (1972) Sex differences in human development. *Human Development* **15**, 153–170

Keeney A.H. (1968) Comprehensive classification of the dyslexia. In *Dyslexia, Diagnosis and Treatment of Reading Disorders*, eds. A. H. Keeney and V. T. Keeney, pp. 174–175. Mosby, St. Louis

Keir G.H. (1959) Behaviour difficulties in slow learning children at a remedial clinic. The slow learning child. *Australian Journal on the Education of Backward Children* **5**, 138–149

Keir G.H. (1964) Teaching reading to older backward readers. *First International Reading Symposium*, ed. J. Downing, pp. 183–200. Cassell, London

Keir G.H. (1974) The teaching of reading–which method? *London Education Review* **3**, 59–66

Moss H. (1967) Sex, age and state as determinants of mother–infant interaction. *Merrill-Palmer Quarterly* **13**, 19–36

Ounsted C. & Taylor D.C. (1972) *Gender Differences–Their Ontogeny and Significance*. Churchill, London

2. DIAGNOSIS

Reid J.F. (1966) Learning to think about reading. Research Note. *Educational Research* **9**, 56–62

Reid J.F. (1969) Dyslexia: a problem of communication. *Educational Research* **10**, 126–133

Reid J.F. (Ed.) (1972) *Reading Problems and Practices.* Wark Lock Educational, London

Reynell J. (1969) *The Reynell Developmental Language Scales.* National Foundation for Educational Research, Windsor

Sampson O.C. (1966) Reading and adjustment: a review of the literature. *Educational Research* **8**, 184–190

Spreen O. (1970) Postscript: review and outlook. In *Specific Reading Disability*, eds. D. J. Baker and S. Satz, pp. 1–15. Rotterdam University Press, Rotterdam

Thompson D. (1971) Season of birth and success in secondary school. *Educational Research* **14**, 56–60

Thompson G.B. (1975) Sex differences in reading attainments. *Educational Research* **18**, 16–23

Tizard Report on Children with Specific Reading Difficulties (1972) Advisory Committee on Handicapped Children. HMSO, London

Vernon M.D. (1957) *Backwardness in Reading.* Cambridge University Press, London

Vernon M.D. (1971) *Reading and its Difficulties.* Cambridge University Press, London

Vilschek E.C. (Ed.) (1968) *A Decade of Innovations: Approaches to Beginning Reading.* International Reading Association, Newark, Delaware

Whitehead F., Copey A.C. A.W. & Maddren W. (1974) *Children's Reading Interests,* Schools Council Working Paper 52, University of Sheffield, Institute of Education. Evans/Metheun Educational, London

Some Typical Academic Problems of Learning Disabled Children

Some Typical Reading Problems

1. Confuses b and d, reads bog for dog and often confuses b,d,p,q.

2. Confuses the order of letters in words—reads was for saw.

3. Doesn't look carefully at the details in a word, guesses from the first letter: reads farm for front.

4. Loses his place on a page when reading, sometimes in the middle of a line or at the end of the line.

5. Can't remember common words taught from one day to the next; knows them one day not the next. Most frequently forgets abstract words: us, were, says.

6. If he doesn't know a word, he has no systematic way to figure it out. Guesses or says "I don't know."

7. Reads without expression and ignores punctuation. The mechanics of reading are so hard for him that he has no awareness of the ideas expressed by the written symbols.

8. Reads very slowly, and reading tires the child greatly.

9. Omits words or adds words to a sentence, attempting to make meaning out of the symbols he has trouble decoding.

10. Reads word by word, struggling with almost each one of them.

Some Typical Language Problems

1. Cannot state something in an organized, cogent way. Tends to muddle, starts in middle of an idea. Cannot organize words properly into a question.

2. Has trouble following directions, particularly long sequences of them.

3. Doesn't enjoy being read to. But does like looking at pictures in book.

4. Becomes distracted in class when instruction is presented orally. Learns from watching, not listening.

5. Very literal. Misses inferences, subtleties, nuances, innuendoes.

6. Poor sense of humor, doesn't understand jokes, puns, sarcasm.

7. Trouble with abstract words. Defines words by their concrete attributes or function.

8. Rigidity of word meanings, can't deal with multiple meaning.

9. Can't tell a story in sequence or summarize, can only recount isolated and highly detailed facts about an experience.

10. Forgets names of things that he knows, has to describe them (word-finding problem). Later, when not under pressure, will recall the word he wanted to say.

Some Typical Spelling Problems

1. Writes b for d and vice versa.

2. Transposes the order of letters, spells was, s-a-w or the, h-t-e.

"Some Typical Academic Problems of Learning Disabled Children," Sally L. Smith, *No Easy Answers--The Learning Disabled child*, Department of Health, Education and Welfare, 1978.

3. Doesn't hear the sequence of sounds in a word and writes isolated parts of it; writes amil for animal.

4. Has no memory for common words that are not regularly spelled. May try to spell them phonetically, writes sez for says.

5. Does not hear fine differences in words, writes pin for pen.

6. Has trouble with consonants, writes wif for with.

7. Often disguises poor spelling ability with consciously messy handwriting.

8. In sentence writing, uses no capitals and no punctuation.

9. Leaves words out of sentences, can't express himself in complete written sentences.

10. Avoids writing whenever possible, at nearly any expense, because it is so difficult and so demanding.

Some Typical Handwriting Problems

1. Holds pencil awkwardly, too tightly, inefficiently. Gets easily tired by writing.

2. Can't write without lined paper. Spacing is poor. Leaves no space between words. Leaves no margins.

3. Writes letters backwards.

4. Mixes lower case letters with capitals. Memory for the forms of letters is poor, so he uses whichever form he can remember.

5. Letters are written above and below the line. No size consistency.

6. Writes in very large hand, can't control pencil enough to write small.

7. Holds pencil too tightly and writes very small. Can't relax hand and pencil. Also hides poor spelling.

8. Process of writing is incredibly slow. Takes 5 minutes to write a sentence. Perfectionistic tendencies—each letter must be perfectly formed.

9. Can't remember how to form letters, uses his own way. Draws letters inefficiently.

10. Erases often and writes over the same letter several times.

Some Typical Arithmetic Problems

1. Counts on his fingers.

2. Cannot commit multiplication facts to memory.

3. Reverses two place numbers—13 becomes 31. Also reverses 5 to Ƨ, etc.

4. Doesn't understand place value.

5. May solve addition and even multiplication problems by counting on fingers, but cannot subtract, which is the reverse operation.

6. Subtracts smaller number in a column from larger number. In the problem $25-7$, he subtracts the 5 from the 7 simply because the 5 is smaller, not seeing the 5 as representing 15, thus he arrives at the answer $25-7=22$.

7. Often understands concepts but can't do it in written symbolic form with paper and pencil.

8. On the other hand, sometimes a child can do rote arithmetic on paper, but it has no meaning and he can't solve problems in daily life, such as making change for a dollar.

9. Can't remember sequence of steps to multiply or divide, has trouble switching from one process to another, such as dividing and subtracting in long division.

10. Solves problems left to right instead of right to left.

Some Typical Thinking Problems

1. Has a hard time sticking to the main point, brings up irrelevant, extraneous points.

2. Doesn't grasp cause-effect relationships. Rarely uses the word "because." Doesn't anticipate and evaluate.

3. Rigidity of thought. A word can have only one meaning. Or knows $5 + 7 = 12$ but can't answer $12 = 5 + ?$. Or knows $8 \times 7 = 56$ but can't reverse gears and solve $56 \div 8 = ?$.

4. Has trouble seeing similarities and differences. Has trouble understanding relationships.

5. Doesn't see patterns. All words have to be memorized as he can't see spelling patterns; all mulitplication facts have to be memorized one by one (that's why he gives up) instead of seeing patterns that simplify the task. He doesn't group ideas together to form patterns of thought.

6. Poor memory. Can't remember names of people or places. Also trouble with faces. Reasoning often gets sidetracked because of poor memory.

7. Doesn't organize the facts and concepts he does have and thus can't mobilize them to solve problems, to predict or foresee consequences.

8. Can't categorize or classify. Each experience is an isolated event. Doesn't summarize. Can't generalize from the concrete to the abstract.

9. Doesn't transfer learning from one lesson to another. Has to relearn each concept from scratch.

10. Understands concepts too narrowly or too broadly. All 4-legged animals are dogs. Only black and white cats (like his own cat) are cats. Or he may call all cats Puff, the name of his own cat.

Some Typical School Problems

1. Erratic. Inconsistent. Unpredictable. Appears to be lazy. Good days, off days. Forgets what was learned yesterday. But without reteaching, he may remember it 2 days hence.

2. Poor attention span—no sustained focus.

3. Works very slowly—never finishes work in allotted time. Or works carelessly, finishing in half the expected time. Feels need to hurry, without thinking.

4. Poorly organized. Desk a mess. Always losing his coat or lunch.

5. Late to class, lingers after class.

6. Loses homework, or hands it in late and sloppily done. Doesn't understand or forgets assignments.

7. No study skills—doesn't know how to organize work, how to plan in regard to deadlines, how to organize time.

8. Low frustration tolerance. Gives up easily, or explodes.

9. Freezes when asked to perform on demand. When he volunteers information, he can tell what he knows; in responding to questions, he appears dull and ignorant.

10. Can't plan free time. Daydreams, acts silly, or repeats same activity over and over when given free choices.

FOCUS

PL 94-142 Part 121a

Procedures for evaluating Specific Learning Disabilities

Effective Date...February 1978

CHILDREN WHO ARE CONSIDERED LEARNING DISABLED: 121a.5

"Specific learning disability" means a disorder in one or more of the basic psychological processes involved in understanding or in using language, spoken or written, which may manifest itself in an imperfect ability to listen, think, speak, read, write, spell, or to do mathematical calculations. The term includes such conditions as perceptual handicaps, brain injury, minimal brain disfunction, dyslexia, and developmental aphasia.

CHILDREN WHO ARE NOT CONSIDERED LEARNING DISABLED:

The term does not include children who have learning problems, which are primarily the result of visual, hearing, or motor handicaps, of mental retardation, of emotional disturbance, or of environmental, cultural or economic disadvantage.

PROCEDURES FOR EVALUATING: 121a.540

In evaluating a child suspected of having a specific learning disability, in addition to the requirements of 121a.532, each public agency shall include on the multidisciplinary evaluation team:

A

1. The child's regular teacher, or
2. If the child does not have a regular teacher, a regular classroom teacher qualified to teach a child his or her age, or
3. For a child of less than school age, an individual qualified by the state educational agency to teach a child of his or her age; and

B

At least one person qualified to conduct individual diagnostic examinations of children, such as a school psychologist, speech-language pathologist, or remedial teacher.

Focus prepared by David Carofano
Consultant: Dr. John Sullivan

CRITERIA FOR DETERMINING SPECIFIC LEARNING DISABILITIES
121a.541

A

A team may determine that a child has a specific learning disability if:

1. The child does not achieve commensurate with his or her age and ability levels in one or more of the areas listed in "Procedures for Evaluating," paragraph a-2, when provided with learning experiences appropriate for the child's age and ability levels, and

2. The team finds that a child has a severe discrepancy between achievement and intellectual ability in one or more of the following areas:

   a. Oral expression
   b. Listening comprehension
   c. Written expression
   d. Basic reading skill
   e. Reading comprehension
   f. Mathematics calculation or
   g. Mathematics reasoning

OBSERVATION
121a.542

A.

At least one team member other than the child's regular teacher shall observe the child's academic performance in the regular classroom setting.

B.

In the case of a child of less than school age or out of school, a team member shall observe the child in an environment appropriate for a child of that age.

PREPARATION OF THE WRITTEN REPORT
121a.543

A.

The team shall prepare a written report of the results of the evaluation.

B.

The report must include a statement of:
1. Whether the child has a specific learning disability:
2. The basis for making the determination;
3. The relevant behavior noted during the observation of the child;
4. The relationship of that behavior to the child's academic functioning;
5. The educationally relevant medical findings, if any;
6. Whether there is a severe discrepancy between achievement and ability which is not correctable without special education or related services; and
7. The determination of the team concerning the effects of environmental, cultural, or economic disadvantage.

C.

Each member of the team shall certify in writing whether the report reflects his or her conclusion. If it does not reflect his or her conclusion, the team member must submit a separate statement presenting his or her conclusions.

the role of testing in the educational process

By Lois E. Burrill

Here, an in-depth look at testing and how it relates to your children and you

What is a test? What role does it play in the educational process? Perhaps you, the readers, will question whether any such role exists, but it's my belief that such a view arises from a misapprehension of what a test really is.

Permit me, then, to submit what I believe to be an appropriate definition: A test is any sample of actual behavior—particularly those samples noted in some sort of standard and defined way—and is usually collected for the express purpose of decision making.

Too often a test is considered simply as a way to *judge* how well a subject has been taught and learned—that is, to measure *success.* Important though this is, it's only part of the decision making process in which teach-

A former classroom teacher, Ms. Burrill is manager of information and advisory services, The Psychological Corporation, New York.

ers are constantly engaged. Teachers must also ask themselves what is *worth* teaching—in other words, what is *important.* Having determined this, they must further decide how *best* it may be taught and learned—what is *appropriate.* We are concerned with these kinds of questions because we are members of a helping profession and our role is to help individual children and groups of children. We must therefore take action and make choices among alternative courses of action.

Our decisions are based on our evaluation of the present situation. An important part of the word evaluation is *value* and our decisions ultimately must be concerned with worth or value as shown by all those italicized words. But sound decisions depend on our being able to evaluate relevant factual information

about the present situation. The more we know, the more accurate and trustworthy our information, the more likely we are to be able to evaluate and make appropriate decisions.

Now it may be clearer why I offered a broad definition of testing. Testing is the appropriate term to describe any and all methods we use to collect that information. Using this more accurate definition, any doubt about the enormous role testing must and should have in the teaching/learning process evaporates.

Indeed, it's clear that, intentional or not, testing is constantly taking place within the school setting. It would not, in fact, be totally out of line to suggest that good teaching and testing are so closely related and intertwined as to be virtually inseparable. Good teachers are constantly testing, just as they are constantly teaching, whether in the lunchroom, on the playground, in the corridors, or in the classroom!

Much testing, of course, is and should be informal. No paper and pencil "test" is necessary or even appropriate for many kinds of situations. Testing covers a wide variety of methods, procedures and techniques, and it must be stated loud and clear that formal paper and pencil testing, even where appropriate, does not, cannot, and should not be allowed to replace other effective methods of testing.

Ways of Testing. What, then, is the role of standardized, norm reference-testing in the educational process? If we accept the stereotyped view generally adopted by students, teachers, congressmen, and, it must be admitted, too frequently test publishers, this sort of "test" might well be used as sole criterion for a definition which would probably be something like this:

A paper document, developed by some unknown persons outside the local school, asking a lot of questions—each with several possible answer choices. Such a test also has a separate piece of paper on which answers are to be recorded by number or letter. That piece of paper, the "answer sheet," will then be scored by a machine somewhere outside the school and another piece of paper with lots of "scores" will be returned to the school some weeks after "testing" has taken place.

It's a shame that our minds jump to such an image, for to limit our notion of such tests to this very narrow definition precludes the positive value of such instruments as appropriate techniques to complement, supplement, enhance and enlarge information gained by other testing procedures.

The most appropriate testing technique or tool to use in each case depends in part on the knowledge or behavior you are seeking to test. Some behaviors lend themselves rather well to direct measurement; others are more difficult to get at. Some knowledges and behaviors can be tested both efficiently and accurately by use of paper and pencil; others may only be assessed by observation of a child's actual behavior.

Here are some of the ways we have of testing:

1. One of the teacher's first sources of information about a child may be a parent, rather than the child himself. An interview with a parent would, by the definition proposed above, be considered testing, as would the more formal completion of a questionnaire or behavior inventory.

2. Observation is probably the most important method of testing in early childhood years. There are numerous techniques of observation, ranging from the most casual noting of behavior to quite systematic and formal methods such as time samples. Observations can be extremely valuable, but they can also lack validity. Teachers need to develop skills in observing children in ways that will not encourage false impressions or lead to conclusions biased by the hopes and wishes of the observer. And many times, without special preplanning, it's difficult to observe any evidence one way or the other about many of the goals teachers deem important.

3. One way to combat certain shortcomings of the usual observation techniques is to create a situation in which the behavior for which you want to test is likely to occur. Such structured situations are particularly useful in testing for behaviors that may not occur often in the classroom or which do not usually occur spontaneously.

4. Closely related to structured situations for observation are structured work samples. The child's own products are cer-

tainly, by the broader definition, tests and should be a valuable source of information about the child's progress and current level of development.

5. Check lists and rating scales are paper-and-pencil testing tools a teacher can use very effectively. In some cases, teachers may develop their own check lists and, less frequently perhaps, rate each characteristic on a scale of one to three, five, seven or ten. However, a number of check lists have been developed by state departments of education, test publishers, textbook publishers, and other external sources, and are readily available.

6. Classroom exercises are also tests. Sometimes these take the form of informal inventories of difficulties, or informal quizzing of students on particular content of the curriculum. Sometimes, of course, especially as a child progresses through the grades, these are paper and pencil tests.

7. Textbooks often include chapter tests, unit tests and review tests. These, too, may be useful sources of information for decision-making.

8. Finally, there are published and commercially available tests. Although publishers provide materials for use in several of the categories of testing mentioned earlier, it is for so-called norm-referenced or standardized tests that they are best-known. Their importance in the decision making function of the teacher is determined to a great extent by the individual, but the fact remains that certain behaviors of children can be accurately and efficiently tested by such methods. By collecting the kinds of information that *can* be collected in this way, teachers may obtain valuable insight into many aspects of student behavior in a relatively short period of time, leaving more time for action based on the decisions the teacher makes using this information.

I think it's important at this point to return to the idea of

2. DIAGNOSIS

evaluating and to make again the distinction between *evaluating* and *testing*. Testing, as we have defined it here, is a tool, a procedure for collecting relevant information. That information is, in isolation, quite neutral—valueless. The results of testing must be processed—evaluated—by teachers, administrators, parents and other decision makers. Testing attempts to answer the question: "What is the present situation?" It does not and cannot go beyond that and answer the questions: "So what? Is that good? Is it good enough? What do I do next?"

And it is also important to remind ourselves that not all test-ing is good or useful or relevant. Tests and testing are tools and tools may be poorly made. Furthermore, like most tools, it takes a certain amount of skill to use testing well.

I have dwelt at length on the role of the teacher in the testing process. What role, then, do I propose for test publishers in the teaching/learning process? I would suggest several. First, we test publishers should continue to try to develop good testing tools for use by the classroom teacher. Not only should we publish paper-and-pencil tests for those purposes for which they are appropriate but also other, non paper-and-pencil procedures for collecting relevant information about children and their development.

Second, I believe we have a role to play in helping teachers develop their own methods of testing and information gathering. Unfortunately, many of the skills necessary to the good use of test results are not now part of the teacher's formal preparation for teaching, especially in the area of using good paper-and-pencil testing information for decision making in instruction. Therefore, a third responsibility of the test publisher must be to help teachers gain proficiency in these areas.

don't be nervous -it's only a test

Many children feel anxious about taking a test and, all too often, it's teacher herself who's partly responsible for the anxiety

By Ruth Wilson

Ruth Wilson is a former corrective reading teacher in the Title I program and is currently assigned to a classroom in Brooklyn, N.Y.

Traditionally, Americans love a challenge. To overcome an obstacle, to excel in some sport, to triumph in the face of adversity, to fight for and win the respect of one's peers are feats that are praised in history books and daily newspapers alike. To be "put to the test" is to call forth the best that is in us, whether we are small boys running a race in a school playground or politicians running for high office. Why, then, is the testing process—so essential to sound pedagogy—an upsetting experience for the vast majority of children?

That this is indeed so is apparent to teachers and parents alike. Too often, both the anticipation and the actual test-taking experience are accompanied by feelings of anxiety and, in some cases, hostility and frustration. Why does this particular testing situation produce such different responses from those experienced by the child in other areas of endeavor? Obviously, we rise to challenges of our own choosing. We run if we think we might win the race. We put ourselves to the test. In the classroom, tests are imposed upon children by teachers; or even worse, they are imposed upon both children and teachers by some external authority.

So, the child shrinks from the challenge of a test through fear of not doing well. He feels that if his performance is poor, he will suffer a loss of prestige among his peers. Often he fears the displeasure of parents and teachers if he should fail to meet their expectations. Moreover, the thought of doing poorly is a threat to his own ego and self esteem.

Too often, such feelings of anxiety are reinforced by the teacher. "Don't be nervous," she warns and, with reason, the child infers that he is about to be confronted with a task that might predictably produce nervousness. "Your scores are very important. Do the best you can," the teacher says, and the mind of the child translates this to mean that he must, at all cost, do well.

There has been a subtle but devastating shift of emphasis. Yes, the scores are very important, but when properly used, a low score is just as important, just as valuable and indicative as a high score. Yes, it's essential that each child do the best he can, but only in order that the test results may be accurate, not so that the child may excel in the test when his performance in class is only mediocre. A classroom test is not a race or a contest; no one wins or loses. Competition may have a place in some school situations, but it has no part in the effective assessment of achievement through testing.

Can we, as teachers, convince our children of this? Can we produce an atmosphere where every pupil is able and willing to "do his best" on tests? We know that feelings of anxiety and inferiority, fear of loss of prestige and of failure to measure up to parental expectations can impair test performances. Can we eliminate or alleviate these pressures? Not unless we, ourselves, have fully understood the true purpose and value of testing.

Common Purpose. All tests, whether they be informal checks on progress or standardized, professionally prepared documents, have as their purpose the accurate assessment of a child's achievement. They are, by their very nature, instruments to be used in furthering that achievement. Standardized tests add an important and unique dimension to this assessment. Not only do they show how much progress Mary has made and where she stands in relation to her classmates, but they evaluate her achievement in terms of widely accepted educational objectives which transcend environmental limitations.

The tests we prepare ourselves are directed toward a specific set of children. We know exactly who we are testing, what we are testing for and how we will use the test results. But when confronted with a standardized test, we are likely to react with anxiety and fears very much like those of our children.

If the teacher herself is insecure, she's likely to feel that it is her own competency which is being tested; and if she feels threatened by the test, it's almost inevitable that her attitude will be communicated to the children. If she's not clear herself as to the purpose and worth of a particular test, she is obviously in no position to show her pupils how it can do them any good. And if she's unsympathetic to the testing program, this attitude will quickly be picked up by her class.

Yet how to overcome these feelings? It's indeed a measure of a teacher's success that her children progress, and it's easy to become disheartened when reviewing a set of test results. "What happened to Carlos? He seems to have fallen completely apart." . . . "I'm sure Susan understands that rule. Why couldn't she apply it?" . . .

"Surely Alex should have scored better." From such reactions, it's an easy step to labeling a particular test "unfair" or "biased." For the teacher, also, a test has become a contest.

Such an attitude is understandable but not justifiable. It arises, for the most part, from a misunderstanding of the proper function of the test. Often the teacher makes the mistake of looking upon the norms of a standardized test as a goal to be reached by all children and feels disappointment when a child does not meet this rigid standard. She fails to realize that the standard is there to help the child, not to judge him; that it represents a stepping stone, not a hurdle.

The teacher, herself, must be persuaded of the value of such objective standards and understand how they can be used to improve the child's performance. At the same time, she must realize that they represent only part of the desired outcomes of the educational program and must not place undue emphasis upon them. She must look to her own attitudes and performance in answering the questions of why Carlos, Susan and Alex scored as they did and be willing to take the necessary steps in preparing her and her class so that test results will be accurate and all her pupils may, in fact, "do their best."

Working Together. Long-range preparation lies in establishing an atmosphere of trust between pupil and teacher, an awareness that they are working together toward common goals. Each child should know that his welfare is of primary concern. Obviously, this can not be established in a few days. It's the outgrowth of an approach that not only includes the pupils in planning activities, but also demonstrates respect and fairness in dealing with them.

The effectiveness of testing is determined by the soundness of pupil-teacher relationships.

Where mutual trust exists, it will not be difficult to convince the child that tests—even if difficult and distasteful—are for his own good. He can be guided to understand that the purpose of testing is not just to assign grades and check mastery, but to help him to profit by his own strengths and overcome his weaknesses.

More immediately, there's need for detailed planning on the part of the teacher. She must remember that if the atmosphere during testing produces tension and anxiety, or if the test is not administered according to the directions given, any real assessment of the pupil's performance becomes impossible.

A practice test, taken a few days before the actual testing, can go far to increase the confidence of both teacher and pupils. The children will develop a more positive attitude toward the test itself through an understanding of the types of items it will cover and through mastery of the mechanics involved. During the practice test, the teacher can determine whether the children are marking the answers in the correct manner, whether they are working quickly and marking only one answer. She can make sure they know what to do if they don't know the answer or want to change it and can clear up any misunderstanding about directions.

A check list is usually provided to help the teacher establish procedures before, during and just after testing. Using such a list can eliminate much of the confusion and frustration that might otherwise arise in the administration of the test. It can give the teacher confidence, not only in her role as administrator, but in the accuracy of the test results.

Using the Results. It is how the teacher uses the test results that will demonstrate their usefulness and reveal her real purposes to her class. If the test papers are not available for review, a discussion will afford each pupil the opportunity to ask questions about material covered. While it's unwise to disclose results in a way that can lead to comparison among pupils, it is desirable that the pupils know where they stand in relation to national norms, both as a class and as individuals. It's important to show that consideration has been given to personal results while, at the same time, making clear that each child has a worth that is not measured by any test score. Through the attitudes the teacher evidences at this time, the children can be convinced that the testing has been done for their own benefit.

However, the teacher must be willing and able to make the benefit an actuality by using the test results as a basis for future instruction. Where results fail to measure up to expectations, an attempt should be made to isolate the cause in each case.

For example, if Carlos "fell apart," it may easily be because of his difficulty in dealing with the language structure and concepts used in the test. In any form of standardized test, these will be those of the standard American-English dialect used in most school textbooks. While the teacher may accommodate classroom instruction to allow for the variety of dialects used by her pupils, it's necessary that some acceptable norm of usage be established. Since ultimately Carlos will have to become proficient in the standard dialect in order to succeed in the educational and business world of our country, it's important that his teacher have a clear understanding of the nature and extent of his deficiency.

Likewise, if Susan failed to apply a well-known rule in a specific example, it may indicate a limitation in language experience arising from Susan's particular environment which her teacher can correct only through understanding its nature.

Finally, since a low score on a standardized test is frequently used as a criterion for admission into special remedial and tutorial programs, it is patently desirable, even essential, that the results be put to proper use.

Teachers have sometimes been accused of teaching "to a test"; in the long run, no purpose is served by this. But insofar as a teacher can teach "from a test" her pupils will gain through her efforts.

Attitudes are the outgrowth of understanding, and where both pupil and teacher understand the purpose and value of a given test, only positive results will accrue.

In an article, "Testing: Bond or Barrier between Pupil and Teacher?", originally published in *Education*, Roger T. Lennon writes: "The taking of tests is a life-long experience for everyone; on the job and in the home, life presents a series of tests, very often under circumstances much less friendly than those the pupil encounters in school. If the child learns to meet these challenges, to face up realistically to his own limitations, to accept success without complacency or smugness, and failure without undue distress or bitterness, he will be that much farther along the way to becoming a well-adjusted adult."

In like manner, if we, as teachers, are willing to meet the challenge of testing, to face our own limitations realistically and look to objective norms to correct and compensate for our deficiencies, to use past experiences for future growth, we will become more effective in our profession.

FOCUS...

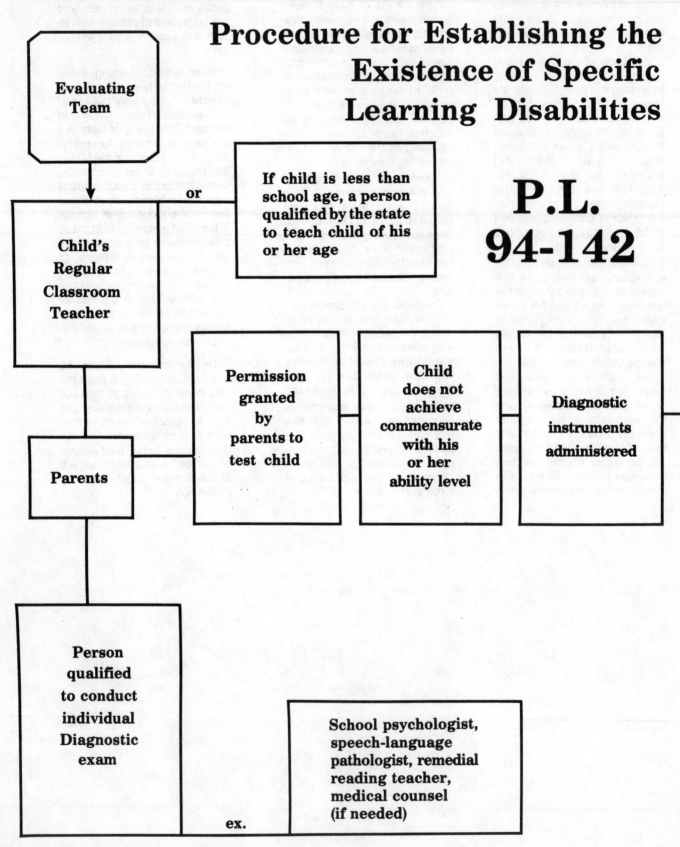

Procedure for Establishing the Existence of Specific Learning Disabilities

P.L. 94-142

Evaluating Team

Child's Regular Classroom Teacher

or → If child is less than school age, a person qualified by the state to teach child of his or her age

Parents

Permission granted by parents to test child

Child does not achieve commensurate with his or her ability level

Diagnostic instruments administered

Person qualified to conduct individual Diagnostic exam

ex. → School psychologist, speech-language pathologist, remedial reading teacher, medical counsel (if needed)

Focus prepared by David Carofano
Consultant: Dr. John Sullivan

Team finds severe discrepancy between achievement and intellectual ability in one or more of seven areas:

1) oral expression
2) listening comprehension
3) written expression
4) basic reading skill
5) reading comprehension
6) math calculations
7) math reasoning

Team prepares report--Results of evaluation

Each team member must certify in writing whether report reflects his/her conclusions

Information is shared with parents and permission of parents is given to place child in a specific learning disability class

If all in agreement, then team prepares an individualized educational program (IEP) in conjunction with the parents and/or the student.

Referral data and testing data collected and analyzed by evaluating team

No Discrepancy is found between achievement and intellectual ability

Child remains in regular classroom

HOW VALID ARE CHILDREN'S LANGUAGE TESTS?

Ronald K. Sommers, Ed.D.
Susan Erdige, M.A.
M. Kathleen Peterson, Ph.D.
Kent State University

Seven independent studies of young children's performances were reviewed. Rather consistently, children's scores on a wide range of popular language tests and measures revealed large numbers of moderately high to high interrelationships which were unexpected, since the authors frequently claimed that their tests measured specific rather than general language skills. Data from two new investigations of different batteries of language tests given to 122 young handicapped children in the first investigation and 44 in the second were subjected to multivariate analyses, including regression analysis and factor analysis.

Results from the first study showed that a few general rather than many specific linguistic abilities characterized the performances of the children; results from the second showed that only one general linguistic factor accounted for the subjects' performances. The construct and content validity of many of the tests studied appears untenable. Implications for use of the tests (accounting for most of the variance in each of the two batteries studied) are presented, along with recommendations concerning the development of more valid language tests.

A plethora of tests can be marshalled to study children's abilities. Of the many available ones, a significant number are published, while a smaller group remains unpublished and can be found in the professional literature. Many new tests are under construction, and the impact of P.L. 94-142 probably will stimulate the development and widespread use of many such tests with preschool and young school-aged handicapped children.

Regrettably, most such tests are underdeveloped and unstudied, their norms either being greatly deficient or nonexistent; many have never been revised, and authors' descriptions of the validity of their tests never investigated. Many tests purport to assess specific linguistic abilities, e.g., syntax, morphology, receptive vocabulary, language complexity, use of simple and complex transformations, etc. Presumably, the consumer chooses a language test to uncover children's specific linguistic abilities and deficiencies, locates the linguistically impaired children, and uses the test scores to assist in planning a remedial program.

Although the validity of many children's language tests has received sparse attention, earlier validity studies of the Illinois Test of Psycholinguistic Abilities (ITPA; Kirk, McCarthy, & Kirk, 1968) frequently challenged the existence of

"How Valid are Children's Language Tests?" Ronald K. Sommers, Ed.D, Susan Erdige, M.A., M. Kathleen Peterson, Ph.D., *Journal of Special Education*, Vol. 12, No. 4, Winter 1978. ©1978 Buttonwoods Farms, Inc.

the many factors claimed to be measured in this instrument. Many investigators reported only one predominant linguistic factor when young children served as subjects (Haring & Ridgway, 1967; Mittler & Ward, 1970; Ryckman & Wiegerink, 1969; Silverstein, 1967; Weener, Barritt, & Semmell, 1967; Wisland & Many, 1969). Disclaimers by Kirk and Kirk (1978) that the ITPA cannot be satisfactorily factor-analyzed seem theoretically unsupportable, and their defense that one investigation identified many factors in older children (mean age, 9 years) does not appear to destroy the many reported findings that only a few factors are assessed when the ITPA is given to young children.

Although many divergent theories of language acquisition can be identified, a popular view has been expressed by Ruder (1972), who stated:

It is apparent that a theory of grammar must include phonology, syntax, and semantics. This is taking a rather broad view of grammar or of language but it is upon such a general viewpoint of grammar that this psycholinguistic model of language acquisition is based. (p. 5)

Others have maintained that three levels of language exist — syntactic, semantic, and phonological — and although each is rule-governed individually, all three are integrated (Roberts, 1964; Smith and Miller, 1966; Solberg, 1973). Perkins (1971), citing Lenneberg (1969), elaborated upon the nature of language and the interrelationships of its four components, consisting of phonemic, morphemic, syntactic, and semantic elements and their changing interrelationships. He wrote:

Not a static product of the mind, it is the dynamic manifestation of the functioning of his brain. Every level of language — phonemic, morphemic, syntactic, and semantic — facilitates the discrimination of relations among classes of objects as they belong to different classes. Never is a word a unique name for a single object. So in the broadest sense, a disorder of language impairs the ability to discriminate relations. (p. 238)

In a discussion of Piaget's Psycholingustic Developmental Model, Sinclair-de Zwort (1973) was of the opinion that early language learning and cognitive development were inseparable; therefore, Piaget's analysis of cognitive structures was most revealing in the context of early language acquisition.

Paradoxically, the belief that the syntactic, semantic, morphemic, and phonemic components of language are inextricably interrelated appears not to have deterred the attempts of some testmakers to measure one or more of the components independently of the others. Since such tests have been developed and used with many young children, the present effort seeks to determine the extent to which testmakers have been successful in assessing specific components of the language of young normal and handicapped children.

The specific purpose here is to review a series of largely unreported studies of many such tests and add to this review the results of two very recent investigations of what batteries of language tests given to groups of preschool handicapped children appeared to measure. It should be emphasized that the present focus is an exploration of the validity of children's language tests. The question of interest is, "Can tests be devised for use with young children that are capable of measuring specific rather than general linguistic abilities?" The broad, ancient, and unresolved issue relating to general versus specific abilities in human functions (i.e., cognition, perception, etc.), while fundamentally important, is not the theoretical issue of the present investigation.

A REVIEW OF SIX INVESTIGATIONS

In the first of the studies to be reviewed, Jackson and Sommers (1972) investigated the language performances of 25 children, aged 5.10 to 10.5 years, from the Akron, Ohio, public schools. Subjects were of normal intelligence, had normal hearing acuity bilaterally, and were generally from lower middle-class American monolingual families. Twenty were attending regular elementary classes; 5 were classified as having learning disabilities and were enrolled in a special class for children thought to have minimal brain dysfunction. Five of

2. DIAGNOSIS

the 20 in regular classes had normal articulation performances, 5 had mildly defective articulation, 5 had moderately defective articulation, and 5 had severely defective articulation.

The battery of linguistic measures given to each of the 25 subjects included the McDonald Deep Test of Articulation (MDTA; McDonald, 1968), the Menyuk Sentence Repetition Task (MSRT; Menyuk, 1969), and the expressive and receptive subtests of the Northwestern Screening Syntax Test (NSST; Lee, 1969). The many high relationships in the subjects' performances are reflected in the correlation coefficients shown in Table 1. The very high r of .95 between subjects' scores on the MSRT and the NSST-E (expressive subtest) may be partially related to the fact that both tests require that the subject repeat the experimenter's spoken message. Thus, both tests involve recognition of a spoken message, storage, retrieval, and a spoken response. However, errors on the MSRT can result from a variety of types of errors in the children's production of the sentences — breakdowns in the semantic components, improper transformations, substitutions, omissions of words, syntactical errors, morphological errors, etc. — while the NSST presumes to measure only errors of syntax. Articulation errors appear to have been more related to expressive linguistic measures than the receptive one assessed in the NSST-R (receptive subscale). However, this receptive measure did correlate to a moderate degree with all three expressive measures in the battery, thus reflecting the probable existence of a general linguistic factor of some significance.

In the second study, Lowry (1973) compared the linguistic skills of aphasic adults and young children. Fourteen female and 6 male normal white children aged 4.2 to 7.2 attended either a preschool or an elementary school in Colum-

TABLE 1
SIGNIFICANT CORRELATIONS FOUND IN THE JACKSON AND
SOMMERS INVESTIGATION (1972)

Tests	MDTA	MSRT	NSST(R)	NSST(E)
MDTA	—	.710	.541	.756
MSRT		—	.540	.946
NSST(R)			—	.663
NSST(E)				—

bus, Ohio. All of the children came from middle-class families, from homes in which American English was the only spoken language. All were considered by the parents and teachers to be normal in all ways.

Each child's linguistic abilities were assessed using a battery of tests, including the Peabody Picture Vocabulary Test (PPVT; Dunn, 1959), the Token Test (TT; DeRenzi & Vignolo, 1961), the Auditory Decoding subtest from the ITPA (McCarthy, 1930), and the NSST-R (Lee, 1969). This battery consisted of tests that required receptive linguistic abilities only, since no speech was required for subjects' responses to test items. The many high correlations demonstrated that subjects' PPVT scores were related to three other receptive language measures which presume to measure receptive syntax (NSST-R) or comprehension of speech (TT and ITPA-D). A strong and very significant general receptive language factor seemed characteristic of these data, presented in Table 2.

The relationships noted in the Lowry study were supported by the findings of a third study, that of Lass and Golden (1975), who studied children's performances on the PPVT and TT. The performances of 20 normally speaking and hearing children, aged 5 to 12 years, were found to correlate .71 on these two tests. They also reported a correlation coefficient of .72 between the performances of 24 speech- and language-impaired children, aged 2.8 to 8.8, on the PPVT and the Auditory Comprehension Subscale of the Preschool Language Scale (PLS; Zimmerman, Steiner, & Evatt, 1969). These results, along with Lowry's, support the contention that the PPVT measures a more general receptive linguistic ability than the "hearing vocabulary" one stated by its originator, Dunn (1959).

In the fourth study, Dukes (1974) determined the effectiveness of two language intervention programs using 13 male and 7 female preschool children. Subjects were judged to be at the same point on a continuum of syntactic development However, 10 of the subjects (mean age of 3.10) were thought to have deviant language, while 10 others (mean age of 3.0) had normal speech and language. A comprehensive battery of linguistic tests was given to each subject and many highly significant relationships were determined. Based on a linguistic analysis of children's spontaneous speech, a general expressive linguistic factor seemed apparent in the many significant relationships found between linguistic measures thought to be discrete, such as subjects' mean length of utterance, number of simple transformations, number

TABLE 2
SIGNIFICANT PEARSONIAN CORRELATION COEFFICIENTS FOUND IN THE LOWRY
INVESTIGATION (1973) OF 20 NORMAL PRESCHOOL CHILDREN

Tests	PPVT	TT	ITPA(D)	NSST(R)
PPVT	—	.727	.846	.829
TT		—	.673	.806
ITPA(D)			—	.820
NSST(R)				—

of correct inflections, number of functions, etc. Dukes further reported a moderately high negative $(r = -.69, .01$ level) relationship between subjects' articulation errors from the Fisher-Logemann Test of Articulation (FTLA; Fisher & Logemann, 1971) and their number of correct responses on the Boston University Speech Sound Discrimination Test (BUSST; Pronovost, 1974). Articulation errors also correlated negatively $(r = -.75, .01$ level) with the number of complete grammatical utterances. The suggestion from this finding is that many elements of young children's spoken language correlate highly enough with each other to suggest the presence of an important general expressive linguistic ability, which includes articulation.

In the fifth study, Landon (1975) investigated the linguistic performances of highly talkative and much less talkative noral preschool children. Twenty children of each type served as subjects, and within each group were 10 males and 10 females, aged 3.0 to 6.5. Landon found that a measure of grammar requiring a spoken response (the Grammatic Closure subscale of the ITPA) correlated highly with a purely receptive test (NSST-R; $r = .75$, significant .01). This finding seems most intriguing since the linguistic processing modalities are different, viz., one is expressive and the other receptive, and the stated intentions of the two tasks appear, superficially at least, very dissimilar. The common variance of 56% reflects the fact that they measured a large amount of a common linguistic factor.

Some additional support for general rather than specific language factors characterizing young children's performances on language tests came from a study by Aram and Nation (1975). These investigators factor-analyzed the scores of 47 language-impaired children, aged 3.2 to 6.11. Their battery of language tests consisted of 14 measures, including the PPVT, Templin's (1957) Picture Sound Discrimination Test (TPSDT), an articulation test, the NSST-R, the Assessment of Children's Language Comprehension (ACLC) by Foster, Giddan, and Stark (1973) and other tests developed or modified by the investigators.

The purpose of the Aram and Nation investigation was not to identify the common factors in their test battery per se but to locate subgroups of language-impaired children who had patterns of strengths and weaknesses on language

2. DIAGNOSIS

factors. Although they successfully identified 6 subgroups of children, only 3 factors resulted from the analysis of children's scores from the 14 language tests. Of the 65% of the total variance accounted for in the factor analysis, 27% came from the first factor. This factor was designated "repetition strength," since its loadings chiefly came from tests that required the subjects to repeat the language presented to them. Factor two was identified as a general linguistic one, while factor three was thought to relate to auditory comprehension of speech.

Aram and Nation's three factors appear to be very similar to those obtained in Investigation I in the present report. Additionally, their "repetition strength" factor seems comparable to the very strong cross-modality factor that emerged from the results of our Investigation II (both investigations will be described below).

SUMMARY

A review of findings from six independent investigations of the linguistic performances of both normal and handicapped children seem in agreement to the extent that many published and unpublished language tests and measures may be assessing a small number of general linguistic factors. Claims of specificity of linguistic factor assessment made by the authors of some of these tests and measures may be both erroneous and misleading. In a holistic sense, all the myriad aspects of validity of many such tests and measures seem in doubt, i.e., construct, content, and predictive validity. The moderately high to high intercorrelations of tests and measures thought to assess different linguistic abilities of children starkly question the assumptions of the test-makers. An implication from a number of these past investigations is that generally receptive linguistic measures correlate more highly with other receptive linguistic measures than expressive ones. This tendency also appears to hold for expressive linguistic measures, since higher correlations appear to exist when expressive test scores are related to other expressive test scores than when expressive scores are related to receptive language test scores.

INVESTIGATION I

In the first investigation of children's linguistic performance, 122 minimal brain dysfunctioning preschool subjects (most of whom had developmental language disorders) were studied on a battery of tests including the PPVT, the Test for Auditory Comprehension of Language (TACL; Carrow, 1973), and the NSST. Most of the authors of these instruments described them as rather specific measures of linguistic abilities. Dunn (1965), for example, said that the PPVT was designed "to provide an estimate of a subject's verbal intelligence through measuring his hearing vocabulary." Researchers have studied the validity of the PPVT (Hammill & Irwin, 1965; Kaufman & Ivanoff, 1968; Shotwell, O'Connor, Gabet, & Dingman, 1969), and some have reported it to be a valid test in some regards, although Williams, Marks, and Bialer (1977) questioned its claim to assess hearing vocabulary. The TACL was designed by its author to assess auditory comprehension of varying language structures. Lee developed the NSST to test both receptive and expressive use of syntactic forms, including comprehension and formulation of basic sentence structure, transformations, and morphological forms (Lee, 1969). In the present investigation, the NSST was divided into its two subtests for study — the receptive portion (NSST-R) and the expressive one (NSST-E).

Method

Subjects. Subjects were 122 learning-disabled children enrolled in classes at the Child Development Center in Norristown, Pa. The 41 females ranged in age from 3.3 to 8.9 years, with a mean age of 6.3 years. The 81 males ranged in age from 3.5 to 9.4 years, with a mean age of 6.5 years. All 122 subjects had a mean age of 6.4 years. Judged by parental occupations, most subjects were from middle-class families, with less than 15% from lower-class families and a small percentage from upper-class families. Each had been examined by neurologists, psychiatrists, psychologists, speech pathologists, audiologists, and occupational therapists; and each was diagnosed as having minimal brain dysfunction with measured or estimated intelligence from moderate retardation to normal. Audiological assessment, using a combination of pure tone and speech audiometry techniques (e.g., threshold, impedance, play audiometry), determined that all subjects had hearing within normal limits bilaterally.

Subjects were administered the 4 language tests before and after a period of 8 months, during which they received language therapy and teaching. The language tests were administered in random order. For the purposes of the present investigation, their posttherapy test scores were used for analysis.

Results

Regression analysis. The means and standard deviations of subjects' scores on each language measure are contained in Table 3. The results of the regression analysis are contained in Table 4. Each of the four tests was used successively as the dependent variable. The remaining three tests, as independent variables, were used to study the extent of their predictability of the fourth test, which then served as the dependent variable. The results show the TACL as the best predictor of the other three tests, with a moderately high degree of linear relationship between subjects' performances on all tests. Interestingly, the NSST-E, the only expressive test in the battery, consistently supplied small amounts of unique variance of significance to the multiple r that predicted receptive language performance.

To estimate the population values of the multiple correlation coefficients in Table 4, the formula for shrinkage (Ferguson, 1976), which takes into account the number of subjects, sample size, and number of predictors, was applied to the data. This resulted in a slight reduction of the multiple correlation coefficients. The multiple r for the PPVT declined to .768 from .775; the multiple r for NSST-R declined to .793 from .799; the multiple r for NSST-E declined to .630 from .641; and the multiple r for TACL to .827 from .829. The reasonably large N of 122 and small numbers of predictor variables appeared to operate to keep the estimated multiple correlation in the sample close to that expected in the population.

Factor analysis. Subjects' scores on the TACL total test, scores on the TACL subtest measuring vocabulary, TACL scores measuring syntax, TACL scores measuring morphemes, PPVT scores, NSST-R scores, and NSST-E scores all

TABLE 3
MEANS, STANDARD DEVIATIONS, AND NUMBERS OF SUBJECTS GIVEN
EACH LANGUAGE TEST IN INVESTIGATION I

	Mean	Standard deviation	N
PPVT	55.55	11.12	106
NSST(R)	29.02	5.07	106
NSST(E)	24.1	9.71	98
TACL	81.44	10.54	106

were subjected to a principal component factor analysis. The eight scores for each subject representing input data yielded four factors; the first two were chiefly responsible for the total measurement of the battery.

The decision to use subtests from the TACL which purport to measure specific linguistic factors — i.e., syntax, vocabulary, and morphemes — was based on an interest in determining whether such measures would load

2. DIAGNOSIS

TABLE 4

SUMMARY TABLE NOTING THE EXTENT OF PREDICTABILITY THREE LANGUAGE TESTS
HAVE ON A FOURTH LANGUAGE TEST

Dependent variable	Independent variables[a]	Multiple r	r Square	Simple r
PPVT	1. TACL	.737	.543	.737
	2. NSST(R)	.775	.599	.714
	3. NSST(E)	.775	.600	.512
NSST(R)	1. TACL	.758	.575	.758
	2. PPVT	.792	.628	.714
	3. NSST(E)	.799	.638	.567
NSST(E)	1. TACL	.624	.389	.624
	2. NSST(R)	.640	.410	.567
	3. PPVT	.641	.411	.512
TACL	1. NSST(R)	.758	.574	.758
	2. PPVT	.808	.653	.737
	3. NSST(E)	.829	.688	.634

[a]The independent variables as predictors are listed in order of importance.

significantly on the same factor that the entire TACL test did or show higher loadings on tests that supposedly measure the same linguistic factors, such as the PPVT for vocabulary and the NSST for syntax.

The many high correlation coefficients contained in Table 5 reflect the probable existence of some general linguistic factors of importance, a finding confirmed by the results of a factor analysis. Factor loadings, based on a varimax rotation, are contained in Table 6.

These results show that two factors, one auditory receptive and the second expressive, accounted for a great portion of the total variance. The auditory

TABLE 5

PEARSONIAN CORRLEATION COEFFICIENTS FOR THE LANGUAGE TESTS FACTOR-ANALYZED
IN INVESTIGATION I (N = 101)

Tests	TACL	TACLVS	TACLMS	TACLSS	PPVT	NSST(R)	NSST(E)	NSST(T)
TACL	—	.900	.964	.759	.739	.780	.601	.740
TACLVS		—	.794	.584	.632	.717	.526	.661
TACLMS			—	.645	.746	.736	.590	.714
TACLSS				—	.538	.617	.438	.557
PPVT					—	.704	.518	.650
NSST(R)						—	.566	.798
NSST(E)							—	.948
NSST(T)								—

TABLE 6

VARIMAX ROTATED FACTOR MATRIX FOR INVESTIGATION I (N = 101)

Test	Factor 1	Factor 2	Factor 3	Factor 4
TACL(T)	.766	.315	.370	.408
TACLVS	.873	.277	.232	.200
TACLMS	.719	.313	.436	.300
TACLSS	.325	.207	.221	.892
PPVT	.338	.255	.856	.191
NSST(R)	.451	.418	.557	.318
NSST(E)	.232	.936	.168	.138
NSST(T)	.343	.845	.337	.223

receptive factor was far more influential than any other, accounting for 73% of what the tests measured. Some of the receptive tests tended to load slightly with the NSST-E, the only expressive test in the battery, to account for 10% of the variance. The two remaining factors were much weaker. The third factor appeared to be a noun/verb recognition or receptive vocabulary one. The fourth factor, also of little importance, appeared to relate to the comprehension of morphemes. Basically, the results indicated that a general auditory receptive linguistic factor was prominent, and a much weaker expressive linguistic factor accounted for most of the variance in the battery of tests.

INVESTIGATION II

Method and procedure

Five months after the Investigation I data were obtained, a new battery of language tests was given to 44 subjects from the Child Development Center, Norristown, Pa. Twenty-two of the 44 served as subjects in Investigation I. Of the 44, 19 were female and 25 male, most were from middle-class families, and most had been classified by the same Investigation I clinical staff as having learning disabilities related (largely) to minimal brain dysfunction. As in Investigation I, many of these children were speech and language impaired. Tests were administered to each subject in a random order by the same staff who had gathered the data in Investigation I. The test battery, however, was different and contained a much larger emphasis on expressive language assessment. The TACL, which proved to be so powerful in accounting for variance in Investigation I, was retained as an auditory receptive measure and pitted against three expressive language tests consisting of the Manyuk Sentence Repetition Test (MSRT), the Developmental Sentence Analysis (DSA; Lee, 1974), and the Mean Length of Utterance (MLU; McCarthy, 1930). Additional tests in this battery, not subjected to factor analysis but studied in terms of relationships to each other, included the Goldman-Fristoe Articulation Test (GFAT; Goldman & Fristoe, 1969a), the Goldman-Fristoe Auditory Discrimination Test in Quiet (GFADTQ), the Goldman-Fristoe Auditory Discrimination Test in Noise (GFADTN; Goldman & Fristoe, 1969b), and the three subtests from the TACL — Vocabulary (TACLVS), Syntax (TACLSS), and

TABLE 7

PEARSON PRODUCT MOMENT CORRELATION COEFFICIENTS[a] OF SUBJECTS' PERFORMANCES ON THE BATTERY OF LINGUISTIC TESTS IN INVESTIGATION II ($N = 44$)

Tests	ARTIC.	SENREP	TACLT	GFWQT	GFWNT	TACLVS	TACLMS	TACLSS	DSS	MLU
ARTIC.	—	.732	.561	.379	.276	.443	.505	.476	.683	.703
SENREP		—	.554	.410	.216	.547	.543	.591	.583	.562
TACLT			—	.639	.631	.944	.970	.849	.527	.599
GFWQT				—	.847	.555	.622	.570	.245	.520
GFWNT					—	.538	.637	.556	.29	.384
TACLVS						—	.920	.840	.437	.513
TACLMS							—	.800	.527	.567
TACLSS								—	.357	.462
DSS									—	.722
MLU										—

[a] $r \geq .29$ required for .95 and $\geq .38$ for .01 levels of significance.

Morphemes (TACLMS). These relationships can be seen in the correlation matrix presented in Table 7. Articulation scores were highly related to subjects' scores on the MSRT ($r = .73$, significant at $< .01$) and to two expressive measures, the DSA and the MLU. For the former, the r was .68; for the latter, the r was .70, both significant at the .01 level. Articulation scores also correlated to a moderate degree with TACL and its subscales, thus showing

2. DIAGNOSIS

some relationship to purely receptive language abilities. Further evidence that the TACL and its three subscales are measuring much of the same auditory receptive factor can be seen in the high intercorrelations contained in Table 8. The high degree of relationship between the DSS and the MLU show the extent to which they may be assessing significant amounts of some general expressive language factor.

Results

Table 8 contains the means and standard deviations of the 44 subjects' performances on each test. The correlations constituted the input data for the principal components factor analysis, using the same computer and computer program as in Investigation I.

Table 9 contains a summary of the factor analysis. The factor was generated following a varimax rotation which accounted for all of the variance. This factor appeared to be one on which both expressive and receptive language

TABLE 8
MEANS AND STANDARD DEVIATIONS OF SUBJECTS' SCORES ON THE LANGUAGE TESTS
FACTOR-ANALYZED IN INVESTIGATION II (N = 44)

Test	Mean	Standard deviation
SENREP	119.98	42.40
TACLT	72.10	19.93
DSS	34.10	22.50
MLU	4.66	2.46

TABLE 9
RESULTS OF THE FACTOR ANALYSIS PERFORMED IN
INVESTIGATION II (N = 44)

Tests	Factor 1	Eigenvalue	Percent of variance	Cumulative percentage
SENREP	−.715	2.38	100.0	100.0
TACLT	−.705			
DSS	−.811			
MLU	−.845			

tests loaded about equally and might be termed a general cross-modality linguistic factor.

In summary, the results of Investigation II were somewhat different from those of Investigation I and the Aram and Nation (1975) factor analysis study in that only one large linguistic factor could be extracted from the test battery even though some of the tests were of singular modality, i.e., only expressive or receptive. The particular battery of tests in Investigation II was weighted heavily with expressive language measures, yet the overriding influence was a general cross-modality linguistic factor.

DISCUSSION

Data from six independent studies and two new investigations of the linguistic performances of young normal and handicapped children raise serious doubts about the validity of many commercial and noncommercial language tests that are commonly used today. There appears to be some consistency in all of these findings centering on the existence of one or more modality-specific linguistic ability on which tests of similar input–output modality show high portions of common variance. An instrument such as Menyuk's Sentence Repetition Test — which may be considered cross-modality since it requires auditory comprehension, storage, retrieval, and reproduction skills — may be one of the most pervasive tests of young children's linguistic skills. General rather than specific auditory receptive and expressive linguistic factors seem to characterize findings from the multivariate analyses completed in the two new investigations, along with the correlational findings of earlier studies. The common finding that many receptive language tests correlated and assisted in predicting of expressive measures, with the converse being true frequently also, seems to support the notion that language processing in young children may be more global than specific.

The high relationships found in the Jackson and Sommers (1972) study between articulation scores and the cross-modality MSRT scores were supported by the results from Investigation II in which children's articulation skills correlated with their MSRT scores to the same degree and also correlated highly with their expressive DSS and MLU ones. Although articulation performances also correlated significantly with some receptive language test scores, the strongest relationships tended to be with MSRT test scores.

Results of the factor analyses in Investigations I and II suggest that a battery of tests designed perhaps as criterion measures for researching the linguistic performances of young handicapped children might do well to include a cross-modality measure, such as the MSRT, a strong measure of a more general auditory receptive factor, such as the TACL, and a purely expressive one such as the DSS or a much simpler and quicker one to administer and score, the MLU.

Although assessment of the validity of children's language tests was of basic concern to the present investigators, a related one was general test construction. Many of the speech and language tests and measures studied had no normative data or very sparse information concerning how young normal and handicapped children performed on them. It is clear that testmakers need to devote more effort to improve the standardization of their instruments, gathering abundant information on both normal children and those with handicaps which their instruments were designed to measure.

As Cattell and his colleagues (Cattell & Cattell, 1969) have repeatedly stated, application of modern multivariate analysis techniques can very effectively serve in test construction in many ways, including item analysis, validity checks, and reliability determinations of various kinds. Many of the language tests reviewed here characteristically appear not to have used such tools and techniques. Further, most of the tests and measures seem never to have been revised, particularly as a result of studies of their validity and reliability.

Data from the studies presented strongly suggest a negative answer to the question of whether children's language tests validly measure specific linguistic abilities. Of course, this is not to state that some of these tests and measures are thus not clinically useful or valuable. Knowing the status of a young handicapped child's language processing, even if this determination is limited to modality processing, is clinically useful. Further, language remediators may find that specific error patterns on specific tests remain useful for the planning of language training. The clinical efficacy of planning and conducting language remediation activities based on specific test findings, however, is a moot question. Results of the present report suggest that the more general linguistic abilities of young children may be just as responsive to a general, modality-based language therapy approach than to many of the specific ones that are widely used today. Perhaps these findings also suggest that remedial approaches of a more general nature might prove more effective than very specific ones. The presence of general linguistic abilities in young children implies that generalization of language structures across language levels (i.e., syntactical, morphological, semantic, and phonological) may tend to occur.

Informal Assessment Techniques with LD Children

Hubert Booney Vance

Hubert Booney Vance, PhD, is director of the Child Study Center, Madison College, Harrisonburg, Virginia 22801.

PERHAPS the one irrefutable characteristic attributed to children with learning disabilities is their wide variability of behavior. Mere classification and/or testing does not necessarily prescribe treatment, complete diagnosis, or assessment of these children. Diagnostic procedures are still, at best, somewhat spotty. Knowledge of IQ, reading grade level, or neurological status, while interesting and useful, does not provide enough information with which either to establish appropriate goals or to construct a reality-based training program for a specific child.[1] Therefore, the implementation in the schools of an effective, educationally oriented evaluation program is of the utmost importance for a successful instructional experience with learning-disabled children.

All activities that contribute information and data to the teacher's knowledge of the child and his problem constitute the total evaluation process. It is this information that is synthesized and used to formulate an appropriate instructional intervention for a particular child. According to D. Hammill, the elements of the total evaluation falls into two divisions: the formal evaluation and the use of informal diagnostic techniques (informal evaluation).[2] It is highly unlikely that a single individual will possess the necessary skills or time to manage the total evaluation. Unfortunately, in actual school practice, even where the team approach is used, the total evaluation rarely reflects an educationally relevant focus and often is accomplished for the sole purpose of labeling, placing, or referring youngsters who fail in school.

Hubert Booney Vance, "Informal Assessment Techniques with LD Children," *Academic Therapy*, Vol. 12, No. 3, Spring 1977, pp. 291-303. Copyright ©1977 Academic Therapy Publications, San Rafael, California. Reprinted by permission.

Teachers of learning-disabled children must assume responsibility for a considerable portion of the total diagnostic effort. This does not mean administering IQ tests or other batteries of formal tests. This *does* mean that the teachers of learning-disabled children must participate meaningfully in the evaluation process. If assessment results are to be used meaningfully in educational programing, then we must recognize that instruction and evaluation are not separate words. Successful teaching is a reflection of a series of effective teacher assessments.

The teacher of learning-disabled children who works in the schools must recognize that in many cases the educational evaluation will be left to him alone. These informal techniques can be used to verify the findings of formal assessment and at the same time be substituted for more formalized test results.

The teacher has a unique opportunity and responsibility for observing the child while he is engaged in learning tasks; hence, she must be prepared to collect data systematically and categorize, store, utilize, and evaluate the information. With the teacher assuming a major responsibility in the assessment procedure, the noticeable gap between the diagnostic process and the prescription process for remediation could be eliminated in most instances. This is accomplished through an ongoing process of teaching the child and analyzing his responses to various instructional tasks. Evaluation then becomes an ongoing teaching procedure, one in which the teacher has the responsible role.

These specific task-oriented tests provide additional evaluative teaching data, many times exceeding the value of information obtained through more formalized testing procedures.[3] Teacher-made evaluative instruments are informal and designed to assess one particular skill (e.g., knowledge of a certain kind, knowledge of specific letter sounds, etc.). Instruments that are included at this level of evaluation include seat work exercises emphasizing one specific task, orally administered exercises, informal teaching lessons assessing various skills, and individually administered written assignments. Below is a partial list of specific informal tests that may be used in different curriculum areas.

Visual-Motor Problems

According to G. Wallace and J. Kauffman, competence in visual motor perception is dependent upon the ability to discriminate the constancy of form, perceive objects in foreground and background and to meaningfully separate them, perceive different parts of an object in relation to the observer, and coordinate vision with movements of the body.[4] Especially, the considerations listed can be helpful as procedures to evaluate particular visual-motor perception problems. Many training activities mentioned throughout the literature are suitable assessment tasks.

1. Observe how the child holds his pencil. How well does he copy and trace?

2. Can he move about the room without bumping into or tripping over objects?

3. Have him walk a straight line forwards, backwards, or on his tiptoes.

4. Observe his hopping, leaping, or skipping.

5. Use "Simon Says" or "Jumping Jacks" to observe certain movement skills.

2. DIAGNOSIS

6. Have the child bounce a ball, hop on one foot, or walk a balance beam.

7. Prepare an obstacle course within the classroom and have the child move through the course in many different positions.

8. Observe the child sorting beads or stringing beads, according to color, size, or patterns.

9. Ask the child to make patterns by having him fold paper—move from direct observation to folding patterns from memory.

10. Observe how children snap or fasten, open locks, buckle, tie or untie shoes and laces.

11. Have children toss bean bags to particular shapes; such as, through square holes, round holes, and small holes.

12. Have children copy various designs from the chalkboard.

13. Observe children playing checkers, dominoes, darts or marbles for hand-eye coordination.

14. Direct children to use tongs or tweezers to pick up a series of objects (beads, etc.) and place them in a small-necked container.

Specific Reading Problems

Difficulties in learning to read have been recognized as the most important single cause of school failure. Many children who encounter reading difficulties experience academic problems in other areas of the curriculum. One of the most important steps in informal assessment of reading problems is observing the child reading both orally and silently as well as providing the best possible basis for diagnostic teaching.[5] The analysis of errors on informal measures provides the teacher with pertinent diagnostic information that may be directly utilized in an instructional program. Listed below are suggestions which the teacher may use in detecting specific reading problems.

1. Have the child match capital and lower-case letters: *Aa, Mm, Pp, Bb*, etc.

2. Present the child with a sight vocabulary list to determine how extensive his sight vocabulary is.

3. Be aware if the child is making consistent work analysis errors.

4. Letter recognition: Say, "Look at the row of letters that begin with a _____. Circle the letter."

        d b p c z e g...
        f j l s t z ...

5. Have the child write the alphabet in capital letters (manuscript or cursive).

6. Have the child write alphabet in lower-case (small) letters (manuscript or cursive).

7. Substitute sounds: Say, "Point to the word *ball*. Say it. Now look below the word *ball*; you see parts of words that end like *ball*. Put a letter in the first blank to make the word *fall*."

ball	*pig*	*tip*
___all (f)	___ig (d)	___ip (z)
___all (t)	___ig (b)	___ip (l)
___all (w)	___ig (r)	___ip (h)

8. Context clues: Say, "Read the first sentence. The missing word begins with *w*."

I like to w_____ in the rain.

The food was too h_____.

I l_____ oranges.

Her doll is red and b_____.

9. Consonant discrimination: Say, "Listen for the consonant you hear in the middle of these words. Write the letter on the list."

butter _____

before _____

lessons _____

10. Beginning consonant discrimination: Say, "Sometimes two letters blend to make a sound. Look at the first row of words. Circle the word that begins like *thing*."

thumb	with	stop	(thing)
wish	shine	slime	(shoe)
blue	show	stub	(black)
fish	fly	shed	(flag)

11. Ending blends: Say, "Look at the first row of words. Circle the word that ends like *perch*."

much	fish	choose	(perch)
three	bath	shoe	(with)
ship	chip	swish	(fish)
sent	tree	send	(mint)

12. Substituted blends: Say, "Look at the word *trap*. Say it. Now look below *trap*. You see parts of words that end like *trap*. Put a letter in the blank to make the word."[6]

trap	*clip*	*wing*
___ap (ch)	___ip (sh)	___ng (thi)
___ap (str)	___ip (fl)	___ng (swi)
___ap (scr)	___ip (str)	___ng (spri)

13. Vowels: Say, "Listen to this word. Write on the line the vowel you hear."

smoke _____

risk _____

use _____

sleeve _____

14. Vowels: Say, "Circle the vowels you hear."

chime

seat

tire

15. Root words: Say, "Circle the root word in each of these words."

looking

longest

return

remodel

2. DIAGNOSIS

16. Prefixes and suffixes: Say, "Circle the prefix and suffix of each word below."

export
disobey
replace
happiness

17. Syllables: Say, "Write the number of syllables each word has on the line beside the word."

reload _____

belong _____ passenger _____ away _____

An analysis of various observed reading skills will often be of help in assessing reading problems. Careful observation of the child may provide answers to the following questions:

1. Does he read too fast, too slow, or word by word?

2. What word analysis skills does the child utilize?

3. What "consistent" word analysis errors are made by the child?

4. Are particular words or parts of words consistently distorted or omitted?

Written Language Problems

Written language is one of the most highly sophisticated high forms of language and essentially the last area of language learned. It is usually preceded by the development of skills in listening, speaking, and reading. Direct observation of written language skills will provide the teacher with exacting data in knowing precisely what a child can and cannot do in this area. G. Wallace and J. Kauffman contend that teachers should be particularly observant of the following: (1) consistent difficulty in copying or revisualizing specific letters; (2) patterns of linguistic errors in the spelling of specific words; (3) pencil grasp and body posture problems; and (4) difficulties with writing form, either manuscript or cursive.[7] Following are a number of teacher suggestions which can be used in assessing written language problems.

1. Put two dots on the blackboard. Does he connect them from left to right?

2. When given paper and pencil, does he begin at the left side of the page?

3. Observe the child to see if he closes letters or has difficulty with crossing, making letters too small, or omitting parts of letter.

4. Determine if the position of the child's hand, arm, body, or paper is correct.

5. Have the child print a series of letters or words to determine:

- Quality of pencil control: kinky, varying?

- Slant of writing: irregular, too many slants, not vertical or too slanting?

- Form of letters: poor circles, places illegible, poor straight slopes, or disconnected letters?

• Spacing within letters, between letters, words, too wide, crowded, poorly arranged on paper and uneven?

• Alignment of letters: off the line in places, uneven in height, capital and loop letters uneven?

• Form of letters: letters too round or thin, beginning and ending strokes poorly made, and strokes not uniform (down)?

Oral Language Problems

The close relationship between language and learning has been recognized by many as extremely important. Children with oral language problems are handicapped in understanding and using the spoken word. Deficits in oral language can be very complicated in nature. There are usually three basic aspects of language acquisition and difficulties which the teacher should be concerned with. There are (1) inner language disorders which prevent the child from acquiring basic language skills; (2) receptive language problems which interfer with the child's ability to comprehend the spoken word; and (3) expressive language difficulties which preclude the development of adequate spoken language. The extensive research and study investigating language problems is not yet reflected in the instruments presently available to assess spoken language deficits. J. Brodie contends there are no available tests which adequately measure all aspects of language ability.[8] Consequently many professionals often rely on informal measures. Diagnostic questions and suggestions which can be used in informal assessment of language difficulties are given below.

Inner Language

Many people who work with language tend to agree that inner language disturbances are probably the most debilitating of all language disorders. Inner language can be defined as the language which one uses to communicate with oneself or the language with which one thinks.[9] Children with difficulties in this area are unable to attach meaning to specific words. Part of the difficulty seems to result from the child's inability to transform any experience with the word or concept into verbal symbols. According to Wallace and Kauffman, inner language development is dependent upon the child's ability to:

1. Establish verbal imagery for sounds, words, concepts, etc.

2. Use the complex maze of skills needed in a logical thinking process.

Some of the following questions and methods may be of help in discovering inner language difficulties:

1. Have the child verbally define such words as train, car, truck, doll, house, etc.

2. Determine if the child can attach labels to familiar objects, etc.; flagpole, doors, windows.

3. Read a series of simple analogies to the child and have him complete each sentence.

4. After reading a story, ask the child specific questions which require interpretation and imagination.[10]

2. DIAGNOSIS

Receptive Language Difficulties:

Auditory receptive language is the ability to understand spoken language of others. Children with deficits in this area usually hear what is said but they are unable to comprehend the meaning of it. Typically children with receptive difficulties will have problems associating names with objects, be unable to name objects, have poor recall of names, and have some difficulty in interpreting environmental language.[11] Diagnostic questions and activities for detecting receptive language problems are listed below.

1. Present various isolated speech sounds to a child and ask him to listen for a specific sound such as /k/.

2. Can the child discriminate among various speech sounds? Ask the child to point to certain objects (in a picture) that begins with the same sounds as a stimulus you provided for him.

3. Can the child classify words into categories such as people, food, and animals?

4. Give the child simple directions to see if he can follow them.

5. Can the child match an object to another object which is basically different in form and physical features but belongs to a similar category?

6. Have the child respond "yes" or "no" to the following questions:[12]

"Do flowers grow?"
"Do dogs bark?"
"Do rabbits hop?"

You also can use true-and-false statements.

7. Have the child select words in a sentence that does not make sense; for example, "It snows during the summer."

8. Determine if a child can follow specific directions after hearing a sentence; for example, "Mother bought some apples at the store. Circle what mother bought at the store."

Auditive Expressed Language

Expressive language can be viewed as the spoken language the child uses in communicating with others. Children with disturbances in this area typically hear what is said to them. The major difficulty these children experience is in using language for communicating with others. The most common type of auditory expressive language problems are expressing speech sounds, formulating words and sentences, and retrieval of certain words for spontaneous usage.[13] The majority of these children are often seen by a speech clinician for remediation rather than a teacher. Activities which might provide the teacher with clues in determining if a child is experiencing expressive language problems are listed below.

Observation of oral language skills will often provide insightful information in regard to expressive language problems. A child might attempt to communicate by gestures only. Delayed responses might also serve as a clue.

1. Can the child isolate sounds such as /p/, /k/, /d/, /n/, /t/, and /l/?

2. Determine the child's sight vocabulary by having him name such objects as fruit, tags, etc.

3. Have the child describe certain activities, such as skipping and jumping.

4. Can the child describe the use of simple tools and kitchen utencils?

5. Prepare a series of sentences with key words missing. Read the sentence and ask him to supply the key word; for example:

"A bird _____."
"A dog _____."
"We have _____ ears."

The careful observation of children in various speaking and nonspeaking situations would be both advisable and helpful. Further informal techniques which can be used for assessing language problems can be found in the works of Nancy Wood.[14]

Arithmetic Problems

Many specific arithmetic deficits may be identified by regular classroom teachers. Three everyday classroom procedures which are suited to informal diagnosis are examinations of written assignments, as answer to oral questions and board work. Written seatwork activities often serve as informal tests. W. Otto and R. A. McMenemy indicate that most problems in arithmetic are due to deficiencies in basic computational skills.[15] According to G. Wallace and J. A. McLoughlin, adequate computational and conceptual skills which are fundamental to successful arithmetic achievement include: (1) an understanding of place value; (2) the ability to add, subtract, multiply and divide; (3) an understanding of fractions; (4) the ability to tell time; and (5) a knowledge of monetary values.[16] Diagnostic questions and informal assessment techniques which may be helpful in detecting arithmetic problems are listed below:

1. Seat work activities can serve as a series of informal tests.

2. Ask the child to describe aloud the various procedures involved in solving a particular arithmetic operation.

3. Interviewing the child often can reveal misunderstanding of basic arithmetic concepts or procedures.

Figure 1

**Example of an informal teacher-made
math-skills test**

_____
                Name

1. Copy these numerals

   1 2 3 4 5 6 7 8 9 10   _____

2. Count these dots. Put answer in box.

   • • • • • • • • • •   ☐

3. Circle the number   4   2
                          ‾‾‾   ‾‾‾
                          XXX   XXX
                          XXX   X
                                       XXX

2. DIAGNOSIS

4. What number comes after

    3 _____   6 _____   11 _____   9 _____   13 _____

5. What number comes before

    _____ 2   _____ 9   _____ 6   _____ 4   _____ 8   _____ 10

6. Write the numerals from 1 through 15.

7. What numeral comes between

    4 _____ 6   7 _____ 9   1 _____ 3   10 _____ 12

8. Circle the numeral that means more.

    8 or 6   11 or 14   52 or 25

9. Work as many additions and subtractions as you can.

    $\begin{array}{r} 2 \\ +3 \\ \hline \end{array}$ $\begin{array}{r} 1 \\ +2 \\ \hline \end{array}$ $\begin{array}{r} 0 \\ +4 \\ \hline \end{array}$ 3 + 4 = _____

    7 + 0 = _____

10. 6 + _____ = 10   5 ☐ 3 = 8   _____ − 2 = 2   9 ☐ 4 = 5

11. $\begin{array}{r} 4 \\ -2 \\ \hline \end{array}$ $\begin{array}{r} 9 \\ -7 \\ \hline \end{array}$ $\begin{array}{r} 5 \\ -0 \\ \hline \end{array}$ 9 − 6 = _____   _____ − 2 = 2

12. $\begin{array}{r} 6 \\ 0 \\ +9 \\ \hline \end{array}$ $\begin{array}{r} 50 \\ 32 \\ +16 \\ \hline \end{array}$ $\begin{array}{r} 45 \\ -15 \\ \hline \end{array}$ $\begin{array}{r} 674 \\ -32 \\ \hline \end{array}$ $\begin{array}{r} \$7.31 \\ -.19 \\ \hline \end{array}$

13. Rename: 175 = _____ hundreds _____ tens _____ ones

    250 = 200 + _____ + 0

14. Complete the following: 12 inches = _____ feet

    36 inches = _____ feet or yard

    _____ ounces = 1 pound

    _____ pounds = 1 ton

    _____ pennies = 1 dime (10 cents)

    _____ nickels = 1 quarter (25 cents)

    5 dimes = _____ cents

    4 quarters = _____ dollar

15. Multiplications and divisions

    3 x 8 = _____   2 x 3 = _____   3 $\overline{\smash{)}9}$

    6 x _____ = 24   7 x _____ = 14   2 $\overline{\smash{)}10}$

    0 x 7 = _____   12 - _____ = 1   _____ - 0 = 0

    6 x 1 = _____   9 - 1 = _____   0 X 5 = _____

    $\begin{array}{r} 23 \\ x2 \\ \hline \end{array}$ $\begin{array}{r} 432 \\ x\ 3 \\ \hline \end{array}$ 5 $\overline{\smash{)}75}$ 2 $\overline{\smash{)}48}$

    3 $\overline{\smash{)}603}$ 5 $\overline{\smash{)}375}$

16. Fractions
    Shade 1/3 of this rectangle

    Circle 1/2 of the apples   ○○○○
    ○○○○

17. Equivalent fractions
    1/2 = __ /4   2/3 = __ /9   3/ __ = 9/12

18. Reducing fractions
    7/21 = _____   12/30 = _____   4/8 = _____   4/6= _____

19. Adding and subtracting fractions s
    3/8 + 1/8 = _____   4/10 + 3/10 = _____
    9/17 - 8/11 = _____   1/4 - 1/10 = _____

Conclusion

Many skill deficiencies can be individually assessed through various informal teacher-made tests. The teacher will then be more aware of the exact difficulties being experienced by the child. These teacher-made and teacher-administered informal tests provide the teacher with exact information that can be used in planning for the specific needs of an individual student. Added advantages of informal tests are usually teacher-made, inexpensive, flexible, rapidly administered, and relatively easy to construct.[17] Informal tests combine the diagnostic values of observation with content that is closely geared to instruction. The purpose of the informal examination is not to label a child, but to prepare an instructional program for the pupil based upon his performance and needs. Informal assessment techniques should, however, be considered as only one part of the total assessment procedure, but a very important part.

NOTES

1. D. D. Hammill, "Evaluating Children for Instructional Purposes," *Academic Therapy* 4:4 (1971): 341-353.
2. *Ibid.*
3. *Ibid.*
4. G. Wallace and J. Kauffman, *Teaching Children with Learning Problems* (Columbus, Ohio: Charles E. Merrill, 1969).
5. B. Strang, *Diagnostic Teaching of Reading* (2nd ed.) (New York: McGraw-Hill, 1969).
6. J. Owen, "Open Education" (Carroll T. Overton School, Salisburg, North Carolina, n.d.).
7. Wallace and Kauffman, *op. cit.*
8 J. Brodie, "Language Tests and Linguistically Different Learners: The Sad State of the Art," *Elementary English* 47 (1970): 814-829.
9. D. J. Johnson and H. R. Myklebust, *Learning Disabilities: Educational Principles and Practices* (New York: Grune & Stratton, 1967).
10 Wallace and Kauffman, *op. cit.*
11. M. McGinnis, *Aphasic Children: Identification and Education by the Association Method* (Washington, D.C.: Volts, 1963).
12. W. J. Bush and M. T. Giles, *Aids to Psycholinguistic Teaching* (Columbus, Ohio: Charles E. Merrill, 1975).
13. G. Wallace and J. A. McLoughlin, *Learning Disabilities: Concepts and Characteristics* (Columbus, Ohio: Charles E. Merrill, 1975).
14. N. Wood, *Verbal Learning* (Belmont, California: Fearon, 1969).
15. W. Otto and R. A. McMenemy, "Corrective and Remedial Teaching" (Boston: Houghton Mifflin, 1966).
16. Wallace and McLoughlin, *op. cit.*
17. T. Stephens, "Directive Teaching of Children with Learning and Behavioral Disorders," (Columbus, Ohio: Charles E. Merrill, 1970).

photo: Office of Human Development Services,
Department of Health, Education and Welfare

REMEDIATION OF LEARNING PROBLEMS

The most important component of a learning disabled child's educational plan is the implementation of effective remedial procedures. During the past few decades various theoretical philosophies for instruction have been offered. Barsch, Kephart and others developed motor curriculums based on the premise that children must be able to move efficiently before optimal learning can result. Frostig and Kirk also developed procedures that emphasized the training of underlying skills.

Medical interventions prevail over the learning disabilities field at the present time. The use of drug therapy, diet control, and massive doses of vitamins have been used to try to improve school related performance. Scattered success has been found with some of these methods.

Recently, research evidence seems to indicate that an academic approach which relies on the direct instruction of a learning problem is most beneficial. Many professionals in the learning disabilities field have challenged the use of perceptual and psycholinguistic techniques and have adopted an academic orientation to their remedial procedures.

Alternative teaching suggestions to the basic regular curriculum are being used. The DISTAR materials and suggestions for instruction given by Beth Slingerland and Anna Gillingham are becoming more popular. Also, learning disability teachers are becoming very skillful in their ability to describe, isolate, and sequence the basic components of academic tasks. This task analytic procedure is crucial if an effective remedial program is to be provided.

The selections that are found in this part of the book focus on academic remediation. Procedures that will assist those instructing the learning disabled child in reading, writing, and arithmetic are suggested. Also a sequential series of steps that could provide structure to good teaching for the disabled learner are listed and described.

Doing It Our Way: Putting the Children First

A Conversation with Beth H. Slingerland

At the most recent meeting of the Orton Society I had the pleasure of talking with Mrs. Slingerland. To say I found her interesting, even intriguing, would seem an understatement to her disciples — yes, disciples! Indeed, it is the personal loyalty and high professional standards of those who have learned from her that prompted me to seek this conversation. As we talked about some of her personal milestones — over fifty years as an educator — both her deep commitment and unique blend of viewpoints emerged. Along with the humble recognition of how much there is to be learned in order to serve children there were strongly definitive attitudes: a rejection of government support, and insistence on "language" and not "learning" disabilities, and hence a rejection in part of special education in favor of regular education. — G.M.S.

JLD: I would like very much to begin by asking where you trace your background, what are your affiliations?

Slingerland: Just to reaching these children — the ones with specific language disability — that somehow or other nobody reaches — all of them.

JLD: You don't see your affiliation immediately as organizations — you see it as the children?

Slingerland: Well, I do, yes. I never think of an organization, to tell you the truth, so much as I do of the youngsters. I really got interested in the private school in Hawaii where I lived. The reason I was hired in the first place was that the school couldn't understand why they had a group of children every year who came from the leading citizens in the territory, and yet who couldn't learn to read, write, and spell the way they were expected. They had bright parents and every opportunity in life. This was in Punahou

School, which is the oldest American school west of the Rocky Mountains, founded in 1841 for the children of missionaries and white people living in Hawaii so they didn't have to send their children on a six-month journey back to New England for their education.

JLD: What took you out there?

Slingerland: We went to live there in 1925 when I was married. I had to come back to the mainland for a little while, and then in 1926 we returned to Honolulu. I wanted children of my own and, therefore, when I was asked to apply at Punahou, I said, "Well, I'm not the one to hire because I don't know how to do what you want. I'm searching for the same thing, but I'm not the right person for you because I can't give you what you want." Even Dr. Orton wasn't known in those days with the exception of a small circle of people. So they said that was all right — and the school's president who knew me felt no one

Reprinted by special permission of Professional Press, Inc. from the *Journal of Learning Disabilities*, May 1978, Vol. 11, No. 5, pp. 263-273. ©1978, Professional Press, Inc.

knew what to do for children who didn't learn to read. He said, "It makes no difference — nobody seems to know, and we would like you to come because you have done a lot of your work under Dr. Frederic Burk," who was the president of San Francisco State Normal College. He was "way out" in his day because, when I was going to school there, you had classes with instructors but it was up to you to say when you were ready to take an examination and you could go as fast or slow as you chose.

JLD: Today it's called "progressive."

Slingerland: Yes; my parents were a little shocked about it — that I chose that. But, anyway, I did. It was a savings for me because I was in very bad health — I could work and be in bed and get well and go back and do some more work and keep abreast of what was going on. I think Dr. Burk had as much influence on me as anybody could because in those days San Francisco State was a small school and I'd meet with him.

JLD: So you're talking about influence now in intellectual terms as opposed to general motivation.

Slingerland: That's what made Arthur Hauck of Punahou hire me. He said, "If you worked with Dr. Frederic Burk, we feel you would have the right attitude toward finding out what we would like to know." So I began my work there and it was wonderful work. I felt very inadequate in that I wasn't doing what I wanted for the children, but I began getting on the right track without knowing I was. Then we heard of Bessie Stillman and Anna Gillingham. The trustees of Punahou said, "Go off and start working with them if you can." But Anna and Bessie said, "We don't have schools, we don't have any summer schools so you can't do that. We take our vacations then and go to Glacier National Park where it is beautiful and we stay there and rest up. But, because you are from Hawaii and if you will come over here, we will give you three hours every morning." So my husband went to fish and I went "to school," and when Anna found out that we hiked every afternoon and on the weekends, she said, "Oh, please, take me because that's my favorite activity." So we worked all day long, in the morning with Anna and in the afternoon we hiked. When we went back and told the school trustees what had taken place, they offered to bring them to Hawaii. Anna had just finished her work with Dr. Orton and wanted to spend all the time writing, but they came and spent two years and I worked with them constantly day and night — or so it seemed. My time was spent in learning from them.

You know, a newcomer has to be very careful — the last thing in the world you want to do is be the "know-it-all." So I had to go slowly and not make myself obnoxious by bringing in a new idea too soon.

JLD: Is that the basis for your interest and training?

Slingerland: That's the basis for my beginning to get knowledge of what to do for these children, and from then on I became more interested. I didn't go back to any classroom work because they didn't want me to — instead I began to do teacher training and direct their lower school. Well, about that time there was a considerable amount of unrest. We sensed that war was coming before it actually did. Well, when it came it interrupted a great many things. It was after the war that I came back to the mainland, and I didn't do any school work for a couple of years but read under a great deal of pressure not to take more time off but to get back with children. So I looked around Seattle and didn't find anything that offered an opportunity to be anything but a stereotyped person.

JLD: Jobs seem to come in categories, don't they?

Slingerland: Yes, and that distressed me, so I went to Renton, Washington, and when I walked into the school administration building somebody I had known in Hawaii walked out of the superintendent's office and introduced me to Mr. [Oliver] Hazen. She told him a little about what I had done in Hawaii, and I said I would like to apply for a position because I had visited some of their classrooms and I liked some of the things they did. He said, "We will hire you right now." So I didn't have to go through all the "building up" because I had been recognized.

JLD: Yes, it's a very different perspective now from what you are describing.

Slingerland: Anyway, that's what got me on my way in Washington State.

3. REMEDIATION

JLD: It's interesting — so much of the field is oriented toward the other Washington.

Slingerland: D.C.? — Yes!

So I decided to break away from the Gillingham-Stillman approach of one-to-one instruction. . . . I'm strong for classroom work, so I made up my mind I was going to adapt the techniques to a classroom approach and meet the needs of all the children.

JLD: You were going to Washington where almost necessarily you were not going to have an immediate impact.

Slingerland: There was no impact at all. You have to look back to see how it came.

JLD: This was in about '45 that you came back to the mainland?

Slingerland: Well, we returned but it wasn't until close to '48 that I went into the schools. And then I knew no one and there was no one to talk with — nobody at all. Of those I met nobody had ever heard of dyslexia. You know, a newcomer has to be very careful — the last thing in the world you want to do is to be the "know-it-all." So I had to go slowly and not make myself obnoxious by bringing in a new idea too soon.

You can detect those that need in-depth testing and refer them immediately — don't wait until they fail. Find them right away.

JLD: Was there a feeling also that on the other side of the "know-it-all" coin potentially was a kook?

Slingerland: You didn't want that to happen at all because they would think you were a member of some cult or something. And as I say, this superintendent was a savior — and that's unusual. This somehow was most fortunate. Lots of people wouldn't believe it, but I have come in my many years to realize that maybe we are meant to do certain things. You see, I never had children even as much as I wanted them, so I was able to give all my time and energy to other

people's children. I got my satisfaction from those children and loved them — and still do.

JLD: You have had many?

Slingerland: Yes; and I think I have been fortunate in falling into Miss Gillingham's work as I did and then coming to Washington and having the superintendent hire me and giving me free rein. Only none of the other people I began work with knew about the concept of dyslexia, or special language disabilities. Once I was in a conference about a child with a group of people. I had been listening to all that had been said by those representing different disciplines. I knew what was the matter with that child right away, but I just kept still and listened. Finally, the mother in desperation said, "Isn't there anybody who can help my child or who knows what is the matter with him." I couldn't hold in any longer. I said I believed I knew what was the matter and mentioned it. With that, the pediatrician, who happened to be a woman, looked aghast and said, "I didn't know anybody in the state knew anything about this." She had learned about dyslexia at St. Louis University. Right away we became friends.

JLD: The "small-world" phenomenon again.

Slingerland: Yes; we became friends and would often meet on Saturdays after her work and would talk about children's problems. From then on things just opened up — and definitely on the track I've followed and have been on ever since. I only worked in the mornings and gave my afternoons in working with one or two or three children — but that was very frustrating because of all who weren't getting any help. So I decided to break away from the Gillingham-Stillman approach of one-to-one instruction. People think we are doing big things when we work with four, five, or six children. I'm not talking about the technique and all the good we do with it. I'm strong for classroom work, so I made up my mind I was going to adapt the techniques to a classroom approach and meet the needs of all the children — providing they can be screened and the teachers trained, because you can't do a thing if you screen and fail to implement what you find out.

JLD: There's no back-up.

Slingerland: Without it there's no reason to screen in the first place.

JLD: But, then again, screening is "group" also. Is this a question of efficiency again?

Slingerland: We don't have any trouble because when you screen you can find the children, this 15 to 20%, and from them you can detect those that need in-depth testing and refer them immediately — don't wait until they fail. Find them right away — send them to the departments of psychology or special services.

JLD: But you are not using teacher referral but rather testing as the first source?

Slingerland: And screening — I like more and more to call them screening procedures because I don't feel that we are really testers. We are doing just exactly what we say.

JLD: What do you think about the use of teacher checklists or even simply teacher referral as the major first screening source?

Slingerland: No, we don't use that. We take every child in the first grade and screen him — and besides you learn how to evaluate much better by doing it that way.

JLD: You screen everybody?

Slingerland: We screen everybody and from the greatest number there are no problems. They are just going to go into the regular, conventional classrooms — and teachers get enough

---

They are placed beyond their ability *at the moment*, which is wrong for the child if you are trying to make him fit into what you think he *should* be doing. This is just backwards — because I am a strong believer in the individual child, not the group.

---

knowledge so that if we should make mistakes, they would refer the child again right away.

JLD: They pick it up *after* screening.

Slingerland: Yes — those who show no disability and those who show no weaknesses. Then from that very small group left over we find a few who have no business being in the classroom they are in. They are placed beyond their ability *at the moment*, which is wrong for the child if you are trying to make him fit into what you think he *should* be doing. This is just backwards — because I am a strong believer in the individual child, not the group.

JLD: Can it be individualized within the group so that the child can still be a first grader, or need he be held back?

Slingerland: Well, for instance, we screen children who come from kindergarten in late April or May so they are all ready for first-grade placement.

JLD: You think that's the best time — not after a couple of months of kindergarten?

Slingerland: No, not when they just enter kindergarten, because the phenomenal part of language is still developing. It is not yet time for the nonphenomenal period of growth when children learn to use symbols to represent the language — during the first six or seven years. But from then on, for reading we would be using the symbols. That is not a phenomenal thing, and it must be taught. So we can screen and find those who seem to have made a perfectly normal development in language skills, understanding, and using the words to express themselves. And then we can find what seems to be happening in the visual modality which is what he is going to have to use for reading and spelling — we can see the children of high risk and the children who are fine. That way we can place the ones who show high risk or already severe disability with the trained teacher in a first grade. All the children in the classroom are children who show high risk or an outright disability and that teacher works with them for the year — then in a continuum they are

---

Our children have no learning problems. They learn, they are quick, creative, imaginative, and they do not have a learning problem per se.

---

moved to the next grade and go on. There are only a few children — there are some, but there are only a few children as a rule — who should not be in first grade at all.

JLD: But you are advocating a grouping of the children with a problem with a special teacher? Of course, as you know the "mainstreaming" effort is contrary to placing them in a special grouping such as that. People are now saying, "Let's get them back into regular classrooms."

Slingerland: We consider ours a regular classroom because the classroom operation is exactly as it is in a conventional class, the only difference being that the child's language arts are taught with a specific approach. There is no

Everybody today must learn to read, write, and spell. We judge people for that, and yet long ago people would nevertheless live a lifetime and become highly successful and nobody would know the difference.

difference whatsoever and there is no stigma because we take only children of average to superior mentality. We don't feel that we should take the mentally deficient because that is not our problem. The government gives money for them you see. We don't get any extra money. We have done all we've done without a penny of help from anyone — and no extra taxes.

JLD: That's so interesting because the learning disability movement was one to try, and successfully so, to get money under a handicap label. I noticed you use the term "language" —

Slingerland: Specific language disability.

JLD: As opposed to learning disability.

Slingerland: In fact, we won't use the term "learning disability."

JLD: Why not?

Slingerland: Our children have no learning problems. They learn, they are quick, creative, imaginative, and they do not have a learning problem per se. They have a *specific* language disability and they can learn when they are taught in a way that helps to put things together for them.

JLD: There is something overly broad about the notion of children who can't learn.

Slingerland: Well, we don't want these children to suffer under any misunderstanding. We want them to feel they are just the same as anybody else. We draw pictures of the brain to show how the language comes in and has nothing to do with the frontal lobe for thought and making judgments. You can be the brightest person in the world and still struggle to read and write. We even point out to them that 200 years ago they probably wouldn't have had any struggle at all — but everybody today must learn to read, write, and spell. We judge people for that, and yet long ago people would nevertheless live a lifetime and become highly successful and nobody would know the difference. They just didn't spend their time on that kind of learning,

and even today we have very successful people who are very poor spellers or writers.

JLD: One of our former Vice Presidents, a Senator —

Slingerland: Sometimes these children from wealthy homes have more opportunity than the children from just average homes.

JLD: Do you believe in the early stimulation?

Slingerland: Oh, I think it helps. The deprivation that some children suffer is not always due to lack of money; it's the kind of attention they get. We see it in Washington — a rich state with so much beauty, opportunity to see ships, animal life, and you'd be surprised how many parents have not taken their children up to Mt. Ranier, haven't taken them to the parks, aboard ships, down to the trains, all those things — and they don't cost any money. Now when our kindergarten group in Hawaii went off on a trip to see things and came back and played with blocks — we have everything under the sun for children, in modern education — we never asked a question and it would be three to four days before they would even start building something they had seen. Not talking about it shows that it was going around in their heads. We waited until it came out and everything was ready.

JLD: I noticed your emphasis on intrinsic motivation so different from behavior modification.

Slingerland: We don't condemn them, we let them know we respect them, and we let them know as soon as possible it is not their fault. As a demonstration, I took a group of boys who were ready to be expelled from school in San Francisco. They did not read, write, spell, or anything — and they were 16. They said these boys were so impossible in school and I said, "Why wouldn't they be impossible?" The only thing I ever ask when I take children without any preparation is, "Give me two or three minutes with the children so I can introduce myself to them privately," whether they are 9 years old or 16. So, I will try to prevent them from saying it is their fault if anything goes wrong. "It is my fault if I failed to reach you in the right way." I get marvelous cooperation. I remember a group in Alaska — they were 12-year-olds and I said to them, "Now remember, it isn't going to be your fault if you should make a mistake; it will be mine for letting you do something before you are prepared for it. 'So whose fault will it be?' And they said, 'Yours.'" And everything went along fine until one boy made a mistake about

> **Everything went along fine until one made a mistake. "Whose fault is that?" and all four boys put their hands out and said, "Your fault." Well, the audience dropped their mouths wide open — they were floored.**

something and I looked at him and said, "Whose fault is that?" and all four or five boys put their hands out and said, "Your fault." Well, the audience dropped their mouths wide open — they were floored. When the children saw the joke and I saw, because they found out what the response of the people was, it just relaxed them.

JLD: It sounds so antithetical to modern university training programs where children have the handicaps.

Slingerland: This is where I realized later what Dr. Burk did for me. He told all of us, but he would talk to me individually too, "If you feel you are going right or you are in a path that has been untrod, don't worry, do it the way you feel is right. Stick to your principles and go ahead because that is the way everything is improved." I can't seem to do anything else. I don't care what people seem to think about me. I care what the children are going to get, and that people you get your support from are wonderful teachers. We get great strength from the parents — they organize, you know. They are the ones who bring the programs into the schools, support them, and provide money. Also, you begin getting your administration to help. Many teachers think they don't know how to teach, that they've never been taught how to teach. Then there are teachers who are so departmentalized they just teach subjects — but we do have other good teachers who are not satisfied with themselves.

JLD: Right, when you are teaching a subject, you almost necessarily are not teaching a child. You lose the texture of the differences in the children. I was thinking of what you said before about the responsibility lying with the teachers. It takes a special kind of teacher to be able to take that much failure because there must be failure in problem-solving all of the time — trying to figure out why a certain child is not progressing.

Slingerland: But, you see we do have a structured plan. We stick to the basic plan which

is to begin with a single unit which is a letter of the alphabet. But that is only the beginning and so often in describing the technique, people fail to realize that the units become increasingly larger. They are of no use to you unless you can use them for some purpose. And alone they aren't of any use so the next thing we must do is learn how they are used to be put into groups. The next larger unit is the word and you start with words that are the easiest kind to blend. You either have to read them to get someone's idea or because you want to express your own thoughts. So you learn to write words which includes spelling, which is not phenomenal learning, by the way — you have to teach it. Unlike the phonetic readers that are published today, we start with just one vowel and the reason for that is neurological. We want to start by creating a pattern of thought, and you must take away all of the obstacles.

JLD: You have them say the same vowel?

Slingerland: Take away the obstacles, make it as pure as you can. Well, if we put in two or three vowels, the child has to stop for discrimination of the two or three vowels, you see. So we want the pattern of how you put single units together to make a larger unit which becomes a word unit — a task not yet requiring discrimination.

JLD: It's so different from the rhyming methods.

Slingerland: One single vowel unit is taught. As soon as the pattern is established, the child knows how to *listen* to the word. To some children, words learned earlier as "wholes" cause trouble. Children understand how sequencing sounds or symbols form words to spell or read. Then you don't need to think of that word as having individual sounds. A sixth-grade boy said to me, "I never knew that. Is that the way sound words are made?" — a sixth-grade boy! Then they learn short-"a" words. As soon as they learn that, the next step is to teach discrimination, which means introducing a new vowel because the pattern of blending is established — putting single units together to make a new word unit. The next larger step is to get your shades of meaning with the use of suffixes, which begins with our first graders about in February, and they get the suffix concept immediately. As an example, after a child has learned to spell "jump," you say, "When I jump, what am I doing when I jump?" and he'll say, "Jumping." And immediately you are ready to teach your suffix. Then, you say, "If I jump now, what did I do yesterday, or before now or this morning," and he says, "Jumped." We don't pay any attention to the sound because we want him to spell through his brain power. What you put there is "ed" and he learns *meaning*.

JLD: The intrinsic motivation?

Slingerland: That's right! Now, if you want him to write some more words, you say, "Write the word that tells what you are doing when you jump," and they write it (one word under the other for perceptual reasons). They always see their root words and know it's the root word.

JLD: The approach is so different say from that linked with the ITPA which is such a strong power in the "language" field — or specific

---

We get great strength from the parents — they organize, you know. They are the ones who bring the programs into the schools.

---

learning disability fields, as it is termed nationally. Are they at all reconcilable?

Slingerland: Well, not exactly.

JLD: You don't train them in the ITPA?

Slingerland: No, we just train them in how to go about this because it takes about two years to learn to be self-reliant. I wish it were something you could do fast, but you just can't. I have deliberately stayed away from making workbooks because teachers are prone to give a child a workbook and say "do it," and we want the teacher to know what she is doing and teach — that's what it means — to teach, and it's up to the child to perform the work under the teacher's guidance.

JLD: That must mean tremendous management training.

Slingerland: It's easy, though we prefer certified teachers who are already trained and know classroom management. Another thing we never do is to have a child who needs specific help attempt something he can't do. We know how to ask him questions to trigger his thought patterns so he can do it, and in the end, though you may have pulled it out like pulling teeth, he succeeds inside. He thinks because you can say to the children, "Who did it finally — he did." And the child knows he did. We never call on

someone who is quick and does things better to do it for him; it humiliates the child too much. That's more of our teacher training — she has to go at it in a different way. We are teaching with the idea that we must conform to our ideas of how fast children learn. Everyone works at a different pace.

JLD: This lack of urgency that characterizes almost all aspects of the interaction process with the child also characterizes the way you go about your own teaching of teachers. Have you ever wondered if the process is fast enough — are there enough people out there to continue this work? There are so many needy children.

Slingerland: There are so many needy children and we need so many good teachers. We have over 22 summer schools now scattered about the United States. It's a matter of getting our people trained so they are capable of teaching other people. We have more and more directors, more staff people. We don't take just anybody — we have to know what they are doing during the year, how they are doing it, so they will use the techniques right. At the moment our organization seems so small, but it's growing faster and faster.

JLD: And yet you don't seek government support.

Slingerland: We don't ask any government support — we get none and we wouldn't get any because it all goes into special ed and they are not about to share anything.

JLD: Is your approach not special ed?

Slingerland: No, it's general education so we are free of government regulation.

JLD: Freedom at a cost!

Slingerland: Yes, but we don't have a lot of time between testing and initial instruction. A child is tested by a half dozen people, and doesn't have to fall on his face in failure. We pick him up before he has any more failures. Maybe he has never had any because you can identify a child when he enters school and you don't let him fail — you *prevent*.

JLD: You certainly could make a case that you are dealing with children who are learning disabled under the law so that you *could* get federal money, and yet you still choose not to.

Slingerland: No, I don't think they would give it to us because we would have to follow all their regulations and that would defeat our whole approach. We wouldn't reach the children we needed to, and we are more interested in the children than we are in anything else.

JLD: It's like Carl Rogers saying, "I don't want to give all those tests, that violates the relationship with my client. I would rather see each as a person."

Slingerland: Well, we do that. I won't even standardize my screening test because I don't want the child to become a number fed into a computer. He is an individual.

JLD: You don't want to standardize — how do you know what is high and what is low?

Slingerland: It's the kind of errors they make. You reach the point that when you test 125 children who are entering first, second, and third grade, they fall into groups themselves.

JLD: You teach the pattern so you know the meaning of the errors?

Slingerland: Yes, definitely. That is a necessary part of evaluation. There is no such thing as written expression until you can write a phrase. There is no such thing as reading until you can read a phrase. If I say the word "horse," there is not one clue that gives you any meaning except what you get out of your head, but if I say "a little black horse," then I have given you something specific. Otherwise, there is no such thing as reading, only word-naming. A phrase leads to a sentence, and a sentence leads to a paragraph. Then comes understanding of a paragraph. We want our children to learn how to conceptualize.

JLD: You're dealing with understanding and not word-naming.

Slingerland: We teach words in phrases. We never let them read one word at a time. But they need to learn to recognize the articles and how they lead into a phrase. Also, they learn concepts from prepositions. They understand what a phrase is if it's *about* somebody or something and then about the ones that show the action and on

---

Teachers are the people I want to "build up," to make them understand that it matters not how much study is needed, how much research is accomplished. If you don't have teachers trained to do the work, it will never get to the children. It's what *they* learn that is so vital.

---

to describe something or *how* somebody or *what*

somebody is doing so they are always looking for how, when, where, or what.

JLD: You speak of neurological plasticity and yet in defining language disabilities you insist that the child's neurological substrata be normal. Is there any reason for that? Wouldn't the reasoning approach work as well or maybe require a somewhat more clever teacher? What if there were some damage, minimal or otherwise?

Slingerland: Damage to the brain you mean?

JLD: Yes.

Slingerland: Well, that would be "impaired." There is considerable difference between impairments and dysfunction. If it's an impairment, we don't claim we can do anything — the break is there, whatever the impairment. So far medical science can't cure or correct it. You may not be able to create a path ever — but if it's a dysfunction, you can pull pieces together or else create a path around. Impairment and dysfunctioning are two totally different things.

JLD: Can research do anything? You seem to have continued your work for decades now with only clinical feedback.

Slingerland: Just on the threshold — I wish I were younger than I am, and knew what I've learned over the years. That's why I keep pouring it into the teachers all the time — and my co-workers and the directors. They will carry on where I leave off because I have gone only so far. They can use that which I had to learn. But there is just no end to what has to be learned.

JLD: Are there questions that you would have wished the researchers had asked that have been overlooked?

Slingerland: I wish some of them, like neurologists, had taken the trouble to learn a little more about pediatrics. There should be more interdisciplinary work being done than there is. Each follows along in his own field and does not know enough about what is going on in another area. Teachers are the people I want to "build up," to make them understand that it matters not how much study is needed, how much research is accomplished. If you don't have teachers trained to do the work, it will never get to the children. It's what *they* learn that is so vital.

JLD: The training programs going on now with funding from the government turn out some whom I think you would really question their abilities. Are there more being turned out who are inadequate than adequate?

Slingerland: Too many, and we know because we're in the business. How many people

3. REMEDIATION

go into that kind of training who are inadequate teachers in the first place? In school districts where the administration wants our programs, the children are screened and they get trained teachers; the children progress from year to year in a continuum through as many grades as the school provides the trained teachers. Everything will be going along beautifully, and then the teacher gets married or has a baby, and we've got some place to fill in again. So there is always change, it never stays put. That's why administration is so important — to make sure that the gaps are filled.

JLD: For the delivery of any strategy.

Slingerland: More teachers are getting their initial experience in classrooms each year so they need in-service guidance which in many places they get. In not all, and this is hard on many teachers because they want the extra guidance. If the districts set it up right, their teachers progress farther and it's from those places that we manage to get our future staff teachers and directors.

JLD: Is your approach in terms of teacher training and in terms of knowledge of the children changing, and if so what is the process?

Slingerland: We feel that we are improving. We not only learn from the medical research but we feel we can improve some of the approaches, not just the basic underlying principles. But we want to keep in mind that we don't want to ever become so in a groove that we think "that's it." We've never reached that point and while we know our techniques, we know that we are reaching children with the various modality weaknesses.

JLD: You know this because you see it, but do you do research on this of a statistical nature?

Slingerland: In the screening tests, we can see it in the children, and then the weakness in the child screams at you. And there is a certain sympathy that children show for each other regardless of the disability. We didn't foresee this — the wonderful patience, tolerance, and understanding they show when they discover other people have the same problem. Just like adults, suddenly they begin to have a common view with them. They always thought they were stupid when they were growing up and then they suddenly discovered. A young man who sat through three of my talks came up to me one day and said, "I saw you look at me so I know you recognized me. I have been following you around and the reason is because I have been

going to a psychiatrist for two years and still feel very inadequate. Now that I have listened to this, I don't need a psychiatrist any more. I know what is the matter. I'm not a dumbbell." He had three little boys coming along and he was going to see that they were sent to the right school.

JLD: There is a direct reward. You don't feel the need to have graphs or charts or data in that sense. There is an article published in the *Journal* (January 1978) about modality preference; it reviews some 28 studies, none of which show the validity of the modality concept. I personally believe in it. I am strongly auditory.

Slingerland: Your business would make me think you were.

JLD: Why are these studies failing to validate such a basic construct? I wonder whether the clinical tools and sensitivities are often much sharper than the research tools?

Slingerland: You know, you asked me a question a minute ago and it ties into this too. You asked if we have changed. Well, we do change. When I began I was led for quite some time to believe that you didn't waste much time with children of low IQs because you can't help them, or it wouldn't be enough help. Over the years, we began learning more about the modality weakness and the auditory modality weakness. I figured that well, in that case, if a child doesn't perceive what he hears, if he doesn't get the meaning or else is slow in getting it, then you can't store words; and if you can't store the words, there is no opportunity to retrieve them in self-expression. What happens when you can't give back and you also appear stupid to your friends and relatives? In Montana, I asked the directors to let us find children who have IQs in the 80s — then we add 10 points to those, and place them accordingly. And it worked because they weren't dumb. Now that changed me. I thought, "We are going to face the facts that we have to reach the children with the auditory modality." Now you see why everybody talks about reading — because nobody catches the disability until they get to school and they have to read. They don't realize that we have a whole flock of kids who are in trouble even before they put a foot inside the school. If these children don't fit into your preconceived notion, you are creating a teacher-perpetuated disability because you make them disabled.

JLD: What you have just suggested is that they come with these problems. Is there any sensibility, is there any potential of finding them earlier? We don't have sufficient social systems, of course.

Slingerland: When you have hundreds of children coming into school, we have to adapt something that will reach these children faster than individual testing and teaching. We don't set ourselves up as the ideal, but we are approaching it the best way we know with the facilities and the fact that we get very little recognition. I know, but I always say I would rather grow as we are than to make a big splash and then have the waves all disappear before you have accomplished anything. So we just grow and grow and more people are seeming to get things done.

JLD: That's a very different and perhaps it is a very nice note to end on because it's very characteristic of the way you give the child learning, the way you do your teacher training, the way you want the program to expand because people want it.

Slingerland: They depend on the money and also are inadequately prepared to handle themselves. They just don't come off and that's why we agreed to go on without money — because whenever the teacher goes, it's in her head and she takes it. This worries me a little bit — I said once to the president of the Board of Trustees, "What if I have to leave, if I die or something happens — you have invested so much in me? What happens?" It bothers me — I feel I have too much responsibility and they said, "Don't feel that way because if you have it, it's yours. We've given it to you. You give it wherever you go and we'll feel it was highly just."

JLD: And you have people who refer to themselves as "disciples" of yours.

Slingerland: Well, I understand that happens frequently, but I think it's because they know that I can't put it in a book. I do write the books, you see, but then they know how to use them. But, that is the important thing that no matter where they go, they will be able to serve children with special language disabilities. They will not need me.

Eleven Steps to Good Teaching

SUSAN HASAZI
ROBERT YORK

During the past decade, the educational rights of handicapped children and their parents have been recognized and affirmed. Perhaps the most important affirmation of these rights was the passage of Public Law 94-142, The Education For All Handicapped Children Act of 1975. This law attempts to insure that all handicapped children are identified and receive a free, appropriate public education. To insure the appropriateness of a child's program an individualized education plan (IEP) must be written for each student. At first glance the requirements for the development of each IEP may appear to be inordinately extensive and/or cumbersome. However, we believe these requirements are not extraordinary, but represent steps typically performed in the course of "good teaching."

In our view, good teaching is comprised of a series of interrelated steps that appear to apply equally to handicapped and nonhandicapped students, all teaching environments, and instruction on any skill. Many of these steps are similar to those required in the development of an IEP. Not surprisingly, these teaching steps have been identified by other authors and might be termed *a common sense approach to teaching* (Christie, Williams, Edelman, Hill, Fox, Fox, Sousie, & York, 1977; McKenzie, Egner, Knight, Perelman, Schneider, & Garvin, 1970). These 11 steps are listed below and described more fully in the following narrative.

Preparation of this paper was supported in part by Special Projects Grant #451 AH6 60351 and Program Assistance Grant #6007306053 from the Bureau of Education for the Handicapped, USOE, HEW.

STEPS TO GOOD TEACHING

1. Meet and learn about the students.

2. Determine what the students want to learn and/or what their parents want them to learn.

3. Determine the students' current skills.

4. Determine the skills needed by the students.

5. Specify the goals of instruction.

6. Break the goals down into smaller, teachable, and measurable objectives that, when acquired, lead to the realization of the goals.

7. Select instructional procedures to teach those objectives.

8. Select materials, tasks, and physical arrangements that fit the objectives and instructional procedures.

9. TEACH—implement the instructional program.

10. Measure student progress on the objectives.

11. Evaluate instruction in light of student progress and make appropriate revisions.

Meet and Learn About the Students

It is essential that every student be viewed as an individual with unique strengths, weaknesses, and learning experiences. Sensitivity to individual differences and knowledge about each student are important to the development of quality instructional programs. Familiarity with students allows a teacher to accurately assess skills and facilitate optimal performance. A teacher's knowledge of his or her students is the best single information source for developing and revising instructional programs.

Determine What the Students Want to Learn and/or What Their Parents Want Them to Learn

The guidance and cooperation of students and parents is necessary in the development and implementation of instructional programs. Since parents have had the greatest opportunity to observe their child's behavior, they can provide valuable information regarding current skills, as well as particular preferences and dislikes the child may have. Further, parents are in the most appropriate position to predict future needs and lifelong goals for their child.

Determine the Students' Current Skills

We believe the best currently available way to determine a student's skills is to compare his or her current repertoire against comprehensive sequences of skills. Such skill sequences consist of hierarchies of behaviors that progress from the most rudimentary level to competent functioning in major developmental and academic areas. Similar to the mathematical concept of a number line, skills can be ordered along a continuum of increasing complexity. However, instead of being comprised of a chain of numbers, skill sequences are comprised of behaviors. These behaviors can be converted into objectives for assessment and later for instruction and evaluation. Placing each student within such a sequence of skills allows the formulation of a basic map of where the student is and what skills might be appropriate for instruction (York & Williams, 1977).

Such assessment procedures are based on the notion that evaluation of a student's performance should relate to the environment in which he or she will be functioning. Further, it suggests that assessment should be closely linked to instruction, thus encouraging the process of on going, continuous evaluation.

Determine the Skills Needed by the Student

Following a comprehensive assessment of a student's skills, a careful evaluation of the current and future environment must be made. This process will assist the teacher in determining "what" skills are or will be needed for adequate functioning. Teachers should provide a rationale concerning the value of a skill to a student once it is acquired (Brown, Nietupski, & Hamre-Nietupski, 1976; Williams, Brown, & Certo, 1975). Questioning the rationale behind the teaching of a specific skill will also assist the teacher in prioritizing objectives.

Specify the Goals of Instruction

Following completion of steps 1 through 4, the teacher is ready to select the goals most appropriate for the individual student (Hasazi, 1976). These goals should be selected using: (1) input gained from interactions with the student and/or the parents, (2) assessment of the student's current skills, and (3) the teacher's assessment of what skills the student needs to acquire in order to function successfully within current and probable future environments.

Break the Goals Down into Smaller, Teachable, and Measurable Objectives That, When Acquired, Lead to the Realization of the Goals

Specifying goals is much easier than developing the carefully sequenced set of objectives or steps that will lead to the realization of those goals. Breaking the goals down requires a careful analysis of the component skills comprising those goals. For example, walking across a classroom within 30 seconds may be an easily agreed on goal. However, generating the sequence of objectives from head control to walking is considerably more demanding and might include steps like: (1) creeps (hand/knee locomotion), (2) pulls to knees, (3) lowers from knees, (4) kneels with support, (5) pulls to standing, (6) lowers from standing, (7) stands supported, (8) stands alone, (9) walks sideways while holding onto a table, (10) walks forward while holding onto a table, (11) walks forward along a wall, and (12) walks forward with support (Williams & Fox, 1977).

The process of breaking goals down into teachable objectives is often referred to as task analysis. The seven basic steps of the task analysis process are listed here.

Seven Steps of Task Analysis

1. Delineate the instructional objective.

2. Review relevant literature and resources (normal developmental sequences, curriculum guides).

3. Derive and sequence the component skills of the objective.

4. Eliminate unnecessary skills.

5. Eliminate redundant skills.

6. Determine prerequisite skills.

7. Monitor student performance and revise the task analysis as required (Williams & Gotts, 1976).

Skill sequences developed through task analysis can be adapted to accommodate varying entry levels as well as differences in classroom environments. They provide a framework upon which teaching procedures can be designed. Importantly, these objectives or steps must be stated so that parents and teachers know what to look for as evidence of progress. For this reason, many teachers now use a format made popular by Mager (1962) that specifies the condi-

3. REMEDIATION

tions under which learning is to occur, the expected student behavior, and the criteria for acceptable performance. This format helps to assure that progress toward achievement can be reliably observed and measured.

Select Instructional Procedures to Teach Those Objectives

While considerable debate exists concerning the "best" instructional procedures, the fact that some procedures are necessary is generally accepted. Even advocates of "discovery" or "self instructional" approaches typically attempt to arrange the educational environment so that "discoveries" may more readily occur. We consider any attempts to arrange or create an environment that produces specified changes in the student's behavior to be instructional procedures (Brown & York, 1974). Primarily, these instructional procedures may be broken down into three components.

First, the educational environment preceding the task the teacher wants the student to perform should be arranged to maximize the likelihood that the student will perform that task. This could include such antecedent events as giving clear directions, providing specially designed curriculum materials, or changing the physical environment to encourage social interactions.

Second, the actual behavior to which the instructional procedure is directed must also be considered. The specific skills, knowledge, and attitudes a teacher hopes to develop must be specified and provisions must be made for the unique physical and behavioral characteristics of each student. Consequently, alternate paths to the same goal must be determined in order to accommodate these characteristics.

Third, the consequences for correct and incorrect performance must be specified so that the student will receive appropriate feedback and continue to work at the task of learning. Feedback and reinforcement must be provided to guide, encourage, and nurture the child's love of learning. What the student learns should be of functional value and assist the child in effecting his social and physical world. Ideally, the learning environment is one that promotes further learning by stimulating curiosity and motivation.

Select Materials, Tasks, Physical Arrangements, and Schedules that Fit the Objectives and Instructional Procedures

The physical environment should be arranged to facilitate active involvement and cooperation among students. Further, the environment should be flexible enough to allow for large or small group instruction, self directed learning activities, and one-on-one teaching. Emphasis should be placed on designing or choosing learning materials that are functional, enjoyable, and have generalized value to the student. This requires that a teacher be able to manage an educational environment designed to encourage diverse learning experiences that are receptive to the unique needs of each student.

Aspects of this step are both conceptual and mechanical. The teacher must both decide that an objective, such as matching numerals, can be taught through a game, and then assemble the necessary materials. If the objective is to develop social interactions, the student needs someone to interact with and a place in which to interact. These opportunities for interaction must be regularly scheduled within the time available for instruction. This step requires many decisions, ranging from how the furniture will be arranged, to how this skill can be taught and tested in a natural setting.

TEACH—Implement the Instructional Program

This is, of course, the most obvious thing a teacher must do and perhaps the most important step. Time engaged in direct instruction of a skill has been shown to be the most significant determinant of whether that skill was subsequently acquired (Fredericks, Anderson, Baldwin, Beaird, Moore, & Grove, undated). However, we have seen teachers become so involved in the other steps of teaching that they apparently forgot to teach.

Measure Student Progress on the Objectives

The two major reasons for measurement of student progress are to determine the success or failure of current teaching efforts and revise or continue those efforts as appropriate; and to document student progress over time so that the students, parents, and others are informed and can assist in updating goals. Thus, measurement or data collection is done to aid and improve decision making. Collection of data that are not used for these purposes is usually of little or no value.

Evaluate Instruction in Light of Student Progress and Make Appropriate Revisions

The importance of writing observable and measurable goals is underscored during the process of evaluation. If the goals have been written in such a way that it is clear whether or not the desired behaviors have been learned, evaluation becomes linked to

instruction. The question teachers should ask is, "Has the student learned what I had hoped to teach?" If no progress has been made, teaching has not occurred.

If progress is not apparent or is less than expected, the teacher needs to carefully reconsider all 10 teaching steps leading up to this point. Examination of these steps usually suggests several possible program changes, e.g., Is progress on objectives slow because some prerequisite skills are missing? Are the teaching procedures ineffective because of unclear instructions or uninteresting consequences? Are we measuring the wrong things and missing progress? Thus, solving problems usually means reexamining the first 10 steps of "good teaching." Often a teacher's own analysis will identify a potential problem and suggest appropriate revisions of that step.

If skills are being learned, a teacher must still ask the questions "Is learning fast enough?" and "what is the quality of learning?" Teachers must be concerned with the quality of their instruction and its effectiveness in preparing students to adequately function in their living and working environments. Thus, effort needs to be expended to measure the durability and generality of instruction. Are the skills that were taught functional to the student as he or she performs the tasks required in his or her daily life? Are the skills durable so that the student is able to use them after instruction is over? Do the skills generalize to new settings, people, and materials? Is skill performance controlled by events in the natural environment?

SUMMARY

The 11 teaching steps that have been presented certainly are not revolutionary. However, we feel they define the basis of "good teaching." Further, the development of an individualized education program requires that many of these steps be followed, and, in fact, specified in writing, for each handicapped student. As simple as they seem, their successful implementation usually requires substantial amounts of hard work. However, their successful implementation appears to lead to that most desirable goal of any teacher . . . students who learn and grow.

REFERENCES

Brown, L., Nietupski, V., & Hamre-Nietupski, S. Criterion of ultimate functioning. In M. A. Thomas (Ed.), *Hey, don't forget about me!* Reston VA: The Council for Exceptional Children, 1976.

Brown, L., & York, R. Developing programs for severely handicapped students: Teacher training and classroom instruction. *Focus on Exceptional Children*, 1974, *6* (2).

Christie, L. S., Williams, W., Edelman, S., Hill, M. G., Fox, T. J., Fox, W.·L., Sousie, S. P., York, R. *A master's level training program to prepare teachers serving learners in need of intensive special education.* Burlington VT: Center for Special Education, University of Vermont, 1977.

Fredericks, H. D., Anderson, R., Baldwin, V., Beaird, V., Moore, W., Grove, D. *The identification of competencies in teachers of the severely handicapped.* Monmouth OR: Teaching Research Infant and Child Center, undated.

Hasazi, S. The consultant teacher. In J. Jordan (Ed.), *Teacher, please don't close the door: The exceptional child in the mainstream.* Reston VA: The Council for Exceptional Children, 1976.

Mager, R. F. *Preparing instructional objectives.* Belmont CA: Fearon, 1962.

McKenzie, A. S., Egner, A. N., Knight, M. F., Perelman, P. F., Schneider, B. M., & Garvin, J. S. Training consulting teachers to assist elementary teachers in the management and education of handicapped children. *Exceptional Children*, 37 (2), 137-143.

Williams, W., Brown, L., & Certo, N. Basic components of instructional programs. *Theory Into Practice*, 1975, *14*(2), 123-136.

Williams, W., & Fox, T. (Eds.). *Minimum objective system for pupils with severe handicaps.* Burlington VT: Center for Special Education, University of Vermont, 1977.

Williams, W., & Gotts, E. A. Selected considerations on developing curriculum for severely handicapped students. In E. Sontag, J. Smith, & N. Certo (Eds.), *Educational programming for the severely and profoundly handicapped.* Reston VA: Division on Mental Retardation, The Council for Exceptional Children, 1976.

York, R., & Williams, W. Curricula and ongoing assessment for individualized programming in the classroom. In R. Minisi & P. Thorpe (Eds.), *Education of severely and profoundly handicapped children and youth.* Hightstown NJ: Northeast Regional Resource Center, 1977.

"KIDS CAN'T SPELL!" claim teachers and parents alike, and the entire country is up in arms wondering what to do about it. But for spelling—more so than for any other subject—teachers need a bag of tricks to get kids involved and motivated.

Here, Carol J. Fisher, INSTRUCTOR's language arts consultant, joins Robert Rubinstein, Valerie Sellers, Shirley Shratter, and Sally Todd, all teachers around the country, to describe their favorite games and those tried-and-true gimmicks that mean superspellers in the classroom!

Robert Rubinstein's word game addicts

I teach word games for a nine-week period. During the first four weeks, students work with crossword puzzles, find-a-word games, weird words, and other challenges. The second half of the course focuses on word-game competition. Each student must complete three crosswords and three find-a-words, with the option of completing as many more as he likes for extra credit. (One student recently completed 267 find-a-words and is still going strong!)

These word games are for the entire class, on one's own, or for the family at home. Some students wind up word-game addicts because the puzzles and games offer unique, personal, and fun ways to build a wide variety of language arts skills. Plus the materials and games are readily available at all skill levels.

How to take the YUK out of SPELLING

Crosswords. Find crossword magazines of varying difficulty at your local newsstand or bookstore. There are crossword puzzles for synonyms, homonyms, and antonyms. Students must spell the answers correctly to solve the puzzles.

Every student then composes his own crossword puzzle of 20 words and 20 clues. The clues must offer clear and logical leads to the answers. The key to creating a crossword is to fill in the answer first and make up the clues to fit. A search in the dictionary may lead to some unusual words.

Find-a-word. These puzzle magazines are also on the newsstands, varying in difficulty and approach. They are especially fun for below-average students who might find crosswords frustrating. A student scans a page searching for a group of key letters and learns to recognize a word whether it's printed backward, diagonally, horizontally, or vertically.

Most find-a-word puzzles focus on particular topics, such as holidays, presidents, or famous people. Students find 20 to 40 words concerning that topic. They are given clues and hints. (Some students may need help with the more difficult ones.)

Each student then constructs an original find-a-word of 20 items on a specific topic; the names of old-time baseball teams, for example, or tennis champions. The encyclopedia is a ready source for words on a topic.

Weird words Do you know what a *fipple* is? *Radix? Helve? Nauplius?* These are "weird words" in the dictionary. A student must find 25 weird words and give for each the part of speech, a definition, and the correct use of the word in a weird sentence. For example, *"Fipple,* noun, a plug near the mouthpiece of certain wind instruments. When the musician saw the monkey, he swallowed his *fipple!"*

The best source for weird words is a dictionary like *Webster's New World.* Junior high and secondary school dictionaries are not good sources.

Other word challenges. You'll find other word activities in these books: *An Almanac of Words at Play* by Willard R. Espy (Potter) and *Word Play* by Joseph T. Shipley (Hawthorn).

There are also games on additives.

For example, add a *d* in front of a kind of liquor *(rum),* and a *b* in front of *eat* to get an African rhythm. Answer: *d* plus *rum* and *b* plus *eat* equals *drumbeat!*

Reverse verses are also intriguing. For example: "In the dark of the night, I may scamper by./Turn me around, I shine in the sky." Answer: *rats* and *stars.*

Students can also attempt alpha-sentences. Write a series of sentences with each word in the sentence starting with a consecutive letter of the alphabet. For example: *A bear called Dan entered five gates happy in jumping Kansas. Lately, Molly needs Oregon peas quietly rolling somewhere to understand various ways xeroderma yaps zithers.* The sentences are often strange but the words are used as correct parts of speech.

Word-game competition. In the second half of the nine-week course students are forced to think quickly. Each student must accumulate 450 points in each of four- or five-word game competitions.

Word games include Password, Ad-Lib, Scrabble Crossword game, Probe, and Anagrams. Every time students play games, they add points to those scored in previous games. Even if they lose, they build up credit points. Several students have broken the 1,000-point barrier in "Ad-Lib"!

"Spill" that word, shouts Valerie Sellers

I realized spelling was more than a little problem in my class when several of my third-grade students labeled their papers "spilling." I decided to tackle the subject with new techniques to make the lessons more enjoyable and worthwhile. I added new games and gadgets to the curriculum. But first I didn't throw out my spelling book entirely. I employed these new tricks!

1. Since students have such trouble understanding even the directions for spelling assignments, I assigned one student to explain the various sections before they are tried. Kids loved it!

2. To make sure each child understands the definitions of words used, the class develops its own dictionary

of spelling words. Each child is assigned one or two words to define and write on a duplicating master. Everyone receives a copy of the material for his notebook. Each week pupils add to the list and use their dictionaries in other subjects as well.

3. An additional weekly spelling test was added. A child who has difficulty on Thursday receives an additional chance to try for a perfect paper on Friday. Those successful the first time are rewarded with extra time to enjoy a game or book. Parents comment that their children show a greater interest in spelling with the extra incentive to achieve a perfect score. The tests with perfect scores are displayed each week.

We added games to the learning experience to capture the children's attention. Here are some games my students particularly enjoyed.

Spelling bee. Vary the traditional spelling bee to give extra practice to poor spellers. When a word is missed, the child does not go to his seat but to the end of the line where he will be called upon again. A point is scored against his team. The game ends at a predetermined time with the winning team the one with the fewest points.

Alphabet game. Letters of the alphabet are distributed to children. A leader calls a word and those having the letters for that word form a line in front of the room, holding their letters to spell the word correctly. Redistribute letters frequently so that all class members get a chance to participate in the game.

Spell around. Ask the pupil in the first seat to spell a word you pronounce. Continue around the room and do not stop when a word is misspelled. If the next pupil who follows notices the error, he corrects the mistake. The one who does correct it has "trapped" all the pupils preceding him.

Spelling tic-tac-toe. This is played like the original tic-tac-toe game except with two teams. Make large tic-tac-toe board on the chalkboard. A leader pronounces a word to the first person on Team One. If the word is spelled correctly, that person goes to the chalkboard and fills in either *X*

3. REMEDIATION

or *O.* If the word is spelled incorrectly, the same word is pronounced to the first person on Team Two. Continue back and forth until a team wins diagonally, up, down, or across.

Ruler tap. A student comes to the front of the room and chooses a word from a spelling list. He pronounces the word to the entire class and then taps a ruler or pointer until reaching one of the letters in the word. He calls on another who must first tell him the letter he stopped at and then spell the whole word correctly. If he does both correctly, he gets a chance to be the "tapper." If he makes a mistake, another child is chosen to correct the mistake.

For example, the word *clock* might be chosen. The child pronounces the word *clock* and taps the ruler three times. He then chooses a child who must tell him that the ruler stopped on the letter *o* and then spell *clock* correctly.

Spelling relay. The class is divided into two or more teams. Each child is given a slate. The leader pronounces a word and the first person on each team writes the word on his slate. The team member who correctly writes the word first (and so that it is readable) scores a point for his team. The team with the most points wins.

With the use of these activities and games your class will enjoy and improve its "spilling."

Dr. Fisher's favorite bag of tricks

Games make subjects requiring repetition practice livable and more enjoyable. Spelling is certainly that kind of subject. Here are some spelling games to try or they may inspire you to invent others. Be sure all your games, though, actually promote spelling. I have three rules of order:

1. Write the words! People do not spell orally except in artificial situations. Words are usually written out or seen in print. Children need to develop a visual image of words, to learn when a word "looks right." A very common game that is sometimes abused is the spelling bee because words are spelled aloud but then are not written, or because poorer spellers generally get the least practice.

2. Poor spellers should participate in games, too! If games are to develop skills, leave no one out!

3. Spell! spell! spell! A game should promote spelling—not phonics for reading or activities for vocabulary development.

Some of the games below are for individuals, partners, small groups of two to five, large groups, or the whole class and a leader. Adapt all the games to the age level and ability of your students.

The Super Square. Super Square, a version of tic-tac-toe, is for two or four players, each with a partner. The object is to get five squares in a row (horizontally, vertically, or di-

HARD

MEDIUM

EASY

agonally) before the opponent.

First, words and sentences are printed on cards or slips of paper. A player draws a card, and reads the word and the sentence. His opponent then writes the word. If the spelling is correct, he marks whatever square he chooses. Then the first player spells a word drawn.

Older children may prefer squares in three colors representing easy, medium, or hard words. Use three sets of words—easy, medium, and hard. Each player tells an opponent which level to select.

As in the illustration, colors are placed so that one would have to spell one hard word, two medium,

and two easy ones to get five in any direction.

Change the words frequently. Use chips, silver and copper paper clips, pieces of colored paper, and so on, as markers. Write the words on small chalkboards, laminated posterboard, or simply old scraps of paper.

Matches. This board game, for two or four players, is a spelling version of a television game. Children call out two numbers to find a matching pair of words.

The top card is plain on one side

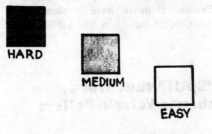

and has a number on the other side. The card underneath has a word on it. If the correct pair is chosen the player gets five points and the cards are reversed to display a plain side.

When one player or team matches they may call another pair of numbers and continue until they fail to match a pair. Then it is the opposing player or team's turn. The game ends when all pairs are matched. The winner is the person or team with the most points.

Make your board out of heavy poster cardboard. Staple or glue strips of cardboard on it to form 20 pockets that hold two cards each. If you can see through the cards, glue two together or cover with a patterned paper. By having the words to be matched on separate cards, they can be changed by rearranging them between games.

In the illustration, the board is shown with a correct match of the homophones *write* and *right,* numbers 8 and 19. In addition to homophones, the game could match different spellings of the same sound or sets of the same words.

The Big Board. This is a game for small groups. Each player has a personal marker to move along as he spells a word correctly. Each child

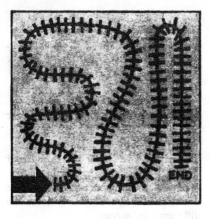

draws a card with a word on it, reads it for the next player who in turn must spell it correctly. If not spelled correctly, that player loses a turn. Each card has a word, a sentence containing it, and the number of spaces to move if correct. Some cards may say, "LOSE A TURN" or "FREE MOVE: FIVE SPACES." Younger children might have a board with 30 or 40 spaces from start to finish with the words giving moves of two, three, or five spaces. Older children might have 50 or 60 spaces.

Ghoti. This card game is like Fish involving two to five children who try to get pairs of cards to match. Each player is dealt seven cards (five if more than four play). The rest are placed facedown and drawn later.

The dealer starts by asking the next player, "Do you have any ....?" If that person has the word, he must give the card requested. Otherwise, the first player must draw a card from

the pile. (You must have one card of the kind you ask for.) The second player asks the next player what he or she wants, and the game continues.

The pairs are various spellings of the same sound. Thus, the cards, like those in the illustration, feature a sound or phoneme at the corner in slash marks, the word below it with the spelling of the sound underlined.

Letter-O. Play this game with small groups of children or the entire class. The object is to spell a word correctly before all the letters are displayed. For example, look at the illustration below. The first three letters of a word are showing. The base has a pocket to hold cards which are arranged in a long row.

Your librarian may have book pockets you can use. Cut and glue to a heavy strip of posterboard. Put 3" x 5" cards in them each with a single letter at the top of one side. Arrange cards, one to a pocket, so the plain side is showing and the letters of the correctly spelled word are on the opposite side.

Players take turns guessing what letters might be in the word. If their guess is correct, the letter is revealed and they may guess again. If it is wrong, they lose their turn to the next person or team.

Findit. Here's a game a large group or whole class can play with a skilled leader. Use rows of pockets like the previous game and 3" x 5" cards.

The game begins with all the letters showing. The leader calls out a synonym or definition of a word. Players try to find it in the maze of letters. They answer by giving the row and

pocket number of the first letter of the word and then they say the word and spell it. For example, the leader says, "opposite of bottom." Players respond row 1, number 7 *top*, T-O-P; or "a curved entry" is row 2, number 20, *arch*, A-R-C-H; or "birds build a ....," is in row 1, number 4, *nest*, N-E-S-T.

Properly structured and varied, games are both fun and good practice for developing spelling skills.

"Spelling chairs" from Shirley Shratter

This game is similar to Musical Chairs and The Boiler Burst, but you use the week's spelling words. In the fourth grade, we use 20 words. Students first become familiar with all the words. Each child takes a turn saying the word, spelling it, and using it in a sentence. Then we begin our game.

Spelling books are left open on the desks. The child who is "it" secretly chooses one of the spelling words and walks around the room telling a story he has made up. Whenever he mentions one of the spelling words, everyone changes seats. During this game, students constantly scan the spelling list in front of them so they will recognize a word immediately and be able to move faster than the others. This is an efficient and enjoyable way to expedite the process of learning to recognize words and learn the meaning of words when first presented.

Sally Todd and her label fanatics

The phrase heard most in my room is "Who Can Spell It?" As a result my second graders are able to spell common words advanced for their years and they *enjoy* spelling!

We start by labeling every object in our room, including the door, window, closet, and so on. We have mini-lessons throughout the day by my merely saying, "Who can spell . . . *closet*, or *carpet*, or *shades?*" Students try without looking at the word and even the slowest spellers feel success with this practice.

This approach grew out of observing children learning to read and

3. REMEDIATION

learning a foreign language. In reading, some words are learned merely by memorization. These are usually words that are not phonetic, such as the word *beautiful*. The more meaning the word has for the child, though, the more apt he is to learn it —and remember it. Children learn to read *Halloween* and *Christmas* very quickly.

Do not use words with which children have little experience. What second grader has ever encountered the word *mansuetude*? But sometimes I add words new to kids just for the sheer fun of it. (Millions of children learned to spell the word *antidisestablishmentarianism* this way.)

The technique can be adapted successfully to intermediate as well as primary situations. Follow these guidelines:

1. Label all objects possible in the room clearly.
2. Begin slowly. Label words of objects in the classroom first and then branch out to include other spelling words.
3. Make sure words are familiar to all children.
4. Use the phrase "Who can spell it?" several times a day for reinforcement.
5. Keep the atmosphere casual. I find that spelling a word on a volunteer basis works well.
6. Have the children work with partners for practice.
7. Call on slower children for easier words like *rug*, for example.
8. Ask students themselves to volunteer words and make up a chart of them.

Make spelling a positive subject with your class, and you will see the difference in success!

FIGURE 1

Cursive writing begins with chalk.

ELSYE HEYMAN

Elsye Heyman is a lead teacher at the Howard School for Children with Special Learning Disabilities, Atlanta, Ga.

■ **A SERIES OF CHALK-BOARD EXERCISES CAN BE FUN AND EFFECTIVE IN TEACHING LEARNING DIS-ABLED CHILDREN CURSIVE WRITING.**

FIGURE 2

FIGURE 3

■ Mastering cursive writing has many benefits for special children. It permits the child to see each word as an integral unit, helps solve spatial problems for students who run all words together, and eliminates serious letter reversal.

It is a rare child who does not enjoy the opportunity to draw or write on the chalkboard. The approach to teaching cursive handwriting described in this article uses this natural motivation plus the thrill of learning "real writing." The child learns cursive writing without tedious paper and pencil drill, and memory of letters is encouraged through the use of blindfolds at the chalkboard. The child becomes at ease with both the feel and shape of the letter before transferring it to paper. Students may also be used as teachers to help each other, which increases social interaction skills.

In this approach, the child is introduced to cursive writing through a series of chalkboard exercises designed to help him achieve a smooth, fluid rhythm. Letters are taught in groups, whose sequence is determined by the motion required to form the letter. There is as little back and forth movement as possible. Each letter starts on the line and returns to the line, preparing the child for writing words in one continuous motion. Very early the child begins to write words dictated by the teacher. He learns immediately that in cursuve writing letters are not isolated, but are always connected to form words.

Instruction starts with a series of pre-writing lessons designed to relax the child's gross motor patterns and eliminate any stiff or jerky movements before he begins to form letters. This enables him to experience immediate success when he starts to write letters.

PRACTICING RHYTHMS AND SHAPES

The teacher should first place the child about one foot from the chalkboard. The student should lean forward so that his nose touches the surface and an *x* should be placed on the spot made by the child's nose. The child should stare at this spot during the exercises rather than follow his hands with his eyes.

Drawing Circles

The teacher should next draw two circles on the chalkboard. The circles should touch each other at the *x* and should be a comfortable size for the child to trace. The child's hands should be placed flat against the chalkboard at the top center of each circle (12 o'clock) and guided so that both hands move outward at the same speed around the circle. After the child feels comfortable with this movement, the teacher should stand back and let him do 10 circles alone. If his hands do not move symmetrically, the teacher should continue to guide them until the child is able to move independently (see Figure 1).

Step 1. The teacher should place chalk (preferably large sized) in both of the child's hands and ask him to trace the circles. He should keep a slow, steady rhythm. If the circles are flat in the center, the child is probably stretching too high and too low to be comfortable and is making the circles too large. The teacher should have the child make slightly smaller circles until they become round. The teacher can also draw directional arrows to help the child (see Figure 2).

The teacher should listen to the rhythm of the chalk on the board; it should not start and stop, but should be smooth and continuous. It is important that the child's arm movements be relaxed and even. Some children will be very stiff at first. The teacher should try holding their arms at the wrists and shaking their hands until they become loose "like puppets." If a child seems to be concentrating too hard and chewing his tongue, the teacher should give him a piece of gum to chew while he works at the chalkboard. This is a good relaxer.

Step 2. The teacher should have the child make the same circles, but with his hands going inward instead of outward. He should be able to switch from step 1 to step 2 without stopping on verbal cue from the teacher, "Now go the other way" (Figure 3).

3. REMEDIATION

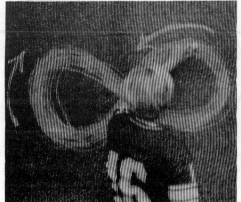

FIGURE 4

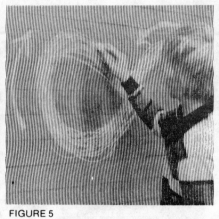

FIGURE 5

Racetracks...

Step 3. "Racetracks" are introduced to help the child cross his midpoint on the chalkboard. The teacher should draw a racetrack on the chalkboard that crosses at the *x*. The child should trace this from one side to the other and back again with his dominant hand. Sometimes a child will gradually shift his position so that the racetrack is either to the right or left of his body. If so, the teacher must help him to cross his midpoint by showing him that his own middle ("belly button") should align with the *x* on the chalkboard (Figures 4 and 5).

There is also the tendency for the child to make the circle on his dominant side larger. If this happens, the teacher should have the child stand back from the chalkboard and let him compare the two sides and then see if he can make them more equal.

Children usually enjoy making the racetracks, but it can be difficult for the child with a severe motor problem to cross from one side to the other. Often this child will make one circle starting and ending at the top and then go to the other side and make a second circle, instead of swinging from one side to the other at the *x*. The teacher will have to guide his hand and may find it advisable to verbalize the movements. "Start at the top, swing down, around, and to the top of the other, and down, around, back to the top, swing down, around . . ." and so on until he can do it alone. As soon as the child can do the racetrack pattern comfortably with his dominant hand, the teacher should have him repeat the pattern with the other hand 10 times.

At this point, the child will start the day's exercises with circles, then do racetracks first with the dominant hand, then the opposite hand.

Step 4. The teacher should have the child place each hand at the top center (12 o'clock) of each circle and instruct him to go right with both hands. This parallel movement is difficult. Frequently the child will sway from side to side, and it will be necessary for the teacher to hold his hips so that only his arms do the work not his entire body. In some children with severe motor problems, both hands will touch and follow each other, making one circle rather than two (usually on the right). The teacher should guide the child's hands until he is able to make separate circles.

Step 5. The teacher should have the child draw parallel circles with both hands going to the left. The child should be able to switch from one direction to the other without stopping on verbal command from the teacher.

At this point, the child should be able to do 10 or more circles in each of the four patterns learned without stopping, as well as 10 racetracks with each hand. This can be very tiring for the child with motor problems; however, it is important for him to increase his ability to sustain arm movement and become strong enough to do at least 40 continuous circles without hesitations or pauses. At this stage, the teacher should call out changes in direction, and the child should respond without hesitation.

...and Lines

Step 6. The teacher should have the child, using both hands, make straight

FIGURE 6

lines starting from his *x* and going out and in, out and in. He should be encouraged to stretch, opening and closing his elbows so that the lines are not short and cramped. Often the lines will curve, and the child should be helped to straighten them out. Again rhythm is important, and the teacher may want to chant "out, in" to help the child keep a steady pace (Figure 6).

Step 7. For the final prewriting exercise, the teacher should instruct the child to make straight lines with parallel arm movements. His left hand starts at the out position with the arm open; his right hand starts at the *x*. The child moves both hands to the right and then to the left so that one hand ends up on the *x* and the other is extended. If the child's hands cross the *x* and follow each other to one side or the other, the teacher should place her hand against the chalkboard at the *x* to serve as a wall that cannot be crossed. Eventually, a vertical line drawn to serve as a boundary that the child cannot cross can be introduced (Figure 7).

Usually a child will be able to master these prewriting exercises within 10 days with an instruction period of 10 to 15 minutes per day. If he is doing particularly well, the child may begin the writing exercises after the fourth or fifth day while continuing to do the circles, racetracks, and lines as a warmup.

"REAL WRITING" AT LAST

Learning Letter Groups

Step 1. The teacher should make a row of cursive *e*'s connected to each other and then guide the child's hand to trace them. The child should then be asked to trace the letters five times alone. Next, he should trace them with his "writing finger" (the index finger or his writing hand) to encourage him to remember the movement. The child should then trace the *e*'s again five more times with the chalk. Then, the child should be allowed to make a row of *e*'s of his own

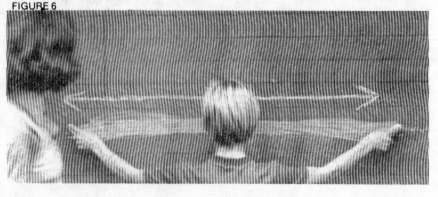

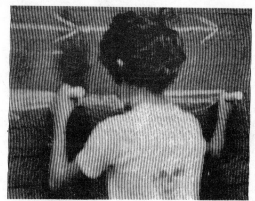

FIGURE 7

beneath the teacher's. The letters should be connected in groups of at least five letters; letters are never made in isolation, but always in a series. If the child makes the letters correctly, the teacher should instruct him to, "Cover the chalkboard with e's. Make as big a mess as you like so long as you move from left to right and connect the letters."

Generally, the children are so overwhelmed at being instructed to make a mess that they will start out making neat rows. Since fluency of movement is important, the teacher should remind the children that they can let the rows overlap, vary in size—whatever they want—as long as the form is correct and they move from left to right. The teacher should watch carefully at first as some children will turn the form upside down without realizing it. Others will go right to left when they reach the far side of the chalkboard and must be reminded that writing goes only from left to right (see Figure 8).

The teacher should point out that the only difference between an e and an l in cursive is size, and the child has now mastered two letters.

Step 2. Next the form of i, t, and u is introduced. The teacher should make a

FIGURE 8

row of u's first. Each new form follows the instructional sequence of step 1 of the writing exercises.

After the child has learned to write the letter u, the teacher should point out that the cursive i and t have the same form, but with a dot over the i and the t crossed. He should then be taught to write these letters as a continuous row, then go back and either dot the i or cross the t.

Each day's work builds on the previous day's lesson. At this point, the child should be doing about 4 minutes of warmup exercise (circles, racetracks, and lines). Then he should review the previous day's lesson before starting on a new one.

Step 3. The letters m and n are introduced. At this stage, the teacher makes a row of either m's or n's, pointing out the difference. It is sometimes difficult for the child to make the slight curve upward from the end of the letter to the beginning of the next one. Therefore it is better to introduce this immediately rather than just make the humped shape in a continuous row.

Now the child is ready to start writing words. The teacher first emphasizes that in cursive writing each letter begins and ends on the line so that the next letter can be started without stopping. It is recommended that the chalkboard be lined with green magic marker that will provide guide lines without being too distracting when other work is being done on the chalkboard.

The teacher should dictate such words as it, lit, let, tell, met, net, men, ten, tin, and nut, which use the letters the child has learned to form.

Step 4. The cursive letter c is introduced. For the first time, the child must reverse his motion. Most children will have a hard time making the curved top of the c;

there is a tendency for the shape to be pointed. This letter usually requires more guidance and tracing from the teacher before it is mastered. It is important to master the curve to the c as it will be repeated in the letters to follow. Sometimes it helps the child if the teacher points out the resemblance to ocean waves. This particular letter probably will require several days practice before going to the next one. Words such as cut and cute may now be added to dictation.

Step 5. Next the letter a is introduced. It is almost a repeat of c, except the letter is closed.

Step 6. The letter d is illustrated—an a that continues upward.

Step 7. Next g is introduced—an a that goes down below the line. This is the first letter to go beneath the line, so the teacher should point out that the loop swings up and crosses at the line, ready to go on to the next letter.

At this stage, a variety of words can be formed with the mastered letters and should be dictated daily. Similar words such as can and cane and mat and mate can be used.

Step 8. The letter o is introduced. The letter itself is not difficult since the letter a has been mastered already. However, the child will need extra work in learning how to connect o to other letters. The teacher should spend some time in teaching him how to write such combinations as oa, oe, ol, oo, and on. The teacher should dictate such words as load, toe, told, ton, not, and moon.

Step 9. Next w is taught. The teacher should point out that w is a u that ends up in the air like the o instead of returning to the line. Therefore, it must be connected to other letters in the same fashion as o.

Step 10. The letters j and y are introduced. These letters follow the form of i and u except that they go beneath the line. The loop on the bottom follows the same direction as the g previously learned.

Step 11. The teacher introduces the letter p—a j that curves back over and then closes at the line.

Step 12. The letter q is introduced—a g with the bottom loop reversed going to the right rather than the left. This is the first letter with a tail beneath the line that closes to the right so the teacher should make sure that the child perceives the difference.

Step 13. The letter *b* is introduced. It follows the form of *l* and ends like a *w*, but there is a tendency for the child to close it or to leave too large a gap. If he does the latter, the letter will resemble the *lr* combination.

Step 14. Next, the letter *f* is taught. This is the same form as *b*, however, it loops below the line then closes at the line.

Step 15. The letter *h* is introduced—as an *l* combined with the curve on the *n*. Most children will have trouble keeping the letter together without a gap.

Step 16. The teacher introduces the letter *r*. This is a difficult letter to make even though it looks simple. The shape is completely new with its slight point at the top and will probably need over-learning.

Step 17. Next comes *s*, an extremely difficult letter. The slight point and outward curve of the *s* (the only small cursive letter with this outward curve) makes this a hard letter to master.

Step 18. The letter *x* is introduced. This is not a difficult letter to master, but the teacher should be careful that the child does not reverse the cross mark.

Step 19. The teacher introduces the letter *v*—the same motion as an *x*—but *v* ends up in the air like *o*, *w*, and *b* and must be connected to other letters from that point.

Step 20. The letter *z* is introduced. Again, *z* is close to the form of cursive *x;* however, it has a loop on the bottom.

Step 21. The final letter, *k*, is introduced. This is probably the hardest letter in the

FIGURE 9

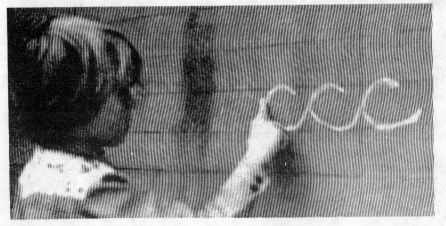

cursive alphabet because it combines several motions.

The child has now been introduced to the entire alphabet and should be writing words daily using both his new and old letters.

At this point, the teacher should check to see if the formation of the letters has been retained. The teacher should place a blindfold on the child (a halloween mask with the eyes blocked out will do) and ask him to write each letter. It is surprising how much hesitation a child will display when he is no longer able to summon visual clues.

Putting Words to Paper

Since writing is a tool skill only—a method for conveying thoughts and knowledge to others—the writer should not have to spend energy on remembering the shape of the letters. The form of the letter should be so completely integrated that concentration can be directed toward putting information on paper. By blindfolding the child, the teacher can determine which letters are internalized completely and which need further work before starting on capital letters.

If possible, the teacher should not introduce paper and pencil until this time. This is difficult because the child is anxious to show off his skills. However, it is advisable to be strict. He may practice letters he has learned on paper if he is doing well. Until the child has mastered all the letters, the teacher should not allow him to do his daily work in cursive because he will attempt to form letters he has not learned and sometimes teaches himself incorrectly. This must then be unlearned before proceeding. To begin on paper, the teacher should make simple dittos of each letter, one letter to a sheet. The top half should contain the letter repeated three times to be traced by the child. Then, the child can copy the

FIGURE 10

letter on the lower portion of the paper. Most children proceed rapidly down to standard size and write all of their work in cursive within 2 weeks. Those with severe motor problems will still need to write larger than normal size for a longer period of time.

Adding Capital Letters

Capital letters are taught following the same procedure used for the lowercase alphabet. Usually the capital *I* is introduced first since it is so important in writing lessons. This is a difficult letter to master because it reverses the direction learned for *e* and *l*. After *I* the capitals are introduced in alphabetical order. The teacher must be careful to point out that many of these do not return to the line to connect with the next letter. Although some of the letters are more difficult than others, by now the child has generally mastered the technique and does not have much trouble. Again check with a blindfold to see if the formation of the letters has been mastered.

STUDENTS TEACHING STUDENTS

Usually there will be one or two children in any group who master each letter with ease. These students make extremely effective teachers of children with more severe problems. Both "teacher" and "student" seem to thoroughly enjoy working together and will continue as long as the regular teacher will permit. Frequently these student "teachers" achieve more success than the regular classroom teacher particularly with some of the more socially isolated students.

CONCLUDING COMMENTS

This method of teaching cursive writing has been used with great success with 7 to 11 year old learning disabled children, many with severe motor problems. For some, it was their first success experience in school. For several it served additionally as the bridge that helped them to comprehend the sound-symbol relationship necessary to learn to read.

MATH FOR THE REAL WORLD OF SCHOOL

3. REMEDIATION

"Consumer math" and "survival math" may be no more immediate to young children than were the old Farmer Brown problems. Here, instead, are more than a dozen ways to relate math instruction to the child's *real* real world.

BY JOAN AKERS

Much has been said—most of it true—about the gap between school mathematics and real-world arithmetic. Many children fail to make the connection between their math work in school and real-life math problems. For these children math is something done during one period of the day, with an emphasis on getting the "right" answers—the answers the teacher wants.

The back-to-basics movement has brought with it an emphasis on "life skills," or "survival skills." These skills deal with the basic math literacy needed for achieving success in work, making consumer purchases and meeting other challenges of adult life. Children no longer deal with word problems about Farmer Brown and the shoe store manager. Instead, students do the mathematics of job applications, family budgets, tax forms, and the economics of running a car or operating a sewing machine.

But wait a minute. That "real world" may be no more immediate to young children than are the beautiful abstractions of numbers. For most children the real problems of 15 years from now might as well be a millennium away.

How about expanding the definition of basic skills? Mathematics *should* be relevant. Why not show how it relates to the children's *real* real world? Major parts of that world are the children themselves—as they are *now*—and the setting, subjects and routines of school *now*. Why not do more to make mathematics a part of the children's lives?

Classroom routines offer an opportunity for children (especially primary-aged children) to use math skills in real situations. Adapting meaningful tasks for young learners takes planning, of course. What everyday chore that adults usually do in the classroom can be done by children? How can jobs be made simple enough so that the children in your class can do them and *learn* by doing them?

Remember that the routines may take longer when done by children than when they are done by adults (particularly at first and with young children). The teacher must look upon the routines as *learning experiences* for the children rather than just as jobs that must be done. Some jobs may need an adult as an assistant.

Monitor Jobs

In most classrooms, monitors are selected for a week, with a child having a particular job once or twice during the year. Although it is harder to keep track of assignments, you might consider changing the jobs each day instead. This provides opportunities for all children to have frequent experiences doing the various tasks. The children will also mature, learn skills and gain confidence as they rotate jobs throughout the school year. To give children more chances to be monitors, you might consider assigning a pair of children for each job. Many jobs need two people to do them. Other jobs can be combined so that there is enough work for two children.

The following is a sample list of monitor jobs that are related to developing and reinforcing basic math skills. The activities are structured so that children can do and learn from tasks usually done by the teacher or an adult aide.

Taking the roll suggests three monitor job possibilities that involve photographs, name tags or group seating arrangements.
• Collect small photographs of the children and write the children's names on the backs of their pictures. This system begins with the photographs mounted on the bulletin board, facedown, at the end of a school day. Children turn over their own photographs (so that their pictures show) as they come into the room each morning. Monitors can fill out a form stating how many children are present (faces showing) and listing those who are absent (names showing).
• Children place their name tags on a daily graph of facts and opinions. The roll monitors fill out a roll form and also make an oral or written report about the graph information. Either the monitors or the class as a whole can determine what the topic of the next day's graph will be. Here are a few possible topics: What time did you go to bed last night? Did you bring or are

you buying your lunch today? How did you get to school today—by walking or by bicycle, car or bus? How many children (or pets) are in your family? What is your favorite color (TV program, food, animal, etc.)?
• If your students sit in groups or at tables, have a group or table monitor report to the roll monitor those children who are absent. Totaling the number of students at each table is good addition practice.

Counting lunch money can be a major math project for children. Students buying lunch (and/or milk, ice cream, fruit, etc.) fill out an order blank and take it, along with their money, to the lunch monitors' table. Each amount is checked (with the help of a money counting chart) as it is received, and the lunch monitors count the total amount collected to see that it tallies with the number of lunches sold. If it's thought necessary, the teacher or students can develop a reference table showing correct totals for all quantities of lunches that might be sold.

Keeping track of time offers a worthy challenge for young children. Appoint time monitors to ring a bell (or give some other signal) at the time the class needs to stop an activity (such as before recess or lunch). The "bell schedule" is posted next to pictures of clock faces showing the appropriate times. A large clock with movable hands should also be displayed so that the monitors can set it to match the next designated stopping time. At the appropriate times, the time monitors ring the bell and announce to the class the time and what the bell signifies.

Caring for classroom animals involves many learning skills, including the math skills of knowing *when* and *how much* to feed the animals. The animals benefit because their meals are controlled by only one or two children at a time. The animal monitors can also periodically weigh and measure the pets and chart their growth as well as follow proper cleaning procedures for the cages and the animals.

Integrating Skills

How can math skills be used in other subject areas or units? That question gets easier to answer as the teacher —and the students—grow more alert to the possibilities. The following are examples of integrating math with other subjects. Concepts, such as symmetry, and units of measure, such as half pints and quarts, are dealt with in contexts that children understand.

Physical education offers one setting for playing the Order-Up game. The materials required are equal numbers of red and green cards, each set sufficient for exactly half the children in the class. Number each set of cards sequentially from 1 and place each card in an envelope. The children begin by drawing one envelope apiece from a box. At a signal, each child pulls the card from its envelope to learn its color and number. The children form two lines by color and in numerical order. The first line completed wins a point. Cards are returned to the envelopes and the box, and the game is played again. Keep track of the number of times each color wins. (And see if the children realize—or care—that teams change each time.)

Science units contain many opportunities for students to apply math skills to real-world situations. Nutrition activities, in particular, teach consumer awareness as well as provide a context for number practice.

• "School lunch versus sack lunch" is an interesting issue for kids to deal with. Survey the class to see how many children buy lunch, how many bring it and how many go home for lunch. Graph the results. Discuss the reasons why children buy or bring their lunches. Discuss how much lunch costs. Children know the price at school. Is lunch brought from home "free"? Who pays for it?

• Compare the cost of milk bought at school with the price paid at a store. Buy a quart. Measure it out in half-pint portions and figure the cost per portion. Discuss why the milk bought at school is cheaper than milk bought at the store (explain about government subsidies).

• Make a lunch and compute the cost. Buy bread and lunch meat for sandwiches. (Perhaps the class can do this on a field trip to a grocery store.) Organize the children into small groups and have them find out how many sandwiches can be made from a loaf of bread and a package of lunch meat. Figure the cost of an individual sandwich. (For young children, use pennies for the total cost of the ingredients and divide the pennies into as many piles as there are sandwiches.) Then compute the cost of other lunch items, such as fruit and cookies.

Social studies lessons should involve math practice as well as a look at the here and now of a child's life.

Mapping is a unit that helps give children a sense of their place in the school and in the community.

• Make a (scale) model of the classroom. Use a cardboard box proportionate to the size of the room and let the children make and put modeled objects (such as furniture, chalkboards and rugs) inside. Be sure to orient the box in the same direction as the room. If the box model is developed as a long-range learning center task that is worked on intermittently, the children will discover the need to use some kind of scale.

• Estimate the distance (in number of walking steps, number of minutes or number of meters) to various school locations by several routes. Then have students actually measure the distances and compare results.

• Where do the members of the class live? Take walking (or bus) field trips to see the homes of all the children in the class. Discuss which children live near each other when planning which houses to see on a particular trip. Discuss how to get to different children's homes. (For example, "Walk three blocks and turn right. It's the fourth house on the block.") Make a graph of the number of students living in houses, apartments, trailers.

All About Me and You is an awareness unit that can truly "personalize" math.

• Ask children to count parts of the body—such as toes, arms, teeth—and to group them according to number. For example:

1	2	10
nose	hands	fingers
face	elbows	toes

• What parts of the body do we have *one* of, and what parts do we have *two* of? Note that the parts of the body we have only one of are all located along a center vertical line and that pairs of parts are divided so that one part is on each side of the vertical line. Our bodies are symmetrical. Make "flip bodies" by tracing along one side of a child (on butcher paper), cutting the traced half out and flipping the cutout over to trace the other half. The child then lies down on the completed cutout to see if it fits. Children can color in the life-size bodies.

• What else about a person can be counted? Have children count the number of buttons they wear on a particular day. Make a class graph and then total the number of buttons in the room. Have children count other things they are familiar with: the number of people in the family, number of pets, number of steps between the child's bed and the TV, number of times each child can write his or her name in a minute, etc. Make class graphs and compare results.

• Measuring is a great way to personalize math. Make a wall chart that stays up all year to show how the children grow. Cut a large sheet of butcher paper into one-inch-wide vertical strips and assign each child a strip. Primary grade children needn't measure in centimeters or inches, but can mark their actual heights with a short line. The children can thus keep track of their individual growth during the year.

• Have children weigh themselves regularly and keep track of their weight gains (or losses) as the year progresses. (Use a scale calibrated in kilograms instead of pounds.)

• Play the nonverbal Find Your Mass Match game. Without talking, each child finds a partner whose weight looks close to his or her own. The partnership's score is the actual difference between the two weights, and the lowest score wins.

• String is a good tool to use for measuring parts of the body. Ask children to:

1. Find body parts that are one half (one fourth, one eighth) their height.

2. Find several body measurements that are about the same (for example, the length of an arm and a waist size).

3. Make individual body measurement charts with string. Have the children cut string to the length of various body parts and label each piece. The strings are put in order according to length and pasted on a chart. Compare charts to see if the body-part order is the same for all children.

• Birthdays, of course, are especially important. Enter students' birthdays on the calendar (in advance). Make a graph showing the birthday months of the students. Determine how many days older one student is than another.

• "Favorites" is a favorite activity. Ask partners (or small groups) to select their favorite Favorite category (such as TV show, food or color) and to survey the class about it. Each pair or group then makes a graph depicting the class choices. Using its graph, each group can make up math story problems, such as "How many more children like pizza than like hot dogs?" The class as a whole can make class preference lists and compare its favorites with those of other classes.

These exercises are not only fun but also relate to the child's world—the real world of children's real-world mathematics.

Joan Akers is a mathematics resource teacher in the Santee School District, Santee, Calif.

It Can Teach Them to Organize Logically

Math As a Teaching Tool for the Learning Disabled

SHIELA C. SWETT

Shiela C. Swett is Learning Disabilities Specialist, Pequenakonck Elementary School, North Salem, New York. Condensed from Academic Therapy, *XIV (September 1978), 5-13.*

MANY educators may be overlooking a potentially significant tool for helping learning-disabled children: mathematics. This particular discipline has the inherent characteristics needed for making it a new key, useful for unlocking educational problems of the learning-disabled child.

In dealing with learning-disabled children, educators have traditionally concentrated on the development of language skills. Recent evidence indicates, however, that only when a child is able to organize his thoughts and activities in a logical, confident way can he go on to master the more abstract demands of language development. The unique quality of math is that it provides just this kind of training. Math offers a variety of visual and concrete techniques for training its students to analyze, to zero in on essentials, to look for patterns, and to classify and organize information in order to solve specific problems.

Most learning-disabled children are boys, and this country still tends to consider math a masculine subject. It is, therefore, not unusual that most boys consider math a "treat" compared to endless work in dealing with our complex English language. The language of math is concise, its symbols few. It is always dependable, for its rules have no exceptions. Math's basic structure makes it safe and secure, not so threatening, perhaps, as our language. Math's many patterns and consistent order help it serve as a haven for the structureless learning-disabled child.

The basic skills of math are really not hard to teach when it is so full of fascinating patterns and irresistible "tricks." It does not require complex auditory perception, for its basic concepts can all be experienced visually and concretely. Math always makes sense and can be logically proved. The potential for immediate success when you know you've "got it" is especially appealing for children with short attention spans or with long histories of failure. There are many ways to succeed in math, not always numerical, not always requiring paper and pencil, but concrete, relevant, and *fun!*

Most resource rooms are oriented toward remediating the underachieving child in the basic language skills of writing, spelling, and reading, with a sprinkling of math as a separate topic. But we can interrelate the Three Rs, using math as a meaningful and motivating tool in handwriting, spelling, vocabulary, and reading for mastering these important and difficult language skills.

Math as a multisensory experience also offers great potential in the strengthening of such vital nonverbal, prereading skills as visual discrimination, pattern-matching, discernment of likes and differences, and classification and sequencing of visual and tactile data. Whatever Piagetian stage of conceptual development a particular child is at—and we can predict that our learning-disabled child is lagging, progressing slower through these stages than his classmates, because of his perceptual difficulties—there are mathematically sound ways to help speed up the child's progress.

Whether in the "preoperational stage" or the "period of concrete operations," any child needs concrete manipulative experiences in measuring, comparing, and eventually understanding quantitative as well as qualitative relationships. Because many

Shiela C. Swett, "Math as a Teaching Tool for the Learning Disabled," from *Academic Therapy*, Vol. XIV, September 1978, pp. 5-13, Academic Therapy Publications, San Rafael, California. Reprinted by permission. Taken from *Education Digest*, Vol. XLIV, No. 5, January, 1978.

perceptually handicapped children can't depend on their visual or their auditory memory, it is of primary importance for these children to "do," to experience the learning of each new concept in whatever discipline, in a concrete way. It has been demonstrated that learning-disabled children learn best when they can touch, feel, and use all their senses together.

Valuable Tools

Math lab materials offer ideal ways to help the learning-disabled child. Organization games that give multisensory experiences with emphasis on sharpening visual-perceptual skills within the solid framework of mathematics are valuable tools which cannot be ignored in the resource room.

In using math lab materials with the learning-disabled child, we are expanding our own vision and recognizing the potential inherent in bringing together the oft-separate worlds of math and learning disabilities. *Use* math lab materials to provide basic Piagetian experiences such as conservation, seriation, and classification. *Use* geometry as a concrete, visual, tactile, and relevant tool for helping these children organize their faulty perceptions of spatial relationships, including sequential and directional concepts. *Use* math games in new ways to sharpen memory as well as problem-solving skills. Math as a built-in source for multisensory remediation materials seems self-evident.

In terms of math for social remediation, there are significant psychological benefits in giving the socially immature learning-disabled child controlled opportunities for game-playing. Children of above-average intelligence who are frustrated because of their inability to express themselves effectively in written work or through speech need opportunities to succeed in nonverbal situations.

Necessity for Success

They may have been "losers" inside of school and out, so that they really need to win for a change. They need to interact with their peers and with adults in ways that are positive and fun. Math games, both chance and strategy, can be analyzed, invented, scored, won, *or* lost by this intelligent but impaired group of children. More than play therapy, math games can be directly tied to the classroom, strengthening specific skills a child needs so that he's aware of the connection. Besides academic benefits gained from learning how to play games involving strategy, planning, foresight, and organized thinking, there are therapeutic benefits as well.

The learning-disabled child is often lonely, struggling to keep up but increasingly aware of his own academic lags. He needs to *want* to take an active role in the learning process, which will happen only if he has positive and meaningful learning experiences *with* his peers or *with* an understanding adult.

Working alone, plugged into some preplanned program, perhaps doing seemingly irrelevant exercises in eye-hand coordination or dull drill, is not always beneficial. He needs a change from the regular classroom, an atmosphere where learning can be fun for him, where he can laugh, talk, and share his fears and learning problems, restoring his confidence in his ability to learn.

Social remediation should be a top priority when working with the learning-disabled. It can happen while the child is learning his needed skills only if we plan the learning experience accordingly: the room, the materials, but, most of all, the teacher.

Is this math-oriented approach to remediating learning disabilities the only answer? Of course not. So much depends on the point of view, the training, and the experience of the teacher, as well as on the individual child's specific needs.

As the field of learning disabilities increases its role in schools, it becomes increasingly important to include all aspects of the complex learning process so that all three Rs work together. For motivation, for basic skill building, for a source of remediation materials, for informal diagnosis as well as social remediation, math offers a new perspective. Math as The Organization Game could play a significant new role in giving our learning-disabled children a variety of new tools with which to structure their learning experiences.

Educational Implications of Dyscalculia

By **Paul F. Flinter**

One of a child's finest attainments in his learning experience is the concept of number—ideas of quantity, weight, time, operation, numerical classification and problem solving. These principles begin early and develop as the individual grows. According to Gessell and Amatruda (1947) generalizations are made as early as in the first year with manipulations of various objects. Piaget (1953) observed acquisition of number concepts through a series of sequential levels depending upon the individual's readiness. A majority of children will acquire understanding of number and will encounter little difficulty. However, some will fail because of language disorders, faulty teaching methods, reading problems, or disturbances of qualitative thinking (Johnson and Myklebust 1967).

Disturbances in arithmetic that result from disorders of quantitative thinking are referred to as forms of dyscalculia. Kozc (1974) believes that "developmental dyscalculia ought to include those disorders of mathematical ability which are a consequence of heredity or congenital impairment of the growth dynamics of the brain centers" (p. 48). The disability is usually characterized by a retarded growth in mathematical skills while the person demonstrates normal auditory abilities and an excellence in reading vocabulary and syllabication. It could also be said that pure dyscalculia exists only when there is a disorder in arithmetic functioning without a parallel disability in general mental aptitude.

Symptomatology and Remediation

In order to focus on what symptoms a classroom teacher should look for and then on what steps that teacher can

Paul Flinter is currently a doctoral candidate in special education at the University of Connecticut. The manuscript for this article was drafted while he was completing a master's degree program in special education; it was revised while he was a teacher for learning-disabled children in the Cheshire, Connecticut, public schools.

take to remedy the situation, specific disturbances need to be identified. The disorders may occur in isolation or in clusters.

Verbal disturbances

Luria (1966) attributes this difficulty to what he describes as an "extinction of the direct meaning of words" (p. 435). When the individual is forced to calculate aloud, he has difficulty in naming the presented quantities. Kozc (1974) referred to it as "an inability to designate verbally mathematical terms and relations, such as naming amounts and numbers of things, digits, numerals, operational symbols and mathematical performances" (p. 49). Johnson and Myklebust (1967) indicate that this type of child will do well in written computations but is inferior in reasoning and word meaning, and will do poorly on an arithmetic vocabulary test. There are times when the child does not understand verbal explanation of relationships. Luria (1969) uses the example of "*n* times greater" (or less). He claims this operation forces the child to abstract relationships and it just might be that this awareness has not developed. Thus, there is confusion with expressions "*n* units greater" and "*n* times greater."

Remedial activities

The dyscalculic child must have command of the proper order of names. Emphasis should be placed on getting this individual to organize and classify similar experiences that would require him to verbalize. Have the child match different quantities to spoken names and present objects or problems tachistoscopically while the child tape records his responses. The tape can be played back for self-reinforcement.

Stern (1949) suggests using a counting board for naming amounts. This counting board consists of ten vertical rows, each containing a groove into which blocks of corresponding size may be inserted. The board could be used with the tens table so that the teens, twenties, thirties, and so on, might be expressed. The child should

continuously repeat the names for amounts until they become automatic.

Kaliski (1962) has found "*more or less* present great obstacles because the child rarely hears or applies the word less" (p. 250). Thus, she feels it is proper to substitute words like *not so many as* for the word *less*. She further believes that the child must be given much encouragement to talk in arithmetical terms. She states, "If the child can say that he wants to find out how many groups of nine jacks (in a row) make (not *are*) eighteen jacks, rather than use the expression 'nine into eighteen,' we can be reasonably sure the concept of division is understood" (p. 250). In problem-solving situations the child has to be taught how to analyze. Breaking down a problem into questions which the child can answer one by one, followed by an illustration of the problem, will aid his progress.

Disturbances of visual-spatial organization

This is characterized by an inability to manipulate objects in the imagination. Differences in shapes, sizes, amounts, or lengths are nondistinguishable. Estimating distances and making judgments related to size often result in error. Kozc (1974) includes single addition of objects and comparison in estimates of quantity. Werner (1968) and Wallach (1963) indicate that a child who has difficulty in thinking of objects that are not physically present will encounter uncertainty in addition, subtraction, multiplication, and division.

Remedial activities

Strauss and Lehtinen (1947) believe that you have to slow the child down so that counting of objects is distinct. They also emphasize that all senses by used simultaneously; touching objects, looking at objects, and counting objects aloud.

Where difficulty in shape and form is encountered, children can begin with puzzles in which only one piece will fit into a space. Outlines of different numerical figures can be placed on the

"Educational Implications fo Dyscalculia," Paul F. Flinter, *Arithmetic Teacher*, Vol. 26, No. 7, March 1979. ©1979 National Council of Teachers of Mathematics, 1906 Association Drive, Reston, VA 22091.

floor with ropes. The child is told to look at the form, say the figure's name, and then, to walk along its edge.

With difficulty in estimating, Kaliski (1962) uses color to teach differentiations of rows and concepts such as *beginning*, *end*, *next row*, *first*, *last* and *middle* of the page. Stern's (1949) comparison activities use two side-by-side rows of blocks. Adding and subtracting of units on one row by the instructor have to be equalized on the other row after the child responds to questions like How much more? or How much should be taken away? At the intermediate level, Kaliski has found graphic representations, such as lineal graphs, bar graphs, and scale drawings, to be more meaningful. Johnson and Myklebust (1967) have proposed using inlay puzzles with ten, 10-inch strips. Each strip is made with pieces of varying size. This demonstrates the stability of quantity, because it helps the child to see different combinations of ten. Cuisenaire rods can be substituted through comparison activities with trains and staircases.

Disturbances of reading and writing numbers

Some individuals can neither read nor write a number, but they can show how many objects correspond to a given number or they can call it out. Luria (1969) discovered that when zeros were not designated in speech, a subject could not write the number properly. One thousand twenty-eight was written as "128" or as "100028". Kozc (1974) disclosed interchanges in similar-looking digits (3 for 8, 6 for 9, 17 for 71, and 96 for 69). He noted, moreover, a disability in reading simple operational symbols ($\times$, $-$, $+$, $\div$). Sometimes a copying of geometric forms, shapes, numbers or letters was not possible. A term commonly used for this area is numerical dyssymbolia.

Remedial activities

Stern (1949) begins with awareness of correct positioning for each number before writing. She uses Bakelite figures from one to ten that are fitted into grooves of corresponding form in a square frame. Tracing is performed with this activity to get the kinesthetic sense of how the numbers are to be written. Dotted number figures on sheets of paper, ruled into a framework of squares, are used for practice. Difficulties in number form are remediated through colors so the child sees that 3 is constructed of two curved lines and 8 is in the form of an "s" to be closed with a straight line.

The teacher is responsible for explaining the arrangement of numbers and indicating where numerals of greater value can or cannot go. Assuming there is an ability for this child to count beyond ten, written numbers can be matched to different concrete or pictorial quantities. Riedesel (1973) recommends using a sheet containing several place-value frames. When presented with a number of objects the child should be taught to write the corresponding number in the place-value frames. Cuisenaire Powers of Ten could be used as the concrete materials for this symbolic mapping procedure.

Other exercises for reading and writing could be developed through cutout numbers that would be used to match symbolic likenesses, which would be written on the board. In this activity, the teacher would check for correct reproduction in arrangement and have the child read the number aloud to reinforce the association between name and written symbol. To differentiate operation signs, write two or three signs (e.g., $+$, $\times$, $\div$) in a row and ask the child to state how they are alike and how they are different. When the child cannot perceive them as separate symbols, draw borders around each sign until they are visualized correctly (Johnson and Myklebust 1967).

Impairment in understanding mathematical concepts while performing mental calculation

This difficulty reveals itself in formation of ideas. For example, the child might know 7 can be written as *seven* and vice versa, but he does not know that it is one less than eight or one half of fourteen, and so on. It can be an inability to quickly identify the number of objects in a group. When adding a set of three with a set of four, a child with this arithmetic disability would begin by counting the objects one by one to determine the total number (Lerner 1971). Even the easiest sums present confusion to an individual unable to understand the mathematical relations. Siegel (1957) indicates a difficulty encountered in shifting from one concept to another. He talks of a child having learned $1 + 2 = 3$, but who then insists that $2 + 1$ are not equal to three.

Remedial activities

The dyscalculic child needs to acquire essential number ideas to work sufficiently in arithmetical procedures. Spitzer (1954) suggests experiences on a number chart. His chart has the first nine numbers in the first row so a ten will begin the following row, and a number of the ten table will begin the succeeding rows. This permits the tens to stand out and this initial position clearly shows eleven is ten and one more, fifty-two is fifty and two more, and so on. If the chart is equipped with movable number chips, a tangible activity of "three more than fifty-eight" can be clearly demonstrated.

Extensive practice with visualizing the number of objects in a group is needed. Johnson and Myklebust (1967) suggest a filmstrip presentation of small groups of dots which are widely separated. The child is given a paper showing groups of dots similar to the presentation on the filmstrip. After a group of dots has been flashed, the child circles on his paper what he thinks is the corresponding group. As the child advances, make the filmstrip presentation with a number symbol, but the child is still to circle the appropriate objects. When he advances from this, present number sentences. This will be the first time he has to calculate in his head in order to find the correct number of objects.

Another project would be to have the child arrange concrete manipulatives into a display, after having been given a written or verbal problem. For example, given a written problem 5 $\times$ 4, the child would arrange the chips into five groups of four. It is also practical to give the child twenty-four chips and ask him to arrange them in two groups of twelve, or four groups of six. "As he gains practice with the parts that form a whole, he becomes more conscious of the visual groupings that are possible" (Johnson and Myklebust 1967, p. 265).

Serial order and relationships may

3. REMEDIATION

be worked at through number lines. When a particular number has been selected on the number line, it is important that the number be represented pictorially or concretely. If twenty-four was the designated number, chalkmarks on the board or sorted-out chips could represent it. Then it is possible to show the number on the number line and, with the chips or chalkmarks, that twenty-four is four groups of six, two groups of twelve, or three groups of eight. Horowitz (1970) would suggest the game "Buzz," if you wanted to count on a number line by fours. The counting procedure would be as follows: 1, 2, 3, buzz, 5, 6, 7, buzz, 9, 10, 11, buzz, ...

Disturbances in operation

The inability to perceive signs, and confusion with arithmetical operations is a frequent mistake. Addition might be done instead of multiplication, and subtraction performed instead of division. Luria (1966) describes a situation where a subject was given an ordinary problem like $5 \times 2 = ?$, and was able to respond 10, but when the same problem was given again with all the numbers but with the sign omitted, $5 \_\_ 2 = 10$, the subject might place a subtraction sign in the blank. The point to be made is that when the operation was made a conscious activity, there was a general inability to understand the meaning of the mathematical process sign.

Remedial activities

In this area the meaning of process symbols has to be explored in detail with the child. Emphasis should be placed on precise vocabulary. If there is a need for a synonym, it should be clarified with the student. Horowitz (1970) discussed important vocabulary that should be stressed in each process:

1. In the operation of addition, *adding* and *plus* should mean putting together. Vocabulary meanings that are significant would be *plus*, *sum*, *total*, *more than*, and *greater than*.

2. The operation of subtraction emphasizes "taking away." Corresponding vocabulary would include *less than*, *subtracted from*, and *minus*.

3. In multiplication the child is re-

sponsible for making distinctions with *multiply*, *times*, *product*, and *multiplier*.

4. When working in division, a literal translation of the division sign is necessary (e.g., $9 \div 3 \neq 3 \div 9$). There are three groups of three objects in nine, not three groups of nine objects in three.

Along with the use of consistent, precise instructional language for operations, exercises can be given that will combine and at the same time isolate functional ideas of addition and multiplication or subtraction and division. In addition and multiplication, a worksheet of squares can be used for shading in or cutting out. (See fig. 1) The

terminology would be as follows:

Cut out three groups of seven squares or $3 \times 7 = ?$

Cut out three squares and seven squares or $3 + 7 = ?$

In comparing or contrasting division and subtraction, it should be noted that subtraction has these types of physical world situations: *take away*, *comparison*, and *how many more are needed*. Division has *partition*, *measurement* and *ratio* (Riedesel 1973). When working with the two operations, make use of the same concrete representation of the quantity for both operations. (See fig. 2)

Fig. 1

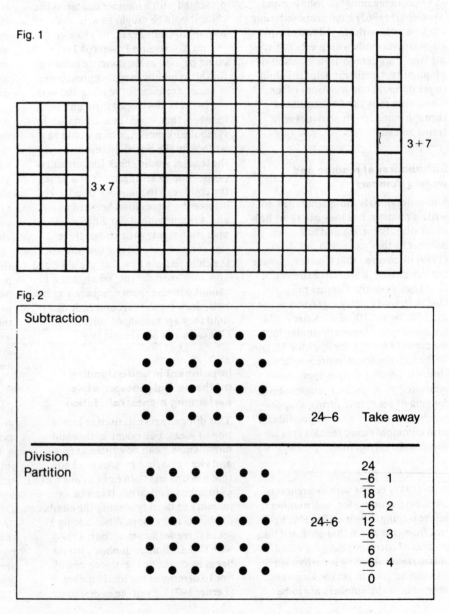

3×7

$3 + 7$

Fig. 2

Subtraction

$24-6$ Take away

Division
Partition

$24 \div 6$

$$\begin{array}{r} 24 \\ -6 \quad 1 \\ \hline 18 \\ -6 \quad 2 \\ \hline 12 \\ -6 \quad 3 \\ \hline 6 \\ -6 \quad 4 \\ \hline 0 \end{array}$$

Confusion of place value and direction in computation

There are many mistakes in calculation which are due to an impairment of the place-value concept. Simple one-digit additions,

$$\begin{array}{r} 5 \\ +6 \\ \hline \end{array}$$

are usually retained but with the introduction of two-digit and three-digit numbers,

$$\begin{array}{r} 14 \\ 17 \\ \hline \end{array}$$

significant difficulties occur. Luria (1969) found place-value impairments particularly in numbers that are presented in a horizontal line,

$$14 + 17.$$

The individuals ignored the place-value meaning and consequently units would occupy the tens place and vice versa. Sometimes the numerals would be gathered into a sum,

$$17 + 14 = 1714.$$

Uncertainty as to the direction in which to work is usually compounded by a total loss of orientation. Affected children are not aware of right/left concepts and thus experience problems in direction (Myers and Hammill 1969). Disturbances in loss of direction have been found in counting numbers, which denotes a loss of forward and backward concepts.

Remedial activities

Unless the child is made to see the reason for writing figures in columns, he will use the figure mechanically, which will lead to error and lack of meaning for remaining numbers. At this level, Stern (1949) introduces the Dual Board. It contains ten rows, each the length of a ten-block, to accomodate the tens up to 100, and a separate unit compartment, which is a single row ruled into ten units numbered from one to nine (fig. 3). No more than nine cubes are allowed in this separate unit. Initial experiments will help the child to see how the step-by-step adding of one more cube will eventually force him to switch from units to tens. When his amount grows to ten single cubes, he replaces it with one solid ten-block.

He is then shown that the next cube will go in the units place until ten single cubes are reached again. This same step-by-step initiation to place-value meaning will eventually bring the child to operations.

Cuisenaire Powers of Ten or Dienes Multi-Based Arithmetic Blocks with the same physical pieces, unit, long, flat, cube, can be substituted. As the child works with either material, he should be writing the figures down. In other words, matching should occur between the child's inner ideas and his symbolic efforts.

The same concrete materials should be continuously used, even with number renaming, until the response is automatic and the child is aware of why he is doing what he is doing (fig. 4). (Riedesel 1973, p. 185)

The student who has a difficult time in recalling the sequence of steps in calculating should be exposed to signals or cues that will guide him. Johnson and Myklebust (1967, p. 269) say, "A green dot might be drawn above the number showing the starting point for calculation, arrows may be drawn to shown the direction in which to work, and written charts can be provided containing step by step procedures for each process." As the child progresses, cues should be gradually eliminated. The concepts of right/left, up/down, top/bottom and forward/backward can initially be taught by drawing a large circle on the floor with direction

Fig. 3

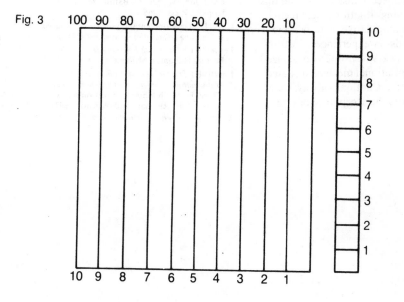

Fig. 4

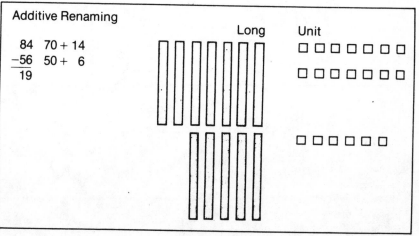

Additive Renaming

$$\begin{array}{r} 84 \\ -56 \\ \hline 19 \end{array} \quad \begin{array}{r} 70 + 14 \\ 50 + 6 \end{array}$$

Long   Unit

labels in the appropriate spots. A child would be in the center of the circle and respond to the different commands of the teacher.

Summary

The information presented in this article is far from a complete description of the difficulties encountered by a dyscalculic child. Children with the disability have a general inability to comprehend methods of mathematics, and to learn and reproduce mathematical ideas and combine them with symbols. The goals for such children are no different from those for normal children. If considerations are to be given to individuals achieving independence in society, an arithmetic program should be kept practical. Concepts have to be made the subject of instruction and this means learning situations must include concrete, manipulative materials and direct, hands-on experiences. Instruction must always be properly organized and compensational mechanisms used to their fullest. Caution is always exercised to avoid the acceptance of rote learning.

References

Chalfant, J. C. and M. A. Scheffelin. "Central Processing Dysfunctions in Children: A Review of Research." Bethesda, Md: U.S. Department of Health, Education and Welfare, Monograph No. 9, 1968.

Gessell, A. and C. Amatruda. *Developmental Diagnosis.* 2d ed. New York: Grune & Stratton, 1967.

Horowitz, R. S. "Teaching Mathematics to Students with Learning Disabilities." *Academic Therapy* 6 (Fall 1970) : 17–35.

Johnson, D. J. and H. R. Myklebust. *Learning Disabilities: Educational Principles and Practices.* New York: Grune & Stratton, 1967.

Kaliski, L. "Arithmetic and the Brain-Injured Child." *Arithmetic Teacher* 9 (May 1962):245–51.

Kinsbourne, M. and E. K. Warrington. "The Developmental Gerstmann Syndrome." In *The Disabled Reader: Education of the Dyslexic Child.* John Money, ed. Baltimore: The John Hopkins Press, 1966.

Kozc, L. "Developmental Dyscalculia." *Journal of Learning Disabilities* 7 (March 1974):46–59.

Lerner, J. *Children with Learning Disabilities.* Boston: Houghton Mifflin Co., 1971.

Lovell, K. *The Growth of Understanding in Mathematics: Kindergarten through Grade Three.* Early Childhood Education series. New York: Holt, Rinehart and Winston, 1971.

Luria, A. R. *Higher Cortical Functions in Man.* Translated by B. Haigh. New York: Basic Books, 1966.

————. "On the Pathology of Computational Operations. In *Soviet Studies in the Psychology of Learning and Teaching Mathematics,* Kilpatrick and Wissup eds., vol. 1. Chicago: University of Chicago Press, 1969.

Myers, P. I. and D. D. Hammill. *Methods for Learning Disorders.* New York: John Wiley & Sons, 1969.

Piaget, J. "How Children Form Mathematical Concepts." *Scientific America* 185 (1953) : 74–79.

Riedesel, A. C. *Guiding Discovery in Elementary School Mathematics.* 2d ed. New York: Appleton-Century-Crofts, 1973.

Siegel, S. "Discrimination Among Mental Defective, Normal, Schizophrenic and Brain-Damaged Subjects on the Visual Verbal Concept Formation Test." *American Journal of Mental Deficiency* 62 (1957):338–43.

Spitzer, H. F. *The Teaching of Arithmetic.* 2d ed. Boston: Houghton Mifflin Co., 1954.

Stern, C. *Children Discover Arithmetic.* New York: Harpers, 1949.

Strauss, A. A. and L. E. Lehtinen. *Psychopathology and Education of the Brain-Injured Child.* New York: Grune & Stratton, 1947.

Wallach, M. A. "Research on Children's Thinking." In *Child Psychology,* 62nd Yearbook, National Society for the Study of Education, H. Stevenson, ed. Chicago: University of Chicago Press, 1963.

Werner, H. *Comparative Psychology on Mental Development.* Rev. ed. New York: Follett Publishing Co., 1948.

DECODING, SEMANTIC PROCESSING, AND READING COMPREHENSION SKILL

Roberta Michnick Golinkoff and Richard R. Rosinski
University of Pittsburgh

GOLINKOFF, ROBERTA MICHNICK, and ROSINSKI, RICHARD R. *Decoding, Semantic Processing, and Reading Comprehension Skill.* CHILD DEVELOPMENT, 1976, **47**, 252–258. To explore the relationship between single-word decoding, single-word semantic processing, and text comprehension skill, a set of decoding tests and picture-word interference tasks were administered to third and fifth graders who were skilled and less skilled comprehenders. While results on the decoding tests indicated that unskilled comprehenders possessed weak decoding skills compared to skilled comprehenders, results on the interference tasks indicated that these groups did not differ on the extraction of meaning from single printed words. These findings indicate that decoding and semantic processing are separable reading processes and that problems in reading comprehension cannot be attributed to a failure to obtain single-word meaning.

Reading comprehension has been defined as the extraction of meaning from printed text (Gibson & Levin 1975). Two skills that may be crucial for comprehending text are (1) decoding, defined here as the ability to pronounce words out loud, and (2) semantic processing, defined here as obtaining the meaning of individual printed words. The present study was designed to determine if decoding and/or semantic processing are problems for the less-skilled comprehender.

While researchers have studied the acquisition of the decoding skill, for example, Gibson, Osser, and Pick (1963), the relationship between decoding and semantic processing is not clear. For example, research by Buswell (1920), Katz and Wicklund (1971), and Perfetti and Hogaboam (1975) has indicated that children who are unskilled comprehenders possess weak decoding skills compared to skilled comprehenders. However, Cromer (1970) and Weiner and Cromer (1967) argue that many unskilled comprehenders possess decoding skills on a par with peers who are skilled comprehenders. It is important to uncover what role the ability to decode plays in semantic processing for beginning readers and less skilled comprehenders.

Another important component of reading comprehension is the access of meaning from single printed words. For average readers semantic processing may occur rapidly, perhaps automatically, and without an intermediate decoding or articulatory stage (Kolers 1970; Rosinski, Golinkoff, & Kukish 1975; Stroop 1935). For example, Rosinski et al. (1975), using a semantic interference task, found that word meanings were being accessed even when subjects were told to ignore words. In this task, subjects were asked to label pictures of common animals and objects on which words (or trigrams) were superimposed. Picture labeling took significantly longer for children and adults when the meaning of the words and pictures conflicted than when they matched. Furthermore, in a control condition in which pronounceable trigrams did not "match" the pictures, subjects experienced significantly less semantic interference. The fact that real words caused more interference than trigrams indicated that the interference effect had a significant semantic component.

While the results of the Rosinski et al. study suggest that no intermediate decoding stage is required for semantic processing, the use of this task with skilled and less skilled

The authors wish to thank Karen Kukish for collecting these data and Sister Leona and the staff of St. Josaphat's school for supplying the subjects for this investigation. Comments on this manuscript by Drs. Alan Lesgold, Frank Murray, and Charles Perfetti are gratefully acknowledged. Author Golinkoff's present address: Department of Educational Foundations, University of Delaware, Newark, Delaware 19711.

[*Child Development*, 1976, **47**, 252–258. © 1976 by the Society for Research in Child Development, Inc. All rights reserved.]

"Decoding, Semantic Processing and Reading Comprehensive Skill," R. Golinkoff and R. Posinski, *Child Development*, Vol. 47, No.1, March 1976.

127

3. REMEDIATION

comprehenders may permit us to distinguish between the two ways that decoding and semantic processing could be related. First, it is possible that the written word is translated into the auditory (or articulatory) mode and then interpreted by existing processes of aural language comprehension. Presuming the decoded word is present in the reader's lexicon, its meaning would then be found. Thus, decoding ability would determine the extent to which the reader obtains single-word meaning. According to this alternative, then, if less skilled comprehenders were unable to readily decode individual words, the decoding process may have actually interfered with getting those words' meaning. For example, since a word may be represented as a complex of features (Gibson 1971), paying too much attention to one set of features (during decoding the phonological and orthographic features) may distract attention from semantic content. In support of this suggestion, Willows (1974) has found that poor readers pay more attention to the physical features than the semantic content of text.

Second, it is possible that semantic processing during reading does not rely on processes of aural language comprehension. In this view, decoding ability is not closely related to the access of individual word meaning, and children who are good decoders may not get the meaning of individual words. Goodman (1973) has asserted that "remedial reading classes are filled with youngsters . . . who can sound out words but get little meaning from their reading" (p. 471). If this is true, unskilled comprehenders should fail to obtain the meaning of individual printed words even if they possess adequate decoding skills. According to this same alternative, unskilled comprehenders may have weak decoding skills which do not interfere with their semantic processing.

The present study assessed decoding and semantic processing in third- and fifth-grade children of two levels of comprehension ability as measured by a standardized test. Decoding was assessed by timing subjects as they read aloud a series of words and trigrams. Semantic processing was assessed with the use of the picture-word interference tasks described above (Rosinski et al. 1975). For average readers, labeling the pictures when real words are printed on them takes significantly longer to perform than the trigram control condition (Rosinski et al. 1975). For the less skilled comprehender, the relative amount of interference in these conditions may depend on the extent to which decoding and semantic processing are separable skills. If the first hypothesis is correct, unskilled comprehenders who have decoding problems should experience significantly *less* semantic interference than skilled comprehenders. Alternatively, if the second hypothesis is correct, unskilled and skilled comprehenders should experience an equivalent amount of semantic interference even if the unskilled comprehenders have decoding problems.

Method

Subjects

Twenty-four third graders (mean CA = 9-4 years) and 24 fifth graders (mean CA = 10-6 years) from several classes in the same school were selected on the basis of whether they were above or below grade level in reading comprehension on the Metropolitan Achievement Test. Children falling in the top or bottom 10% were not used. Sex distribution was approximately equal in all groups. The average grade equivalent score for the skilled comprehenders was 4.25 and 7.09 for the third and fifth grade, respectively, and for unskilled comprehenders it was 2.23 for the third grade and 3.59 for the fifth grade.

Materials

Decoding tests.—Twenty common first-grade-level nouns naming an animal or object were used in the word decoding test. For the trigram decoding test, 20 pronounceable consonant-vowel-consonant trigrams with association values ranging from 35% to 65% (Archer 1960) were used. The words and trigrams were printed on two separate sheets of 8½ × 11-inch paper. Each sheet was divided into 20 equal size cells. Depending on the test, either a word or a trigram appeared in each cell.

Picture-labeling warm-up task.—To make certain subjects could readily label the pictures to be used in the interference tasks, subjects were asked to name the 20 pictures. For this test, each cell of an 8½ × 11-inch sheet contained a line drawing of one of the animals or objects on the word sheet.

Interference tasks.—In the three interference tasks, a word or trigram was superimposed on the line drawing in each cell. In the 100% condition, the word matched the drawing, for example, picture of a pig with the word "pig" printed on it. In the 0% condition, the drawings and words did not match, for example, picture of a pig with the word "cat" printed on it. Drawings and words in this condition were randomly paired with the restriction that semantic categories, that is, animal versus object, were not crossed. In the trigram condition (see fig. 1), a trigram was superimposed on each of the drawings.

Procedure

Each subject was tested individually by a female experimenter who did not know whether the subject was classified as a skilled or unskilled comprehender. The testing was conducted in January of the school year.

Decoding tests.—Subjects were told to read the words or trigrams on a test sheet as rapidly as possible without making mistakes. The experimenter timed the subject's reading of the entire sheet with a stopwatch (to the nearest 0.1 second) and corrected pronunciation errors. The order of the decoding tests

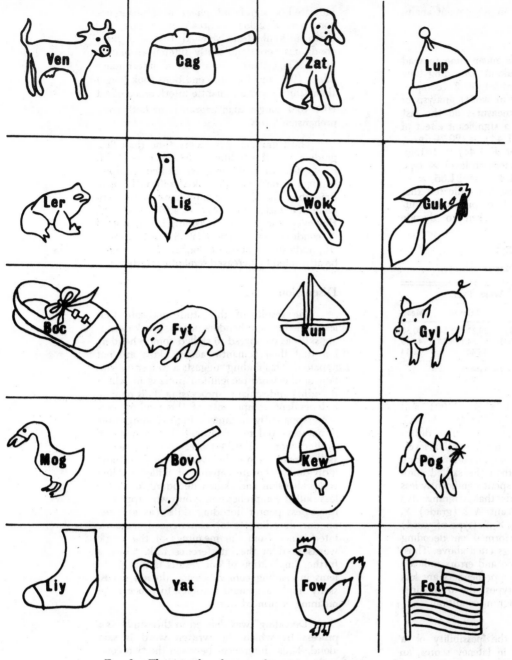

FIG. 1.—The stimulus sheet in the trigram interference task

was counterbalanced with the picture-labeling task across subjects.

Picture-labeling warm-up task.—Subjects were told to name the pictures on the stimulus sheet as rapidly as possible. The experimenter timed each subject with a stopwatch (to the nearest 0.1 second) and corrected errors.

Interference tasks.—One day later, subjects were given the three interference tasks (100%, 0%, and trigram). The procedure followed was identical for all interference con-

ditions: subjects were told that they would be given a sheet with words *and* pictures on it. They were told that their job was to name the pictures as fast as they could and to *ignore* the words. The interference tasks were presented in counterbalanced order. The experimenter timed (to the nearest 0.1 second) the subject's picture naming in each interference task and recorded errors.

Results

Preliminary analyses yielded no effect of sex on the decoding or interference tasks and

3. REMEDIATION

that variable was pooled in subsequent analyses.

Decoding Tests

Table 1 presents the mean time to read the trigrams and words aloud. Decoding time was analyzed in a 2 (grade) × 2 (comprehension level) × 2 (type of word) analysis of variance with repeated measures on the last factor. Results indicated a significant effect of comprehension level, $F(1,44) = 20.79$, $p < .001$, and semantic content, $F(1,44) = 101.99$, $p < .001$, and a comprehension level × type of word interaction, $F(1,44) = 21.65$, $p < .001$. A test of the interaction indicated that the skilled and less skilled comprehenders differed only on the time taken to decode

TABLE 1

MEAN DECODING TIME IN SECONDS

COMPREHENSION LEVEL	WORD TYPE		
	Word	Trigram	Mean
Skilled	11.74 (2.03)	29.27 (11.04)	20.50
Less skilled	20.04 (12.03)	67.54 (38.56)	43.79
Mean	15.89	48.40	32.14

NOTE.—Standard deviations in parentheses.

trigrams, $F(1,44) = 70.64$, $p < .001$, and not on real word decoding, $F(1,44) = 3.33$, $p > .05$. Thus, trigram decoding time distinguished between the two comprehension levels with the less skilled comprehenders taking significantly more time than the skilled comprehenders. Both groups spent significantly less time decoding real words than trigrams. No other effects were significant. A 2 (grade) × 2 (comprehension level) × 2 (type of word) analysis of variance performed on decoding errors mirrored the findings cited above. Thus, analyses on decoding time and errors indicate that, while less skilled comprehenders are less capable on both word types, the differences are heightened in the trigram condition.

Interference Tests

To insure against the possibility of a speed-accuracy trade-off in latency scores, an a priori criterion of 75% correct, that is, a maximum of five errors where the word instead of the picture label was supplied, was adopted for inclusion of a subject's data in the analysis. All subjects tested met this criterion. In fact, too few errors of this kind were made to analyze the error data. Mean errors per subject ranged from 0.25 to 1.7.

The mean time to label the pictures in the three interference conditions is presented in figure 2. A 2 (grade level) × 2 (comprehension level) × 3 (interference condition) analysis of variance with repeated measures on the last factor was performed on these times to determine if both comprehension groups experienced more interference from the meanings of real words than from trigrams. Results

indicated a significant effect of interference condition, $F(2,88) = 56.45$, $p < .001$, and Newman-Keuls tests showed that the three conditions were significantly different from each other. Thus, there was a general interference effect (0% and trigram conditions took longer than 100%) and a semantic interference effect (0% took longer than trigram) for both comprehension levels.

Third graders spent more time than fifth graders in all conditions, $F(1,44) = 7.34$, $p < .01$. In addition, less skilled comprehenders in both grades took significantly more time than the skilled comprehenders to complete the tasks, $F(1,44) = 4.67$, $p < .05$. However, the lack of a comprehension level × condition interaction, $F(2,88) = 2.03$, $p > .10$, indicates that these longer times cannot be attributed to increased semantic interference.

Discussion

The results of this study indicate that less skilled comprehenders possess weak decoding skills as compared to skilled comprehenders but that their semantic access skills are not impaired. This finding suggests a conceptualization of the word-recognition process in which decoding and semantic-processing skills may be independent components of the reading process. Apparently an intervening decoding stage is not essential for obtaining the meaning of printed words. Furthermore, meaning access skills do not seem to be available only to those individuals who are capable of skilled reading comprehension and skilled decoding; even the less skilled comprehension group who appeared to possess poorer decoding skills (as assessed on our decoding tests) experienced semantic interference from the meanings of the single words used in the interference task. Thus, a further implication of our results is that problems in reading comprehension do not necessarily imply a general inability to process the meaning of printed words.

"Decoding" was defined in this study as a process by which the written word is said aloud. Thus, differences between the two comprehension groups on our decoding tasks can only reveal some general decoding problem and cannot distinguish between problems in using spelling-to-sound correspondence units versus the skills involved in rapid oral production. The finding that our population of less skilled comprehenders suffered from inadequate decoding skills suggests that statements questioning this relationship may not be founded on sufficiently sensitive decoding data (Cromer 1970; Goodman 1973). Latency or rate measures on unfamiliar or nonsense words may be more sensitive indices of decoding skill than error rates on common words.

Although the results indicated that the comprehension groups differed in decoding skill, both groups experienced semantic inter-

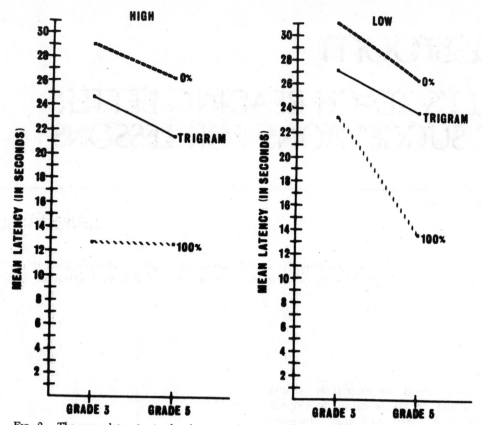

FIG. 2.—The mean latencies in the three interference conditions. *High* refers to skilled comprehenders, *low* to less skilled comprehenders.

ference on the picture-word interference task when their scores in the trigram and real word conditions were compared. A recent model of automaticity in the reading process (LaBerge & Samuels 1974) supports the explanation we have given of our present findings. These authors suggest that with practice the reader comes to be able to process the graphemic stimulus into the visual word code and then to activate the meaning code for that word in semantic memory. On common words the reader can bypass the "phonological code," or the word's acoustic representation. With the common first-grade-level words used in this study, even unskilled comprehenders accessed the meanings of the distractor words in semantic memory and experienced interference. Furthermore, the fact that no differences were found in the extent to which third and fifth graders experienced semantic interference replicates the results of Rosinski et al. They found that with these same simple words, second graders, sixth graders, and adults demonstrated virtually identical amounts of interference, even though the younger subjects were slower over all tasks.

While the comprehension groups did not differ on the extent to which they experienced semantic interference on the interference tasks, there was a main effect of comprehension level. On all the interference tasks, the less skilled group took longer than the skilled group to complete the task. As Rosinski et al. argued, interference in these tasks is the result of a variety of developmental factors such as children's ability to ignore irrelevant stimuli. It is not possible to determine exactly from this experiment which factor the less skilled group was deficient in or what effect that deficiency may have on the reading process. Apparently though, that deficiency does not affect semantic processing as studied in this experiment.

In conclusion, our results suggest that decoding and semantic processing are separable processes and that, although less skilled comprehenders have difficulty decoding, this does not result in difficulties in accessing meaning. This finding may have important ramifications for the study of the reading process for it suggests that less skilled comprehenders can automatically pick up the meaning of printed words. The source of difficulty, then, may not be located in single-word semantic processing but in some other component of the reading process.

The Classroom

LET'S TEACH READING BETTER!
20 SPECIFIC SUGGESTIONS FOR LESSONS

Laura Bursuk

Laura Bursuk, PhD, is an associate professor at the York College of the City University of New York, Department of Teacher Preparation, Jamaica, New York 11451.

Pupils' reading proficiency and how to develop it are primary concerns of teachers as they seek to assure pupil development and progress in this very important curriculum area. The suggestions given below are designed to assist teachers in their endeavors to teach reading more effectively.

1. Teaching should proceed through a three-phase cycle: (1) development of understanding of what is being taught; (2) the actual teaching of the skill; and (3) the application of the skill in a natural reading situation. The largest proportion of the time should be in the teaching phase—which also includes teacher-supervised practice with reading exercises.

2. Every lesson should have specific objectives. If a lesson has more than one objective, the objectives should be related and compatible.

3. Teach skills in appropriate developmental sequence. Helpful guides may be found in curriculum bulletins published by local and state educational agencies and professional groups. Published materials usually have their own guides for the sequence of the particular programs.

4. All reading lessons should fit into an overall, comprehensive plan of reading goals developed for the particular school term or year. However, teachers should be flexible and responsive to demonstrated needs of pupils, and so should organize lessons in skills needed even if these do not fall within the original plan.

5. Provision should be made for ongoing evaluation of pupils' acquisition and application of skills taught

Laura Bursuk, "Let's Teach Reading Better! 20 Specific Suggestions for Lessons," *Academic Therapy*, Vol. 14, No. 2, November, 1978. ©1978, Acaemic Therapy Publications, San Rafael, California. Reprinted by permission.

and reviewed. Such evaluation can be built into the lessons themselves, as well as form a separate activity.

6. Pupils should always be aware of what they are doing, why they are doing it, and how well they are doing, and should be given guidance in how to improve their performance when this is necessary.

7. Proceed at the pupil's rate of learning—no faster, no slower. This means working with small groups, if not using complete individualization.

8. It is better to teach a little bit thoroughly than a lot superficially. Therefore, do not attempt to teach too much at one time. There is a big difference between "covering" and "teaching."

9. All activities within a lesson should be focused on the development of the specific skill being taught. Do not clutter your lesson with unrelated and/or unnecessary activities.

10. Review of previously learned skills can be and should be incorporated into lessons on new skills.

11. Do not *tell* any more than you have to. Structure your lessons so that you *elicit* information from the pupils. Use questioning to lead them to discover the relationships, associations, and generalizations involved.

12. Teaching and practice activities should entail active pupil participation and overt responses.

13. Be a diagnostic teacher. This means teaching with a pencil and paper at hand so that you can make notes concerning pupil's errors and diffficulties. Future lessons should incorporate work designed to overcome these deficiencies.

14. Materials used should be appropriate in regard to the reading achievement level of the pupils, the difficulty level of the skill(s) being taught, the interests and concerns of the pupils.

15. Know the pupils' independent and instructional reading levels. Word identification lessons should use instructional level materials; comprehension, fluency, and study skills lessons should use independent level materials, for teaching purposes. Subsequent practice and application of skills should be in instructional level materials. "Free" reading and at-home reading should be at independent level.

16. Materials used should center on the skill(s) being taught and should permit the application of these skills.

17. All teacher-prepared materials should be clear and legible. Use black felt pens and manuscript print for hand-made materials. Use a primer typewriter for typing primary-grade materials. Double or triple space typewritten materials.

18. Know the difference among:
    a. reading
    b. teaching reading skills
    c. reviewing

      d. supervising pupils as they do exercises

      e. checking and testing

19. Be aware of what is teaching and what is application or practice. Exercises enable pupils to practice and apply—they do not teach. Be certain that exercises used do indeed provide for the practice or application of the skill being taught, and not something else. Design your own exercises or modify published ones if you cannot find published material that focuses on precisely the skill(s) of your particular lesson.

20. Be particularly aware of the difference between *reading* and *teaching reading*. The reading of stories is the practice and application of skills in reading, within a natural reading situation. But it does not teach reading skills. It is also the hoped-for outcome of the learning of reading skills in the first place. Both reading and teaching are important aspects of the reading instructional program; both need to be included in the program, in proper balance. Be specific in teaching reading skills and then provide opportunities for the use of those skills in reading.

The Basic Basic: Getting Kids To Read

What one system did—and what you can do—to motivate children to read.

BY BERNARD A. FALLER, JR.

I couldn't help noticing the fourth grade boy who sat closest to the door. His hair was a wild thatch of sun-soaked straw. He was wearing a grass-stained Dallas Cowboys T-shirt with the left sleeve all but ripped away from where the seam should have been. Under his desk he had shoved aside a pile of rumpled papers and loose crayons to provide a safe resting place for his football.

Here was a boy, I thought, that no schoolroom would ever tame. And yet he was totally absorbed, listening to his teacher read aloud Joseph Krumgold's book *And Now Miguel*, an exceptionally fine piece of children's literature.

I looked around at the other 30 fourth graders. Only two gave me a fleeting glance when I entered, and then they, like the rest, were back in that other world with their new-found friend, Miguel, a boy from northern New Mexico who desperately wanted to become a man so he could tend the family's sheep as his older brothers did.

Across the hall another teacher was reading John Steinbeck's *The Red Pony* to his fifth graders. Two doors down, third graders were crossing the prairie with Laura Ingalls Wilder and her book *Little House on the Prairie*. And over in another wing of the school, Robert McCloskey's *Make Way for Ducklings* was delighting first graders.

Reading to children has become almost a way of life in the North East schools of San Antonio, Tex. And it is paying off handsomely. Growing numbers of teachers in the district's 22 elementary schools are reserving 10 to 15 minutes a day for this special time with good books.

Said one school librarian: "This might be the greatest thing we've done for boys and girls in a long time. Whenever a teacher finishes reading a book to her class, there's a run on it in the library. I simply can't keep enough copies on hand." Other books of a similar nature or by the same author are snatched up quickly. It's not uncommon during peak periods of heavy reading that school librarians begin phoning one another as well as the public libraries to borrow books to replenish their empty bookshelves.

How did the idea of taking time every day to read to children take hold in so many classrooms? The spark came from Rand Dyer, an elementary school principal. He still remembers his second grade teacher who read to her class when he attended the old Milliard Elementary School in Beaumont, Tex.

"Her name was Miss McMaster, Miss Helen McMaster," Dyer recalls. "She's retired now, but when I was in her class she had an empathy for kids that was unreal. And she read to us nearly every day. She instilled in me a love of reading and a love for books that has stayed with me all my life. She read to us in a way that made us feel part of the story. There was a dog book I'll never forget. I wanted a dog just like the one in the story, and I wanted to be just like that boy too. Later when I could handle it, I read that dog book from cover to cover."

Inspiration to Implementation

As principal, Dyer became convinced that children today need more teachers like his Miss McMaster—teachers who take time from a busy school day schedule to read books to their students. He cornered Yvonne Ross, coordinator of library services for the district, and the two of them gathered together a core group of classroom teachers, elementary school librarians and a principal or two. In the first few sessions the group brainstormed and jotted down ideas, trying to get a handle on the best possible way to launch a read-aloud program.

In the end the group nailed down just five points, none of which seemed profound at the time. In fact, four turned out to be questions. Nevertheless, these five points eventually proved to be the critical ingredients for success:

1. How can we learn more about children's literature and what it can do for boys and girls today?

2. If the read-aloud idea is as good as we think it is, how do we spread the good word?

3. What is the best way to get as many teachers and administrators involved in the planning as possible?

4. We recognize that we are inspired, but how do we help other teachers become inspired to devote precious time each day to read to their children?

5. The surest way to kill the program will be to make it a command performance. No teacher should be forced to participate in it.

Focusing on points 1 and 2, Ross assured the group that all of the district's librarians were well-versed in children's literature. "Each school, in effect," she told them, "has its own expert resource consultant right there on campus. It's just a matter of asking librarians to help us develop the plan."

They moved to point 4 and the group asked Ross and Dyer to embark upon

3. REMEDIATION

a search-and-find mission for some-one who would be, as Dyer would later put it, "the best durned inspirer for children's lit and reading motivation in the country."

They found him in Massachusetts. "I traveled a good many miles with Mrs. Ross to check him out," Dyer re-called. Bill Halloran was a fired-up, former elementary school teacher turned traveling consultant.

"Trying to get the money to bring him to our district, we ran into a few problems at first," Dyer explained. "The district's budget was already locked in." But when the word got out that Dyer wanted Halloran so much that he was passing the hat to his fel-low principals after committing $100 from his own school's fund, the dis-trict stepped in and provided the necessary funds.

Halloran flew in from Massachusetts one morning in late August. Having just returned from their summer vaca-tions, the teachers were busy—press-ing hard to get their classrooms in order, putting up "welcome back" bulletin boards, preparing plans for that first day when the children would troop in. They wanted to be back in their rooms. Instead, more than 250 of them sat restlessly in a large assembly room waiting, as one teacher was overheard to say, "to hear some lec-ture on how to motivate kids to read."

Dyer frowned. "This may be bad timing," he said.

And then Halloran popped up, sur-rounded by tables and tables of chil-dren's books, teacher-made materials, motivation gimmicks of all sorts, chil-dren's posters and children's original stories. He flitted from table to table, picking up a book here and there, holding it high over his head for every-one to see while he recited passages from it, or telling how one book or another stimulated his own students. For more than two-and-a-half hours he flooded the room with a kind of story-book magic that inspired this audience "to go out and to do likewise."

Dyer knew that this kind of inspira-tion, like a Sunday sermon, could all but wither away by Monday morning unless a quick follow-up strategy was planned to renew the enthusiasm. Ross and Dyer immediately called their planning team together, and the group agreed to send invitations to all schools to join the read-aloud project. Each school deciding to "join up" was asked to send a three-member team made up of a classroom teacher, the librarian and the principal to an after-school meeting. Not one of the 22 schools missed the chance to send a team.

This meeting generated the idea of a cooperatively developed read-aloud resource book called "Reading Is . . ." Every interested teacher in the district had the opportunity to contribute and every teacher had access to the re-source book when it was completed.

"Any teacher who wished to volun-teer," Ross explained, "was asked to go to the school library and browse around a bit, then choose a book that he or she felt was appropriate for reading aloud to a class. We wanted the teachers to read the selected book first to get a feeling for it, and then read it aloud for the children's reactions."

Once books were chosen, teachers filled out a concise review form de-signed by Ross. An example (from a first grade teacher's review of Howard Knotts' *The Winter Cat*):

SUMMARY: *Knotts, Howard*. The Winter Cat. *Harper,1972, 32 pages. A story told in prose form about a stray cat who gradually learns to ac-cept love and attention from chil-dren as he learns what winter is.*
RATING: *Highly recommended.*
SPECIAL VALUE: *Creative writing, art, poetry. Good in teaching imagery.*
RECOMMENDED GRADE LEVELS: *Kin-dergarten–second grade.*

More than 400 reviews flooded Ross' desk; some teachers sent in two or three. A triple-decked cross index was tabulated by Ross for quick reference to titles, recommended grade level and subject (which includes such per-sonal traits as perseverance, self-es-teem and kindness). Books are listed alphabetically by authors. Though teachers are not restricted to the 360 books included in the "Reading Is" guide, the guide is a useful resource, especially for the classroom teacher whose background in children's litera-ture is sketchy. For any busy teacher it serves as a quick retrieval system for selecting the right book for a particular class.

Spin-offs and Variations
Now that the North East district's ele-mentary schools have had two years' experience in the read-aloud venture, teachers are discovering related activi-ties. Children write to their favorite authors and often receive replies that they read again and again before proudly tacking them up on the bulle-tin board for the whole school to see. It is an exciting bond between author and reader that isn't soon forgotten.

Such correspondence between stu-dents and authors sometimes leads to exciting personal visits. Ross currently is compiling a list of authors who re-

side within a reasonable distance of San Antonio—a list that will be dis-tributed to all schools. She remembers the time, even before the read-aloud program, when the boys and girls from Castle Hills Elementary School wrote to Fred Gipson, author of *Old Yeller*. They discovered that he lived only 100 miles from their school, invited him down, and he accepted. Students still talk about that morning when Gipson strolled into the school's auditorium wearing his cowboy boots.

"I like to write in the mornings," he told the students. "But sometimes I don't like to write in the morning or anytime at all—but I do anyway. I make myself. Just like you. Some mornings you don't want to come to school . . ." (loud applause and cheers from the students) ". . . but you come anyway," he said. (Low groans.)

Later Gipson met with several small groups of students and they asked him question after question. How did he get his ideas? What was it like to be a writer? Did he know Walt Disney?

Yes, he knew Disney. "When they were making the film of *Old Yeller*," Gipson told them, "they had a scene where a jack rabbit jumps in a hole. Now, jack rabbits don't jump in holes; cottontails go in holes, not jack rab-bits. But I could never get those movie people to understand that."

The students and Gipson chatted well into the afternoon and then Gip-son left for home. The following day there wasn't a single copy of *Old Yeller* available at the libraries or at the book-stores in the entire city of San Antonio. The Castle Hills students had them all.

A variation on the read-aloud program in some schools is what one teacher calls "Our Time To Enjoy Reading Silently"—nicknamed the "OTTERS" hour. It really doesn't last an hour (more like ten minutes a day), but it's a time when the whole school reads—students, teachers, the principal, the custodians. It's a time when everyone enjoys reading what they want to read—a newspaper, a fairy tale, a novel, a professional journal, a magazine, even a comic book.

At Walzem Elementary School you walk in the front door, down the corri-dor to the spacious, carpeted learning resource center and you see everyone reading—some readers lounging on the floor, some rocking away in minia-ture rocking chairs, some in a rainbow-colored reading loft.

Walzem's principal, Roger Lawrence, who administers the exemplary dem-onstration school for the state, doesn't miss many silent reading sessions with his students.

"When the boys and girls see us all reading together," Lawrence tells visitors to the school, "it says more to them than we ever could in words that reading *is* important, and it can be fun too. You'd be surprised how many of our students don't want to stop reading when the time is up. After two years we've noticed a big change in children's attitudes toward reading."

The read-aloud program has had an impact on other subjects as well as reading. One fifth grade teacher declared: "I can teach more about the Western movement in a social studies unit by reading to the kids from Mary Calhoun's *High Wind for Kansas* or Sid Fleischman's *Bullwhip Griffin* than I can with all the textbooks in the school."

Other teachers use the read-aloud sessions to stimulate open-ended class discussions, to work on oral language development, even to provide a little bibliotherapy. As one teacher put it, "It's just good to have a special time set aside every single day when we can all sit back with a read-aloud story and smile together with the book's characters."

Looking back at his two years' experience with the read-aloud venture, Rand Dyer summed it up: "We've come a long way since those beginning meetings. We stumbled some along the way, but we picked ourselves up and kept going, and it has been worth it. We've put reading back on top where it should be." He paused and smiled. "I think Miss McMaster would like that."

Bernard A. Faller, Jr., is director of elementary education for the North East Independent School District in San Antonio, Tex.

photo: Office of Human Development Services,
Department of Health, Education and Welfare

EDUCATIONAL SERVICES

Providing effective and appropriate educational services to the learning disabled child is certainly the goal of the majority of personnel in the field. Unfortunately, deciding upon the types of educational models and who should deliver these services can often become both frustrating and confusing.

Once a child's educational objectives have been identified, placement may usually be chosen. On occasion, a child's needs may be so mild that the necessary help may be provided by a regular classroom teacher. On the other hand, a child may require a great deal of educational instruction from a specialist in learning disabilities. Therefore, the primary consideration for educational services must be the nature and severity of the child's learning disabilities.

After the degree of educational support that the child requires has been established, two essential factors must be considered: the chronological age of the child, and the degree of social development. Chronological age becomes important due to the fact that learning disabled children are often functioning at a grade level much below the level expected for their age. It is often inappropriate to place them with children who are younger, as they often react negatively to materials that are identified with younger children.

The lack of interpersonal skills which learning disabled children often demonstrate may also make certain placements inappropriate. A regular classroom may prove to be a difficult environment for such a child, who needs to ignore distractions and function within a different system of reinforcement.

Careful diagnosis and assessment, coupled with appropriate instruction is of primary importance to the learning disabled child. Many options for delivering services, including screening, diagnosis, educational planning, teaching, and evaluation are available. The most viable alternative for these children appears to be regarding the regular classroom as the first consideration to avoid the child's unnecessary isolation from peers and mainstream education. The roles and competencies of L.D. teaching and the perceived status of their students will be discussed in this section.

COMPETENCIES FOR PROFESSIONALS IN LEARNING DISABILITIES

_____ *Phyllis L. Newcomer*

A major role of any professional organization is to establish standards by which professionals and practices in the field can be evaluated. DCLD has taken a major step in this direction by developing a set of competencies for teachers of learning disabled children and youth. This article presents the rationale behind the development of these competencies as well as potential uses of the competency statements. The development of this set of competency statements underscores the Division's commitment to upgrading current practices. Readers are strongly encouraged to provide feedback to Dr. Newcomer's Committee on the scope, format, and content of the competency statements. Meaningful standards can best be derived from these statements through a broad base of input from professionals in the field. — D.D.D.

This article is to introduce the DCLD document, *Competencies for Teachers of Learning Disabled Children and Youth,* which recently was completed and which shortly will be disseminated to the membership. I am pleased to write this article, since it permits me to brag, just a bit, about a hard working committee, a supportive and cooperative board of trustees, and an interested membership, all of whom combined to make an idea into a reality. I will proceed first by providing some background information; second, discussing the rationale for the competencies; third, presenting examples of the competencies; and fourth, outlining some suggestions for the document's future use.

BACKGROUND INFORMATION

Most people would agree that the field of learning disabilities has undergone rapid development in the past ten years and has experienced many of the "growing pains" which usually accompany development. In a remarkably short period of time, professionals in the field have had to come to terms with a variety of controversial issues, not the least of which were the standards of competence required of those who serve the learning disabled

PHYLLIS L. NEWCOMER, Ph.D., is Associate Professor of Special Education, Beaver College, Glenside, Pa.

"Competencies for Professionals in Learning Disabilities," Phyllis Newcomer, *Learning Disability Quarterly,* Vol. 1, No.2, Spring, 1978.

population. Not surprisingly, therefore, a certain amount of confusion was generated by legitimate differences of opinion about this topic and by the ever pressing demands for personnel to provide immediate services to children. Consequently, very little consistent policy existed regarding the types and levels of knowledge and skill which practitioners must demonstrate. It became increasingly clear that the future development of the field depended upon the ability of the professional community to formulate a representative position document regarding standards of competence. As an organization representing approximately 10,000 professionals associated with LD, it was both logical and appropriate for DCLD to undertake such a task. Thus, two years ago, during the presidential tenure of Dr. Donald Hammill, DCLD officially began work on the development of a competency document.

The initial step was the formation of a working committee on competence which I was asked to chair. Committee members were solicited from the membership through personal persuasion and through the DCLD Newsletter. Ultimately, the following three enthusiastic persons comprised the committee:

> Dr. Patricia Ann Magee, Diagnostic-Remedial Specialist, Philadelphia School District
>
> Dr. Judith Ann Wilson, Assistant Professor and Materials Laboratory Director, University of Kansas
>
> Dr. Linda Lou Brown, Assistant Professor, University of Texas

These three women, who have extensive and varied expertise in the field, deserve particular credit for the accomplishment of the task. They donated vast amounts of time and energy to the job and kept their sense of humor throughout the two-year period (well, most of the time).

UNDERLYING RATIONALE

In attempting to respond to Dr. Hammill's charge, the committee had to make a series of important decisions regarding the rationale which would provide the basis for the document. These can be presented most clearly in the form of questions which we tried to answer.

1. **What format to use?** We had all previously been exposed to a seemingly endless variety of competency lists pertaining to some aspect of special education and presented in varying formats. In some cases the competency statements pertained to general knowledge, while in other instances a multitude of specific skills were listed. After considering the problem, we agreed on a format which incorporated both general information and application skills for assessment and instruction. It was reasoned that a competent professional in the field of learning disabilities must *know* and *do*, i.e., must have both theoretical and applied skills, Also, unlike other areas of special education, learning disabilities is closely associated with a diagnostic-remedial model for serving children, thus necessitating an emphasis on assessment as well as instructional skills.

2. **What type of statements to use?** The DCLD charge specifically requested the development of a comprehensive document. "Comprehensiveness" was interpreted in light of the wide variety of skills and knowledge areas in which professionals in learning disabilities must be competent. Their professional roles may cast them in varied instructional settings such as resource rooms, preschool classes, and self-contained classrooms, and may emphasize specific role functions such as educational diagnosis, teacher consultation and materials modification. Also, LD professionals may be required to work with individuals whose ages range from 3 to 21 and whose learning deficits span the spectrum of academic and developmental areas. In short, the specialist in learning disabilities must be an educational generalist, capable of developing comprehensive, individual instructional programs for each learning disabled person, yet must also possess the depth of expertise necessary to provide specific services in children's deficit areas.

4. SERVICES

Thus, it was decided to generate relatively generic statements which would subsume a wide variety of content areas and would include all aspects of the assessment, instructional, management, and consulting skills currently deemed necessary for successful practice in any role function within the field.

3. **What areas to include?** As we were committed to formulating generic statements applicable to all possible roles associated with teaching learning disabled persons, we obviously needed competency statements pertaining to a wide variety of topics, Thus, we included the basic areas of an academic curriculum: *reading, arithmetic, written expression,* and *spelling;* general developmental areas: *oral language* and *cognition;* as well as areas pertaining to affective behavior: *behavior management, counseling and consulting.* In addition, because of our belief that practitioners in the field must be able to incorporate career/vocational education into their instructional plans, must have knowledge of the unique historic-theoretical perspectives associated with the field, and must apply optimal educational operations, competency statements in these three areas were included.

Naturally, we understood that not every practitioner would evidence the same degree of competence in each of these areas and that levels of competence would pertain to role function. For example, a teacher of preschool learning disabled children could be expected to have greater training in the oral language area than a secondary-level teacher of the learning disabled.

We also recognized that many of the competencies which we specified for the learning disablities specialist were not exclusive procedures to be used with learning disabled persons only, but were applicable to all individuals who would teach effectively. This approach reflected our philosophy that the ability effectively to use specific remedial techniques must be based upon a foundation of knowledge and skill which pertain to good general instructional procedures.

4. **Where to get information?** It was understood that if the competencies were to be representative of the current status of learning disabilities, they had to reflect the attitudes and opinions of knowledgeable people within the field and could not simply reflect the combined knowledge of the individuals comprising the working committee.

To begin our quest, we solicited competency documents from a variety of sources. We used the DCLD Newsletter (Vol. 3, No. 1, March 1977) to ask the membership for assistance and also made direct contact with other professional organizations, teacher training institutions, state departments, etc. Input was also solicited from the DCLD Board of Trustees, particularly from the current president, Dr. Steven Larsen. Finally, current text books, curriculum manuals and assessment instruments were examined in order to extrapolate information from those sources as well. Upon completion of these steps, we were able to formulate a first draft of competency statements.

To make this and other succeeding drafts available to members of the field, we continued to use the DCLD Newsletter (Vol 3, No 3, December 1977) as well as direct mailings to a variety of other sources in the country. The response was encouraging as we received suggestions from individuals in a wide variety of professional roles including teacher trainers, state and local education department officials, teachers and students. Those individuals who took the time to help by responding have our thanks, since their ideas enabled us to make modifications which we believe expanded the scope of the document.

Finally, when we reached the fifth revision, the competency statements were submitted to the DCLD Executive Committee in a special meeting at Kansas City in March, 1978. The Executive Committee accepted the document with minor corrections and additions and voted that it be published as a DCLD monograph and distributed to the membership.

We realize that despite our efforts to encompass a wide variety of ideas in the content of this document, some individuals will not find it acceptable. Although we integrated input from the field, we made decisions for the inclusion or omission of statements which, to some extent, reflected our personal biases. However, those individuals who would have done the task differently may take heart since the statements are not chiseled in stone. In fact, they would hardly constitute a valuable document if they were not conceived of as representing *prevalent current* opinions which are subject to modification. Prevailing attitudes change rapidly with the passage of time and these statements must be altered continuously to reflect such changes.

5. **Where to stop?** We were aware that a competency document can be extended to include far more than general statements. Each statement can be operationalized to include such pertinent data as (a) a delineation of the abilities which are required for specific occupational roles in the field, (b) levels of proficiency in each competency area which are necessary for successful performance, and (c) plausible methods of establishing competence in each area.

At this stage, however, we decided not to attempt such an elaborate development of the competency statements. Our decision was based upon two important factors: First, we believed that specific, operationalized competencies must be developed in the field by the various institutions and organizations that have an interest in serving learning disabled persons. Such competencies must reflect local needs and specific frames of reference.

Second, we believed that the further development of the competency document must be based upon sound data, not inferences and opinions. Thus, issues such as the competencies necessary successfully to perform various role functions in schools and clinics, the capacity of teacher training programs to train these competencies, and the anticipated requirements for future occupations in LD must be subjected to empirical investigation before specific operational competencies are developed. Hopefully, this document will provide the impetus for such research by the membership who may then contribute to the further development of the DCLD competency statements.

THE COMPETENCIES

The best way to discuss the competencies is to consider selected examples from each area. As noted previously, the format for most areas included the categories: General Knowledge, Assessment, and Instruction. In the areas of Counseling and Consulting, Educational Operations and Historical-Theoretical Perspectives, however, the format was found to be impractical and consequently not used. In the interests of space, only the first competency in each category will be presented. In some cases where General Knowledge was divided into a number of subcategories, the first competency in each subcategory will also be presented.

Future Uses

DCLD's ultimate goal behind the development of LD competency statements is to provide a document which will be of direct use to the field. Several areas of eventual application can be identified. First, *the competencies may be used as guidelines for the development or modification of teacher training programs.* The rapid development of college and university programs training either categorical learning disabilities teachers or generic special educators who function in the diagnostic-remedial roles usually associated with learning disabilities creates a pressing need for external criteria to provide a basis for program evaluations and comparisons. If there is a baseline of minimal competencies, which all teachers of the learning disabled should possess, it follows that there are baseline curricula for all training programs.

Second, *the competencies may be used to establish certification standards for LD professionals.* At present there is substantial variation among states in their certification requirements. Many do not issue separate certification for LD specialties and those which

ORAL LANGUAGE

I.	General Knowledge	The teacher:
		1. understands the association learning, linguistically oriented, and congnitive theories of language.
II.	Assessment	1. can administer and interpret standardized language tests in the areas of phonology, semantics, morphology, and syntax.
III.	Instruction	1. can select and use appropriate commercial developmental materials and programs.

Reading

I.	General Knowledge	The teacher:
	A. Developmental Reading	1. understands basic theories related to the field of reading.
	B. Specialized Reading 　1. Corrective Reading	1. understands that corrective reading instruction is a system for planning and delivering classroom instruction to students who experience minor deficiencies in the elements of developmental reading.
	2. Remedial Reading	1. understands that remedial reading instruction is a system for delivering intensive individualized instruction to students who have major reading problems in word recognition, comprehension, and fluency.
II.	Assessment 　A. Screening	1. has knowledge of the appropriate instruments and techniques for general screening for reading.
	B. Evaluation	1. has knowledge of the appropriate instruments and techniques for specific assessment of the students' level of reading achievement and the areas that warrant specific attention.
	C. Diagnosis	1. can select and administer formal and informal diagnostic instruments for specific skills related to reading.
	D. Formative/Summative	1. can develop and use tests to monitor students' ongoing and final level of mastery.
III.	Instructor 　A. Corrective Reading	1. can plan and implement instruction for minor problems associated with gaps or deficiencies in the developmental reading process.
	B. Remedial Reading	1. can plan and implement intensive individualized instruction in the skill areas associated with remedial reading.

Written Expression

I.   General Knowledge

The teacher:
1. recognizes written expression as a method of conveying ideas or meanings.

II.   Assessment

1. can administer and interpret standardized achievement tests of written expression.

III.   Instruction

1. can plan and implement an instructional program incorporating the basic components for writing.
   1.1 purpose of composition
   1.2 arrangement of ideas
   1.3 compare and contrast skills
   1.4 organization of ideas
   1.5 types of prose, e.g., narrative, descriptive, expository, argumentation
   1.6 poetry

Spelling

I.   General Knowledge

The teacher:
1. understands the nature and rules of English orthography.

II.   Assessment

1. can administer and interpret the spelling sections of standardized achievement tests.

III.   Instruction

1. can teach spelling skills using a planned sequence of activities.

Mathematics

1.   General Knowledge
    A.   Number Theory

The teacher:
1. understands all the concepts involved in numeration and counting.

    B.   Addition and Subtraction

1. understands the computation process involved in adding and subtracting whole numbers.

    C.   Multiplication and Division

1. understands the computational process involved in solving multiplication and division problems.

    D.   Fractions, Decimals, and Percentage

1. understands all the operations involved in adding, subtracting, multiplying, and dividing fractions, decimal numbers, and numbers expressed as percentages.

    E.   Geometry

1. understands simple common plane geometric figures, e.g., circle, square.

    F.   Measurement

1. understands all concepts involved in measurement of: time, linear planes, weight, liquids, and temperature.

    G.   Money

1. understands the U.S. monetary system.

    H.   Verbal Problem Solving

1. understands the variables that contribute to difficulty in verbal problem solving, e.g., reading level, level of syntactic complexity, distractors, etc.

4. SERVICES

| II. | Assessment | 1. | can administer and interpret the mathematics portion of standardized group achievement tests. |
| III. | Instruction | 1. | can teach a specific mathematical skill by developing and following a planned sequence of activities. |

Cognition

I. General Knowledge   The teacher:
    A. Nature of Thought   1. understands various theories regarding thought and process of thinking.

    B. Piagetian Theories   1. understands the implications of a stage theory such as Piaget's and can compare it with age theories.

    C. Association Theory   1. understands the implications of association theory and can analyze learning situations into stimulus and response components.

    D. Information Processing Theories   1. understands the implications of information processing theory as a model of human intelligence.

    E. Gestalt Theories   1. understands theories which view learning wholistically and can analyze:
       1.1 discovery learning
       1.2 perceptual arousal
       1.3 creative or original responses

    F. Theories of Intelligence   1. understands Q factor theory, "g", and special abilities.

II. Assessment
    A. Formal   1. can administer and interpret standardized tests of intelligence.

    B. Informal   1. can devise tasks which reveal children's skills at problem solving, inferential thinking and concept development.

III. Instruction   1. can incorporate information regarding cognitive development into general instructional programming.

Behavioral Management

1. General Knowledge   The teacher
    1. understands general theoretical positions related to:
       1.1 theories of learning
       1.2 theories of personality and psychopathology
       1.3 child development (normal and atypical)

II. Assessment   1. can define target behaviours.

III. Instruction   1. can use remedial instructional procedures to modify behavior.

Counseling and Consulting

I. Consulting with Teachers and and Administrators

The teacher:
1. must have knowledge about working with exceptional children in school settings involving handicapped and nonhandicapped students.

II. Counseling and Consulting with Parents

1. can establish and maintain rapport with parents.

III. Counseling and Consulting with Children

1. must establish and maintain rapport with children.

Career/Vocational Education

I. General Knowledge

The Teacher:

    A. Knowledge of Individual Characteristics

1. is aware that each individual has unique patterns of abilities and limitations which affect career/vocational decisions.

    B. Knowledge of Career and Occupational Opportunities

1. has comprehensive knowledge of a wide variety of occupational families.

II. Assessment

1. can administer and interpret standardized vocational/career interest and aptitude tests.

III. Instruction

1. will provide information pertaining to a wide variety of career opportunities.

Educational Operations

I. Assessment

The teacher:
1. is able to establish rapport during assessment.

II. Materials

1. can determine student needs to be met by curricula.

III. A/V

1. can identify and select media appropriate for stated instructional objectives.

IV. Environment

1. can identify variables which influence learning in the school and classroom environment.

V. Instruction

1. can plan and implement a sequential remedial program for a student.

Historical-Theoretical Perspectives

I. History of Learning Disabilities

The teacher:
1. can identify early contributors to the field of learning disabilities.

II. Program Models

1. can explain various program models used to deliver services to learning disabled children.

III. Professional Organizations

1. is aware of various professional organizatic is in learning disabilities.

4. SERVICES

do frequently have little objective basis for their particular regulations. Consequently, certification standards would seemingly be improved by the availability of a document reflecting the type of knowledge and skill required successfully to teach LD children and youth.

Third, *the competencies can be used as criteria for employment.* School administrators often must select personnel for teaching positions without having specific knowledge of the types of skills necessary for success in those positions. At the very least, the DCLD competency statement should indicate general areas in which the LD specialist should be proficient and should aid administrators in defining school service positions in terms of the competencies required to fill them rather than simply by an occupational title.

Fourth, *the competencies are significant as standards for monitoring ongoing professional practices.* Obviously, special education is not a profession to be pursued by those disinterested in the issue of accountability. Practitioners must demonstrate that they have planned and implemented an optimal individualized educational plan for each handicapped child. The best method of evaluating the quality of services being offered is to utilize external standards of competence which depict what could or should occur and for this purpose the DCLD competencies would serve an important function.

Clearly, these possible uses of the competency document suggest a direction toward the institution of higher standards and greater quality control within the profession with the ultimate goal of insuring that the educational services rendered to LD persons are of optimal quality.

Concluding Remarks

In introducing the DCLD competency document, I have attempted to project it as representative of the organization's firm commitments to an upgrading of current practices and to the establishment of a clearer perspective for future development in the field. These commitments are made possible only by the interest and cooperation of the membership and other interested professionals. Members will soon receive their competency documents while non-members may obtain copies by contacting Dr. Donald Hammill, Chairperson, Publications Committee, 8705 Merion Circle, Austin, TX 78754. When you receive your copy of the competency document, please take the time to provide feedback to the competency committee. Specifically, let us know how the competencies correspond to those emphasized in your teacher training program or those which comprise your state or local educational guidelines. Please contact Dr. P. L. Newcomer, Coordinator of Special Education, Beaver College, Glenside, PA 19038. Thanks in advance.

Actual and Desired Roles of the High School Learning Disability Resource Teacher

Bruno J. D'Alonzo, PhD, and Douglas E. Wiseman, EdD

Bruno J. D'Alonzo *is an associate professor in the Department of Special Education, Arizona State University, and is currently the project director of Arizona Project RETOOL. His interests are high school programming, methods, and research for adolescents with specific learning disabilities, mental retardation, and behavioral disorders.* **Douglas E. Wiseman** *is an associate professor in the Department of Special Education, Arizona State University and is the project director of the Model Demonstration Center for Secondary Learning Disabled Pupils. His interests are adolescents with specific learning disabilities and nonreading curriculum.*

Job satisfaction and job performance go hand in hand. A major determinant of job satisfaction involves performing tasks related to one's training and interests. If learning disability specialists are to achieve in these critical roles, they reasonably must be trained for the roles they perform and be employed to undertake the roles for which they are trained. Though a reasonable expectation, the resource teachers surveyed said this was not the case. Results of this survey should be of interest and use for teacher trainers, practitioners, and school administrators. — G.M.S.

To investigate the role expectations of the high school learning disability resource teacher, a behavior scale was developed to which incumbents responded as to their actual and desired role performance. Inspection of data from the 134 resource teachers indicates that there are few areas of consensus among the respondents.

The importance of an understanding of teacher roles, specifically that of the high school learning disability resource teacher, cannot be lessened in contemporary education. The emphasis on accountability in educational institutions has added new dimensions to role actualization. The authors believe that administrators, fellow teachers, and parents fail to appreciate the fact that the high school learning disability resource teacher is (1) a *teacher* who must be among the best, (2) a *curriculum specialist* with a comprehensive understanding of a variety of subject areas, (3) an *expert in methods* of working with students who are difficult to instruct and reach, (4) a *technician* competent in the use of the "tools of the trade," both hardware and software, (5) an *administrator* who keeps reports, records, and arranges schedules of others, (6) a *counselor* who deals first-hand with educational, social, occupational, and personal problems, (7) a *public* and *human relations* expert in working and communicating with administrators, colleagues, students, and parents, and (8) a *diagnostician* whose competence plays a major part in student learning.

The behavior of such teachers will be determined by the role expectations as perceived by the incumbent as well as the expectations of parents, general and special education adminis-

4. SERVICES

trators and teachers, state departments of education representatives, and, of course, local school boards. With knowledge of this role, the high school learning disability resource teacher may be more effective in selecting problems to be overcome, ranking these problems by priority, and considering alternative solutions to the problems. Role clarification, therefore, becomes imperative.

Despite the importance of this teacher in the schools, a review of the literature found no studies dealing specifically with the role of the high school learning disability resource teacher. A study was conducted by McLoughlin (1973) in which he observed a number of resource teachers of the learning disabled and of the mentally retarded as they performed their roles. The role of each type of resource teacher appeared to be very similar. Several authors have expressed an opinion regarding the resource teacher's role (Adelman 1972, Bauer 1975, Lerner 1976, McLoughlin & Kass 1978, Reger & Koppman 1971, Reger 1972, Smith 1974). Studies have been completed on the perceived role behavior expectations of educational personnel (Aceto 1971, D'Alonzo 1971, Dillehay 1969, Flannigan 1970, Hencley 1969). In these studies a behavior scale was developed to identify perceived role behavior expectations. This study essentially followed this format, but included an additional component that requested incumbents to indicate their desired roles. In essence, the responses to the behavior scale indicate what incumbents were doing and what they thought they should be doing.

DEVELOPMENT OF THE INSTRUMENT

To investigate the role expectations of the high school learning disability teacher, the High School Learning Disability Resource Teacher Behavior Scale was developed. This scale was developed from information obtained from a review of the literature, and interviews, discussions, and observations with special education directors and supervisors, state department staff, special education faculty in institutions of higher learning, and high school learning disability resource teachers. A jury of experts from the field of learning disabilities in Arizona established the content validity of the scale. The reliability of the scale was determined by the split-half method and corrected by the

Spearman-Brown formula (Ferguson 1966); a split-half reliability of .95 was yielded. The scale comprised 38 items, placed within 12 major categories by the authors. Each category included three to five items. The analysis of each category was general and descriptive.

COLLECTION AND INSPECTION OF DATA

The scale was sent to principals of all (124) public high schools in Arizona. Each principal gave the questionnaire to the learning disability resource teacher(s) on their staff. A total of 134 high school learning disability resource teachers responded. The data were inspected and collapsed into three distinct response modes from the seven-point scale used in the survey instrument. The three response modes were high frequency, moderate frequency, and low frequency. Each behavior was rated in terms of one's actual and desired roles. Table I presents a compilation of the data.

INSPECTION AND INTERPRETATION OF DATA

Inspection of the data shows that there are few areas of consensus among the respondents. Consensus implies that most resource teachers (arbitrarily established at 75% or more) agreed that their actual role does include a particular responsibility. However, only six of the 38 questions demonstrated consensus regarding actual role. The consensus responses suggested that resource teachers actually do the following:

(1) Select their own curriculum materials and media for individualized teaching (Question 1, 82%),

(2) Set individual behavioral objectives based on each student's learning problems (Question 17, 78%),

(3) Work to change student attitudes and behaviors to develop positive self-concepts and social acceptance (Question 19, 82%),

(4) Use materials and strategies necessary to meet individual needs in the areas of reading, math, spelling, handwriting, and language (Question 20, 83%),

(5) Rarely plan, secure, and supervise on-site job training (Question 33, 75%), and

(6) Rarely serve as liaison between the school and state vocational agencies (Question 34, 79%).

It is interesting to note that considerably more desired behavior reached consensus than actual behavior (see Table I). In general, resource teachers desire a more intense and complete involvement in the overall program for secondary learning disabled students.

Program Planning

Information was solicited regarding the secondary learning disability resource teacher's independence in program planning. It appears that most teachers are free to select their own curriculum and materials, organize their classrooms, and establish guidelines for their programs. It is interesting to note that though most teachers feel they have some independence in program planning, their desired responses indicate a desire for even greater independence.

In-service Education

Information was requested on the role resource teachers play in in-service training of regular and supportive staff. Apparently there is no uniform policy regarding this role. Only 16% perform in-service roles on a regular basis, while 38% very seldom or never perform this role, and only 7% feel they should perform this function on a regular basis.

Processing Referrals

Questions in this area explored the role of the resource teacher in approaching parents and support personnel, consulting with other professionals regarding referral desirability, and collecting and interpreting relevant data. Role expectations seem to be relatively unestablished in this area. A surprising 37% of the resource teachers do not contact parents regarding referral, and 24% do not feel this should be part of their responsibilities. Interestingly, 25% do not contact support personnel for referral data.

Evaluation and Student Placement

Information was requested concerning the resource teacher's role in evaluation and placement of students. In actuality, only 39% of the teachers indicated that they very seldom or never observed students in the regular classroom, and 9% of this group felt it should not be a responsibility. Apparently 18% of the sample population do not perform placement testing.

Student Staffings

This area dealt with the resource teacher's role in preparing staffings, assuming a leadership posture in the staffing, and maintaining a current filing system on staffings and referrals. No uniform policy seems to exist regarding the role of the resource teacher in staffing — 38% of the teachers very seldom or never organize staffings and 18% feel they should not; 45% of the teachers feel they provide leadership in the staffings; 67% feel their responsibilities in this area should be increased. A surprising 69% of the resource teachers felt they should be responsible for a current filing system on referrals and staffings. This could be an expression of the need for a central, rather than a dispersed, record-keeping system.

Student Diagnosis

Questions in this area explored the role of secondary resource teachers in performing individual diagnostic tests, developing individual behavioral objectives, and working out integrated programs with regular teachers. Generally, resource teachers do perform individualized diagnostic testing and develop behavioral objectives, but apparently not as many plan cooperatively with the regular teachers (56%). Some 82% felt their role should include closer planning with the regular teachers.

Remedial Instruction

Data were solicited concerning the resource teacher's role in developing positive self-concepts, individualizing instruction with adequate materials, and being free to select the educational approach best suited to an individual. The results show that the vast majority of teachers work to improve self-concept and social acceptance and use materials and educational strategies necessary to meet the needs of individual students. Apparently the freedom to select the educational approach desired is less widespread.

Consulting and Resource Role

This category contained items which examined the role of resource teachers in consulting, informing, and performing resource activities with regular education personnel. Over 90% of the resource teachers perform consulting and resource responsibilities to some degree, but the regularity of this role varies considerably. The vast majority feel this role should play a more important part in their responsibilities.

TABLE I. Reponses to the Learning Disability Resource Teacher Behavior Scale by percentage.

	High frequency		Moderate frequency		Low frequency	
	Actual	Desired	Actual	Desired	Actual	Desired
Program planning						
1. Effectively selecting curriculum materials and media necessary to meet individual needs of the student population	82	91	17	9	1	0
2. Responsibility for organizing the physical structure of my classroom to meet individual needs	73	91	22	9	5	0
3. Establishing a set of guidelines on how my program is to operate	66	88	30	12	4	0
In-service education						
4. Devising a checklist to aid regular staff and support personnel in identifying students who may need LD services	29	54	36	39	35	7
5. Presenting an ongoing in-service program to regular staff and support personnel, with the responsibility of setting guidelines on how the program is to operate	16	2	46	96	38	2
6. Constructing systems and forms for referral that are clear and concise	31	47	35	46	34	7
Processing referrals						
7. Being able to contact parents to explain why their child has been referred for testing and to obtain their permission	37	48	26	28	37	24
8. Contacting the necessary support personnel who can provide testing and information needed for a preliminary staffing	48	55	27	33	25	12
9. Consulting with professionals from related disciplines and interpreting their records	37	68	48	32	15	0
Evaluation and student placement						
10. Observing student in the regular classroom; setting and compiling information regarding the student's present and past performances	21	43	40	48	39	9
11. Using informal and formal testing to evaluate student's performance for possible program placement	57	63	25	29	18	8
12. Developing a profile of the child's abilities, interests, special developmental needs and learning styles to serve as a basis for educational decisions	55	76	32	21	13	3
Student staffings						
13. Organizing a multidisciplinary team staffing for each completed referral and formulating an agenda	31	45	31	37	38	18
14. Interpreting test results, observations, and assuming leadership in decision making as a member of a multidisciplinary team	45	67	36	31	19	2
15. Keeping an up-to-date file system on all referrals and multi-disciplinary team staffings which affect my program	52	69	28	24	20	7
Student diagnosis						
16. Administering individual diagnostic tests to determine which areas of learning need remediation	64	76	25	21	11	3
17. Being able to set individual behavioral objectives based on the assessment of each student's learning problems	78	87	21	13	1	0
18. Being able to work out individualized programs based upon existing school resources, to be implemented by classroom teachers, the learning disability teacher, or a combination of both	56	82	37	17	7	1
Remedial Instruction						
19. Effecting changes in attitudes and behavior of students to help develop positive self-concepts and social acceptance	82	92	17	7	2	1

	High frequency		Moderate frequency		Low frequency	
	Actual	Desired	Actual	Desired	Actual	Desired
20. Using materials and teaching strategies necessary to meet individual needs in the learning areas of reading, math, spelling, handwriting, and language	83	92	15	7	2	1
21. Being able to use different task analysis approaches: child-centered (modality-processing) and/or materials-centered (skills-sequencing)	66	88	31	11	3	1
Consulting and resource role						
22. Dealing with specific requests from regular classroom teachers regarding the instruction of individual students	48	75	42	23	9	1
23. Keeping regular classroom teachers and other team members informed of the student's ongoing progress	56	81	36	19	8	0
24. Consulting with administrators, classroom teachers, other specialists, and paraprofessionals, so that all elements of the program will operate in a coordinated fashion	49	86	41	14	10	0
Team teaching and counseling						
25. Explaining or demonstrating methods all teachers can use to individualize instruction within their classroom	11	48	49	46	40	6
26. Working with classroom personnel to devise instructional programs that will assure coordinated efforts with the special education program	22	63	51	36	27	1
27. Counseling students in cooperation with guidance counselors	53	69	38	29	9	2
Program evaluation						
28. Evaluating my program according to guidelines and criteria established by the high school	48	63	38	35	14	2
29. Conducting an ongoing needs assessment to identify students needing special education	36	60	48	34	16	6
30. Demonstrating the overall worth or effectiveness of the special program	52	72	41	26	7	2
Career education and work experience						
31. Planning and implementing a career-education program	16	40	46	43	37	17
32. Screening, evaluating, and approving all referrals to a secondary work-experience program	12	34	28	40	60	26
33. Planning, securing, supervising on-the-job training sites	7	21	18	42	75	37
34. Serving as liaison between the school and the state vocational agencies	7	23	14	41	79	36
35. Maintaining work evaluation records and interpreting the work-experience program to parents, school personnel, and community	7	24	20	44	73	32
Parent counseling						
36. Keeping parents informed of their child's ongoing progress	65	86	29	13	6	1
37. Working with parents to devise instructional programs or behavior-management programs they can use at home with their child to assure coordinated efforts with the special education program	27	60	51	38	22	2
38. Consulting with parents so that all elements of their child's program will operate in a coordinated fashion	42	72	45	27	13	1

Always — very often = high frequency
Often — sometimes — seldom = moderate frequency
Very seldom — never = low frequency
N = 134

4. SERVICES

Team-teaching and Counseling

Questions in this area explored the responsibilities that resource teachers have in demonstrating techniques for individualizing instruction and in developing instructional programs with regular teaching personnel. Only 11% of the teachers reported they always or very often perform this role. A surprising 40% never or very seldom perform this role. Most felt, however, that this should be an important part of their duties. When asked if they counseled students in cooperation with the school counselor, over half responded that they always or very often do counseling, but 69% felt this should be an important component of their work.

Program Evaluation

This area dealt with the role of the resource teacher in determining needs assessment and overall effectiveness of the learning disability program. The large majority of the respondents participate to some degree in the evaluation of the program, but generally feel they should participate more.

Career Education and Work Experience

This category had five statements regarding the various roles that secondary resource teachers might perform in career education or as a work-experience coordinator. Fully 37% of the teachers seldom or never function in the role of planner or implementor of career-education programs. Only 16% performed this duty on a regular basis, but 40% felt they should. And 17% felt this should not be part of their responsibilities. Only 12% of the respondents always or very often are involved in the process of referring students to work-experience programs, while 60% very seldom or never are involved in placements to the work-experience program. Approximately 26% do not feel this should be part of their responsibility, but 73% feel they should be involved to some degree.

A small number of resource teachers participate regularly in securing and supervising job-training sites (7%), serving as liaison between the schools and the state vocational agencies (7%), and keeping records and interpreting the programs to the larger community (7%). Approximately 75% of the teachers very seldom or never perform these roles with more than one-third of the respondents feeling that these should not be part of their responsibilities.

Parent Counseling

The majority (65%) of resource teachers responded that they regularly informed parents of the progress of their children, while 6% did not. Approximately one-fourth of the teachers worked regularly with parents on programs of instruction or behavior management that could be effective in the home. However, nearly 60% felt they should. Most resource teachers involved the parents to better coordinate the total program for the students.

DISCUSSION

Inspection of the actual roles data provides information on the current role of secondary learning disability teachers. The desired roles data suggest what the resource teachers feel their role should be. The data appear to indicate that the role of the secondary learning disability teacher is not generally agreed on or defined. Each district apparently develops role descriptions independently, and it would appear this is done without consulting the learning disability teachers. To further compound the issue, apparently there is no consensus regarding role behaviors among the teachers themselves. A clear trend does exist, however, indicating that secondary resource teachers do want to be more involved in the total program for the secondary learning disabled student. All 12 categories showed results that support the desire for greater involvement in nearly all aspects covered in the High School Learning Disability Resource Teacher Behavior Scale. The marked difference between actual performance and desired performance indicates that resource teachers are not performing the roles they feel are most needed. Categories that tend to support a consensus regarding resource teachers' current roles include program planning, individualized diagnosis and cooperative planning, individualizing instruction, developing positive self-concepts, and participating in career and vocational education.

Another generalization that seems especially relevant is that most resource teachers see the cooperative planning and interface with regular-education personnel as a problem area. The inadequate relationship between regular- and special-education staff appears to be a constantly recurring theme. It would seem that extraordinary efforts from both fields are necessary to correct this problem. The foundation of mainstreaming is based on the premise of cooperative effort on the part of all involved personnel. Failure of cooperative involvement jeopardizes the spirit of mainstreaming and has a negative effect on the educational growth of learning disabled youths. Numerous secondary level learning disabled students are rapidly completing their education to enter the impersonal world of work. They have a right to an education that will enhance their position in society. Whatever the reasons that inhibit cooperative involvement, whether they be territorial imperatives, anal retentiveness, or the sanctity of the content area, the issues must be reanalyzed and ultimately resolved for the good of all.

Programs for secondary learning disabled students are relatively new and have received little attention within the field of special education. It has seemed logical to emphasize elementary-level programs, on the premise that the sooner learning problems are dealt with the more likely they are to be solved. The problems have not been successfully ameliorated at the elementary level, for secondary schools have been receiving many students with severe and moderate learning disabilities. It is reasonable to assume that special programs at the secondary level should receive the same emphasis and support as elementary programs.

Another perhaps unwarranted practice is that learning disability models, procedures, and materials used at the elementary level have been generalized to the secondary level. Researchers should examine the needs of the secondary schools to determine if indeed the elementary procedures are appropriate. Teacher-training institutions have perpetuated this condition by expecting their programs to certify prospective teachers from the kindergarten level through twelfth grade.

Solutions and problems encountered at the secondary level may be very different from the problems identified in elementary programs. For example, should learning disability teachers be involved in career and vocational education, and, if so, to what degree? How much time and effort should be consumed in counseling learning disabled students? Are current screening and identification procedures appropriate for adolescent students? How much time should be expended in the complicated task of scheduling at the secondary level? Should regular teachers be expected to modify their offerings for learning disabled students? Indeed, should regular education alone accept the responsibility of redefining normalcy? Should content courses be taught without reading to the adolescent learning disabled student? Should the emphasis of resource teachers be on tutoring the student in content areas or on remediation and development of the student's basic skills? Should reading be taught with the goal of acquiring academic knowledge or should the emphasis be placed on life skills? Should teacher education programs have separate content and certification requirements designed specifically for the secondary learning disability teacher?

Until these and many other questions are addressed, the role of the secondary learning disability teacher will remain unclear and programs will lack direction.

RECOMMENDATIONS

The authors suggest that the reader use the behavior scale as a guide to better understand the role of the high school learning disability resource teacher. Further refinement of the behavior scale should be undertaken to reflect recent changes in state and national legislation. A factorial analysis of items on the behavior scale would provide a more empirical placement of those items. After refinement of the behavior scale, a national survey could provide additional data related to the perceived and expected role behavior of the high school learning disability resource teacher.

ACTUAL AND PERCEIVED PEER STATUS OF LEARNING-DISABLED STUDENTS IN MAINSTREAM PROGRAMS

Virginia L. Bruininks, Ed.D.
University of Minnesota

Those few studies which have examined the peer relationships of learning disabled (LD) students in mainstream educational programs have not investigated the ability of such students to assess their own social status, a factor that may affect social interactions with peers. Further information would help in understanding the status of LD students in mainstream programs and in planning educational experiences, if needed, to enhance their relationships with peers. This study, therefore, investigated the peer status of these students in regular classrooms and the accuracy with which they perceived their social position in the peer group. Results showed that LD students in mainstream programs were significantly less socially accepted than their classmates in regular classrooms and that they were less accurate than their classmates in assessing their own personal status in the group. Implications of these findings for instructional planning and further research are discussed.

Although substantial numbers of LD students are now in mainstream educational programs, little is known about their social integration in regular classrooms. Such information is needed, for Lewis and Rosenblum (1975) have noted that peer relationships may be as influential in a child's social development and learning as associations with important adults. In addition, a positive relationship has been found between children's peer status and academic achievement (Gronlund, 1959; Lilly, 1970).

Few studies have examined the peer relationships of LD students in regular classrooms. Bryan (1974, 1976) did find that in fourth and fifth grade classrooms they were significantly less socially accepted than their classmates, and this finding was confirmed 1 year after an initial study, even though most of the LD children had transferred to new classrooms and teachers. However, these studies did not investigate the ability of LD students to assess their own peer status, a factor that may affect social interactions with peers.

Adjustment of an individual to his peer group may be affected by how accurately he can perceive the relative status of its members, including his own status (Ausubel, Schiff, & Gasser, 1952). Ausubel et al. found positive correlations between actual and perceived status at all grade levels from 3 to 12. This relationship may be lower among LD students, however, since poor social perception has been discussed as characteristic of those students by a number of writers (Wiig & Semel, 1976). Thus, in studying the peer relationships of LD students, it would seem important to assess the accuracy with which they perceive their own and others' social status.

"Actual and Perceived Peer Status of Learning Disabled Students in Mainstream Programs," Virginia Bruininks, Ed.D., *The Journal of Special Education*, Vol. 12, No. 1, Spring, 1978. ©1978 Buttonwood Farms, Inc.

The present study, therefore, aimed to investigate both the peer status of LD students in regular classrooms and the accuracy with which they could assess their status within the peer group. Based on limited findings, it was predicted that these students would be significantly lower in peer status than their classmates and comparatively less accurate in estimating their own social status.

METHOD

Subjects

The study included 410 elementary school-aged children from four school districts in Minnesota. These districts had mainstream programs for LD students and represented a range in socioeconomic levels (one rural school district and three suburban school districts). Sixteen LD students were randomly selected from the special education rolls in these school districts. Students met this study's definition of learning disability if they had qualified under State guidelines for special services as an LD student in their district.[1] All received most of their instruction in a regular classroom and an average of 45 minutes of daily instruction in a special education resource room. No student was away from his regular class peers for more than approximately 1 hour daily. Ten of the 16 students were in grades 1–3, while 6 were in grades 4–5. Average grade placement was approximately 4.21 at the time of the study. Twelve of the students were boys; four were girls.

Comparison subjects were 394 regular classroom peers (188 boys and 206 girls), including a sample of 16 subjects composed of 1 student chosen at random from within the regular classroom of each of the LD students. This sample was selected in order to permit comparisons on a measure of perceived social status, while the total group of classmates was used for the peer status analysis.

Table 1 presents academic achievement for the LD students and the comparison sample. Achievement was surveyed by means of the Addition, Subtraction, Multiplication, and Division subtests of the Key Math Diagnostic Arithmetic Test (Connolly, Nachtman, & Pritchett, 1971) and the Word Identification subtest of the Woodcock Reading Mastery Tests (Woodcock, 1973). Grade equivalents were used in these comparisons.

LD students were achieving on the average of 1.5 grades below actual placement in reading at the time of the study, and all these students were appreciably below standards for their particular grade level (Bruininks, Glaman, & Clark, 1973). In reading achievement, the LD students were significantly lower than comparison students. Although some of the LD students were achieving poorly in mathematics, on the average, the group did not differ significantly from grade placement or from the comparison group in arithmetic computation skills. Differences between groups which have only 16 subjects must be very large to reject the null hypothesis.

Procedures and measures

All testing was conducted in the spring of the school year by trained examiners. The Peer Acceptance Scale (Bruininks, Rynders, & Gross, 1972) was used to assess peer status and perceived peer status. This instrument was

[1]Minnesota uses the definition of learning disabilities provided by the USOE, Bureau of Education for the Handicapped, 1961, and Public Law 91-230, dated April 13, 1970. In applying this definition, to qualify a child for services, psychological assessment and staffing teams must discover:

1. Learning problems . . . so dysfunctional as to seriously interfere with the child's own school progress or the educational rights of other children and which require attention and help beyond that which the regular instructional program can provide.

2. Sufficient sensory integrity, motor skill and general mental ability to make educational consideration as a mentally retarded, hearing, vision, or motor impaired child unnecessary (State Department of Education, 1973, p. 7).

TABLE 1
DESCRIPTIVE STATISTICS ON LD AND
COMPARISON STUDENTS

Score	Learning-disabled group			Comparison group			
	N	Mean	SD	N	Mean	SD	t
Word recognition	16	2.76	1.15	16	4.45	2.72	2.32*
Key math	16	3.59	3.73	16	4.70	2.29	1.02

*p < .05.

designed to measure the social status or popularity of students in a group setting. It is a forced-choice scale on which every group member rates every other group member by circling the appropriate number on a line drawing adjacent to the name of each person in the group. Figure 1 shows the response format for the Peer Acceptance Scale.

Each child in the regular classroom of an LD student completed the Peer Acceptance Scale. Peer acceptance scores were computed for each LD and comparison student by totaling the ratings they received within the classroom from (a) all children of the same sex (same-sex ratings), and (b) all children of the opposite sex (opposite-sex ratings). These scores were also produced for the total group of 394 students.

Perceived social status was assessed, using the Peer Acceptance Scale in an individual testing situation with LD students and comparison students. The same instrument was presented, but this time both groups of students were asked to indicate how they felt each of their classmates regarded them. A mean rating for each student was computed.

A STUDENT'S NAME   ʻFriend   All right   Wouldn't like

Figure 1.   Response format for peer acceptance scale.

RESULTS

Statistical comparisons on measures of peer status and perceived peer status were made between the LD students and two comparison groups (identified comparison subjects and all classmates) by means of t tests for independent groups. The .05 level was used as the criterion of statistical significance in all comparisons. Since peer status measures are relative to particular classroom settings, all comparisons between LD students and the total number of classmates in the study were made with classrooms as the statistical unit of analysis.

Findings on the actual peer status and perceived peer status of the LD and comparison groups are summarized in Tables 2 and 3. These tables present information on peer status ratings derived from children of the same sex and ratings of children of the opposite sex. Although data are summarized for boys, girls, and the total sample, primary attention should be given to the results for boys and the total sample, since the sample included too few girls to make powerful comparisons. Ratings on children of the same sex are generally regarded as the most sensitive measure of status within the child's peer group (Gronlund, 1959).

Peer status

Table 2 presents information on same-sex ratings. LD boys produced significantly lower peer status scores relative to both the comparison group and the total class ($p < .01$ and $p < .005$, respectively). The total sample of LD boys and girls combined also achieved significantly lower peer status scores than children in the comparison and total class groups ($p < .01$ and $p < .02$,

TABLE 2
PEER STATUS AND PERCEIVED PEER STATUS SCORES —
SAME-SEX RATINGS — FOR LD AND COMPARISON STUDENTS

Scores/group	Learning-disabled group		Comparison group		Total class		t^a	t^b
	Mean	SD	Mean	SD	Mean	SD		
Peer status								
Boys	2.22	.33	2.64	.23	2.50	.12	2.80***	3.50****
Girls	2.01	.57	2.50	.39	2.44	.25	1.54	2.39*
Total	2.17	.39	2.55	.33	2.45	.16	2.92***	2.55**
Perceived status								
Boys	2.38	.32	2.64	.50			1.13	
Girls	2.35	.52	2.52	.31			.68	
Total	2.37	.37	2.57	.38			1.25	

[a]Learning-disabled vs. comparison group.
[b]Learning-disabled vs. total class.
*$p < .05$ (one-tailed test).
**$p < .02$ (one-tailed test).
***$p < .01$ (one-tailed test).
****$p < .005$ (one-tailed test).

TABLE 3
PEER STATUS AND PERCEIVED PEER STATUS SCORES —
OPPOSITE-SEX RATINGS — FOR LD AND COMPARISON STUDENTS

Scores/group	Learning-disabled group		Comparison group		Total class		t^a	t^b
	Mean	SD	Mean	SD	Mean	SD		
Peer status								
Boys	1.50	.32	1.70	.33	1.66	.32	2.40*	1.33
Girls	1.76	.50	1.72	.36	1.72	.27	.17	.22
Total	1.56	.38	1.73	.33	1.69	.26	1.31	1.08
Perceived status								
Boys	1.63	.45	1.70	.82			1.42	
Girls	1.70	.73	1.72	.59			.05	
Total	1.65	.53	1.75	.66			.40	

[a]Learning-disabled vs. comparison group.
[b]Learning-disabled vs. total class
*$p < .025$ (one-tailed test).

respectively). LD girls were significantly lower in peer status scores than the total class of girls ($p < .05$), but not in relation to the comparison group.

Peer ratings given by children of the opposite sex are summarized in Table 3. Only one comparison between LD students and their classmates reached statistical significance: LD boys were rated by girls significantly lower in peer status than boys in the comparison group ($p < .025$). It is not surprising to find little variation in opposite-sex peer ratings, since elementary school-aged children tend to accord consistently low, stereotypic ratings to children of the opposite sex (Gronlund, 1959).

4. SERVICES

Perceived peer status

LD children perceived their status as comparable to the perceived status of children in the comparison group on same-sex ratings and opposite-sex ratings (see Tables 2 and 3). As expected, peer ratings on the randomly selected comparison children differed very little from those of the total class group.

The more interesting question related to perceived status involves comparison of self-perceived status to actual status as rated by classroom peers. Comparing perceived status and actual status within the LD comparison groups gives an indication of whether or not the LD children in this study were more or less accurate than comparison children in evaluating their social position with classmates. Table 4 presents statistics on actual status and perceived status for both LD and comparison subjects separately, using t tests for related measures. These data reveal that both LD boys and the combined sample of LD boys and girls rated themselves as significantly higher in peer status than the actual status awarded them by children of the same sex ($p < .05$ for each comparison). No significant difference between actual and perceived status scores occurred with opposite-sex ratings, but these ratings are generally less reflective of the child's actual social position than ratings given by peers of

TABLE 4
ACTUAL PEER STATUS AND PERCEIVED PEER STATUS FOR LD AND COMPARISON STUDENTS

Group	Same-sex ratings	Opposite-sex ratings
	Actual status and perceived status t	Actual status and perceived status t
Learning-disabled group		
Boys	1.99*	.78
Girls	1.02	.23
Total	2.05*	.58
Comparison group		
Boys	.00	.21
Girls	.65	.00
Total	.12	.17

*$p < .05$ (one-tailed test).

the same sex. In the comparison group, there were no significant differences between actual and perceived status scores, indicating that comparison children were generally more accurate than LD children in perceiving their social status in the classroom.

In order to further explore these findings, a product moment correlation was computed between actual peer status scores and perceived status scores for both the LD and comparison groups using same-sex ratings. For the LD group, the relationship between actual status and perceived status was not statistically significant ($r = .41$). The relationship between these measures for the comparison group was statistically significant ($r = .51$; $p < .05$), which supports the finding that comparison children were generally more accurate than LD children in perceiving their social status in the classroom.

One possible reason that LD children are less accurate is that they may be inclined to give higher social ratings generally to themselves and other children. In order to assess whether or not this finding of lower social perceptiveness among LD students was an artifact of response bias, comparisons were made between these students and all their classmates on ratings of children in the comparison group. Data in Table 5 reveal no significant differences between status scores given by LD children and classmates to children in the comparison group, indicating that possible response bias did not account for the different pattern of results between LD and comparison students in analyses of actual status and self-perceived status.

TABLE 5
COMPARISONS OF LEARNING-DISABLED AND CLASSMATES ON
PEER STATUS RATINGS OF THE COMPARISON SAMPLE

| Scores | Learning-disabled | | Classmates | | |
	Mean	SD	Mean	SD	t
Same-sex ratings	2.17	.98	2.50	.38	.77
Opposite-sex ratings	2.25	.71	1.75	.41	1.72

DISCUSSION

As predicted, LD students in regular classrooms were significantly lower in peer status than a randomly selected comparison sample and lower in status when compared with all their classmates. As a separate group, LD boys rated significantly lower in status than the comparison sample of boys on both same-sex ratings (which are seen as the most sensitive measure of status within the child's peer group) and opposite-sex ratings. They also rated significantly lower in status when compared with all their classmates using same-sex ratings. The study included too few LD girls to make meaningful comparisons as a separate group.

Although the actual peer status of LD students was significantly lower than their classmates, no difference was found between LD and comparison students in self-perceived status scores. This was true for the total sample of LD students and for boys as a separate group. Both the total sample of LD students and the group of LD boys rated themselves significantly higher in status than their actual position in the group. Among comparison students, there was no significant difference found between their actual peer status and perceived peer status, indicating that they were more accurate than LD students in assessing their social position in the classroom.

In summary, this sample of LD students in mainstream programs was significantly less socially accepted than their classmates in regular classrooms, confirming the results reported by Bryan (1974, 1976). In addition, it was found that such students were less accurate than their classmates in assessing their own personal status in the group. These findings have important implications for instructional planning and further research.

Peer relationships are important because they appear to influence social development and learning (Lewis and Rosenblum, 1975). If LD students do not perceive their poor status in the classroom, they may not see a need to alter their interactions with peers in order to achieve more positive relationships. Perhaps teachers, therefore, should provide experiences that enhance peer relationships in the classroom. For example, much evidence shows that providing small-group, cooperative learning activities fosters the social integration and academic achievement of students. Johnson and Johnson (1975) review this research and explain how to implement cooperative activities in the classroom. Future research might suggest additional techniques to influence the social integration of LD students.

Further investigation of the factors associated with the poor status of these students in regular classrooms is needed. Important areas for study include (a) social perception, (b) patterns of reinforcement for social contact (Hartrup, Glazer, & Charlesworth, 1967), and (c) the interest of the student in social contact and relationships (Northway, 1944). Further study is also needed to determine why LD students appear less perceptive than their peers in assessing their own status in the group. We must also explore the relationships among poor social perception and other aspects of human development and behavior. Identifying the factors that contribute to poor peer status may then lead to the design of appropriate educational interventions which would enhance the acceptance and adjustment of LD students in mainstream programs.

FOCUS...

What must a school
record for a Handicapped Child?

A step-by-step checklist to achieve a current file-in view of PL 94-142

_____ Record of parents' Document of Rights

      _____ Proof that parents received rights

      _____ Proof that rights were communicated in the language of the home

      _____ Proof that rights were understood by parents

_____ Written permission of parents to test child

_____ Record of testing results

_____ Proof that testing information was shared with parents

_____ Record of who participated in evaluation of student

_____ Record of IEP

      _____ Record of invitation to parent to participate

      _____ Record that IEP was completed and specified as to the diagnosis, objectives, services and evaluation

      _____ Record of school personnel who participated in the IEP development, along with the signature of an administrator and the teacher

      _____ Record of parents approval or disapproval of the IEP
If IEP was disapproved, what action is being taken and what is the temporary placement for the child

      _____ Schedule for future evaluations of the IEP and evidence that this and all other meetings with parents are scheduled at a mutually convenient time

      _____ Record showing that parents were informed of the confidentiality of their child's records and their right to limit access to the records, and their right to determine final disposition of the records

Teachers' Preferences for Resource Services

EDWARD E. GICKLING
LEE C. MURPHY
DOUGLAS W. MALLORY

Abstract: An open-ended Delphi type questionnaire was distributed to administrators and teachers of regular and special education throughout the state of Tennessee. Responses obtained from the questionnaire were used to construct a second, forced choice questionnaire. The second questionnaire was distributed only to regular and resource teachers who had voiced a positive commitment favoring mainstreaming exceptional children. The results show many of the preferences of regular and resource teachers regarding inservice training, cooperative planning, and resource service topics. As such, they represent an initial needs assessment of those closest to the actual teaching situation.

EDWARD E. GICKLING is Associate Professor, Department of Special Education, University of Nevada, Reno; LEE C. MURPHY is Director of Continuing Education, Rochester Institute of Technology, Rochester, New York; and DOUGLAS W. MALLORY is Resource Teacher, Munford, Tennessee.

THE 1970's have seen a realignment of special education priorities, a realignment that has called for massive involvement of exceptional children within regular classroom programs. Mainstreaming impetus has become so pervasive that it represents the major vogue in the field of special education today (Brenton, 1974). Enactment of laws at the state and federal levels accentuates the degree of commitment toward maintaining this movement.

The impact of the movement has hit with such force, both philosophically and legally, that educators are, as Hewett, Artuso, and Taylor (1970) said, "playing catch-up." In retrospect it is quite evident that time was not adequate to inventory this complex phenomenon or to prepare for its implementation. This is not to imply that mainstreaming per se has been a mistake, but it is an acknowledgement of some of the inevitable consequences associated with rapid growth. Paraphrasing Martin (1974), educators should have been more concerned about the pell-mell and naive mad dash to mainstream exceptional children; mainstreaming should have been approached with a full recognition of the barriers ahead. A lack of organizational readiness, negative attitudes of teachers and administrators, and a growing body of evidence concerning the equivocal effects of resource service itself (Cruickshank, 1974; Gickling & Theobald, 1975; Harris & Mahar, 1975; Jenkins & Mayhall, 1976; Payne & Murray, 1974; Shotel, Iano, & McGettigan, 1972) illustrate some of the problems of which Martin spoke.

Hindsight has only solidified the realization that the mechanism for implementing main-

4. SERVICES

streaming, namely the resource teacher movement, faces a dilemma. Professional appeals for the improvement of teachers' attitudes, service delivery systems, assessment, teacher training, and inservice education have provided little help, at least in terms of immediate need. At present, the resource movement is caught between trying to help teachers and children and dealing with many of the recurring problems associated with resource services. This study is one means of providing input into some of these unresolved problems. More specifically, the present study serves as a needs assessment of regular and resource teachers' preferences regarding inservice training, cooperative planning, and resource programs. It was felt that persons closest to the actual teaching situation, namely regular and resource teachers, primarily determine the degree of success of any mainstreaming effort. Because of their importance to mainstreaming, the study included only teachers who had shown positive commitments toward working with handicapped students in regular classroom settings.

Procedure

In order to generate ideas relevant to mainstreaming exceptional children, an open-ended Delphi type questionnaire was developed and distributed to both regular and special educators. The information obtained from the questionnaire was then used to construct a second, forced choice questionnaire. Responses to the second questionnaire are reported here.

Questionnaire 1 contained four sections: Section 1 covered specific demographic information, for example, regular or special teacher, urban or rural system; Section 2 dealt with methods used for selecting inservice sessions and for encouraging teacher participation in inservice sessions; Section 3 considered options regarding scheduling and planning time; and Section 4 addressed case load and placement considerations. Questions in the last three sections asked for multiple suggestions concerning ways to facilitate mainstreaming.

Questionnaire 2 contained the same sections as the first questionnaire. Sections 2 through 4, however, consisted of items that represented either frequently made or novel suggestions acquired from the first questionnaire. A total of 62 suggestions were selected and incorporated into 13 questions, with each question containing from three to seven items.

In order to obtain initial input into the study, five copies of the first questionnaire were mailed to 20 special education administrators and 15 regular education administrators throughout the state of Tennessee. The names and addresses of these individuals were se-

lected from the *Tennessee Directory of Public Schools.* All selections were made in an attempt to equalize the distribution of the questionnaire throughout the eastern, middle, and western parts of the state and to help ensure both urban and rural participation. Each special education administrator was asked to fill out one copy of the questionnaire and to distribute the other four copies to four special education resource teachers. Regular education administrators were also asked to complete one copy and to distribute the other four copies to four regular classroom teachers who had demonstrated positive attitudes toward mainstreaming exceptional children. The names of all participants were kept, and after three weeks a followup letter and accompanying questionnaire were mailed to encourage each nonrespondent to participate.

The first questionnaire was completed by 60 teachers and administrators, which represented a 34% response. Of those who responded, one-third were from urban school systems and two-thirds were from rural systems. Among the respondents, 55% were from eastern Tennessee, 28% from the middle area of the state, and 17% from western Tennessee.

The second questionnaire was sent to those teachers who had responded to the first questionnaire and to additional regular and special education teachers across the state who also voiced support for mainstreaming. Of the 80 teachers who were contacted, 76% responded, including 20 regular and 41 resource teachers; 41% of these respondents worked in urban situations, and 59% were employed in rural systems. Most were concentrated in eastern Tennessee, with 71% coming from that area.

In filling out the second questionnaire, the participants expressed their personal preferences by ranking the options for each question numerically. The priorities of regular classroom teachers were tallied separately from those of special education teachers. The totals for each statement were converted into percentages reflecting the priorities held by each of the two groups of teachers. Specific statements that showed the highest percentages for each of the 13 questions are reported in Table 1.

Results

Inservice Training

The first concern of the study was to determine teachers' preferred topics and schedules for inservice sessions. The first section of Table 1 shows that both regular and special education teachers preferred to take an active role in determining the content of inservice sessions regarding mainstreaming (see question 1); 40% of the regular teachers and 49% of the resource teachers chose inclusion on program committees as their first priority. Direct program participation appeared to be the second overall inservice choice among regular and resource teachers. Resource teachers were more in favor of providing input during the planning stage than actively participating in the program. Classroom teachers, however, did not demonstrate such a clear preference, but indicated that they wanted active involvement either as committee members or through program participation. Fewer than 5% of either group wanted to take full charge of inservice programs.

The results of question 2 indicate that 61% of the resource teachers and 35% of the regular teachers wanted to discuss the scope of the roles of resource and classroom teachers. Classroom teachers also showed a strong desire to discuss an issue of more direct curriculum concern: What should be taught to handicapped children and who should teach it? This curriculum issue was not viewed as important by resource teachers, with only 7% selecting this topic as their preferred choice. As a combined first and second priority, only 31% of the resource teachers saw this topic as important, compared with 70% for regular teachers. These findings suggest that both teacher groups recognize the importance of discussing role descriptions, but that resource teachers should also consider curriculum as a primary inservice topic. A less frequently cited topic was that of providing an overview of different exceptionalities and their accompanying expectations, a critical issue for teachers never before exposed to exceptional children.

An area of overwhelming agreement among regular and resource teachers was the subject of individualizing instruction. As seen from the responses to question 3, both groups felt that demonstrations of how to individualize curriculum were the best procedure for implementing mainstreaming. Devoting time and energy to developing special materials or to adjusting class schedules for conferences with as little disruption as possible were not as important to either regular or resource groups. This overwhelming preference (70% and 61%, respectively) for inservice training on individualized instruction seems to reconfirm the positive attitude of the sampled population.

Concerning the scheduling of inservice sessions, classroom teachers again voiced a stronger preference than their special education counterparts. Responses to question 4 show that 65% of the classroom teachers wanted inservice sessions to be maintained at regularly scheduled intervals. Resource teachers did not demonstrate a clear preference, with 49% preferring regularly scheduled inservice sessions and 51% preferring several inservice sessions

at the beginning of the year and fewer later in the year. This desire for regular and predictable activity on the part of classroom teachers represents a pattern that was repeated on other questionnaire items. The fact that special teachers did not appear quite so concerned with regular schedules also showed as a slight pattern.

Cooperative Planning

The second part of the questionnaire investigated teachers' preferred methods for establishing cooperative planning, which included both time and curriculum concerns (see the middle section of Table 1). Question 5 asked how time could be made available to allow regular and resource teachers to plan together. The two alternatives most frequently mentioned were (a) to use aides, volunteers, or other school personnel to oversee classroom activities during planning sessions and (b) to obtain a floating teacher to oversee classes as needed. As a first priority, 40% of regular teachers and 37% of resource teachers chose using aides, volunteers, or other personnel as the preferred method of gaining planning time, compared with the 20% and 27%, respectively, who indicated the need for a full time floating teacher as first choice. Neither teacher group appeared to show overwhelming support for having to take extra time to plan, as indicated by the general lack of high percentages on any option as a first priority. Apparently, teachers did not like the idea of using their own planning time, meeting before or after school, or dismissing school early to gain planning time on top of the planning responsibilities they already held.

Question 6 concentrated on scheduling problems. Three choices were offered: (a) to have a resource teacher available as the need arises; (b) to meet one hour per week; or (c) to meet one hour every two weeks. Regular teachers appeared to prefer meeting as the need arises (first choice of 45%), whereas resource teachers preferred to meet one hour per week (first choice of 34%). Daily planning sessions were not recommended, nor was there a high percent of responses in favor of meeting less than once a week.

Question 7 looked at the problem of bringing special curricula into the scope of regular classroom programs. The majority of regular and resource teachers (60% and 54%, respectively) preferred adapting as many materials as possible from the regular teacher's instructional program when working with a mainstreamed child. Neither teacher group acknowledged that peer and cross age tutoring should be the primary vehicle for facilitating

4. SERVICES

TABLE 1

**Comparison of Regular and Resource Teachers' Priorities
Regarding Certain Aspects of Mainstreaming**

Questions and response items	Percent of teachers listing item as first priority	
	Regular	Resource

Inservice training

1. How can teachers be encouraged to provide input into inservice programs on mainstreaming?

a. Include teachers on the program committee.	40	49
b. Give teachers an active part in the program.	35	29

2. What issues need to be discussed during inservice sessions on mainstreaming?

a. The scope of both the regular and resource teachers' jobs.	35	61
b. What should be taught to handicapped children and who should teach it.	30	7

3. What procedures or mechanics for implementing mainstreaming need to be addressed during inservice sessions?

a. Demonstrations on how to individualize curricula for children in need.	70	61
b. Developing special materials for the mainstreamed child.	5	15
c. Adjusting class schedules for conferences with as little disruption to regular classroom programs as possible.	15	12

4. What is the most efficient schedule for holding inservice meetings on mainstreaming?

a. Several at the beginning of the year with fewer in the middle and at the end.	25	51
b. Regularly scheduled intervals between inservice sessions.	65	49

Cooperative planning

5. How can time be made available to allow regular and resource teachers to plan together?

a. Use aides, volunteers, or other school personnel to oversee classroom activities during planning sessions.	40	37
b. If budgets permit, obtain a floating teacher to oversee classes as needed.	20	27

6. What would be the most efficient schedule for cooperative planning between regular and resource teachers?

a. Have a full time resource teacher available as the need arises.	45	24
b. One hour per week.	30	34
c. One hour every two weeks.	25	24

7. How can special curricula be geared to fit within the scope of the regular teacher's programs?

a. Adapt as many materials as possible from the regular teacher's instructional program for the mainstreamed child.	60	54
b. Use peer and cross age tutoring.	10	7

Resource programs

8. What should the recommended case load for a resource teacher be?

a. 20 children directly served and 10 served through teacher consultation.	75	73
b. 10 children directly served and 20 served through teacher consultation.	20	22

9. What alternative methods of assigning resource teachers are preferred?

a. Set a maximum case load and hire enough teachers to serve the number of identified students.	85	54
b. Have one resource room teacher and one resource teacher consultant per school.	15	15

Table continued on next page

Table 1-Continued
Comparison of Regular and Resource Teacher's Priorities
Regarding Certain Aspects of Mainstreaming

Questions and response items	Percent of teachers listing item as first priority	
	Regular	Resource
10. How much instructional time should be devoted to mainstreamed children in order to provide for a positive educational experience?		
a. One hour per day.	50	44
b. Two hours per day.	25	41
11. What are the problems related to itinerant services?		
a. All schools will present enough problems for a full time resource teacher.	35	37
b. Valuable teaching time is lost in travel.	20	34
12. How would you prefer to implement a mainstream program through the use of resource personnel?		
a. It would be the job of the resource teacher to work with the regular teacher on a one to one basis without administrative restrictions.	80	54
b. Mainstreaming procedures are to be developed by the local school building staff.	10	17
13. What factors should be considered in speaking of categorical or noncategorical programs?		
a. Teachers who individualize can teach a variety of students with varying problems.	75	59
b. Noncategorical services reduce the harmful effects of labels.	60	46

special programing for special children. Providing oral work or seat work, rewriting materials, and using aides, volunteers, tapes, or films all received minimal support as methods for enhancing mainstreamed efforts within regular classroom programs.

Resource Programs

The final section of Table 1 shows teacher responses regarding certain aspects of resource service, namely case load size, categorical versus noncategorical service, and itinerant service. Concerning case load size, question 8 asked what the recommended case load for a resource teacher should be. In answer to this question, three-fourths of all the teachers preferred a ratio of 20 children served directly and 10 children served indirectly. This predisposition for direct service shows that both groups of teachers wanted special teachers to teach special children, while also providing some limited consultation. Neither group preferred a large indirect service case load accompanied by less direct teaching. In fact, when asked about providing service solely through resource consultation, less than 3% of regular and resource teachers preferred this approach.

The question of case load size and its relationship to hiring practices was also reviewed (see question 9). The preferred method of hiring resource teachers was to set a maximum case load size and hire enough resource teachers to serve the number of identified special students; 85% of regular teachers and 54% of resource teachers indicated this hiring procedure as their preferred option. The second, but less desirable, choice (15% of each group) was to provide one resource room teacher and one consulting resource teacher per school. None of the regular classroom teachers and only four special teachers preferred hiring only one resource teacher per school. A more novel response—hiring one resource teacher for every 200 students—was also preferred by a small percentage of both groups of teachers surveyed.

Question 10 asked how much instructional time should be devoted to mainstreaming handicapped children in order to provide a positive educational experience. Responses indicate that 50% of regular teachers and 44% of resource teachers favored a minimum of one hour per day of direct teaching service. A strong but essentially second option was the preference for a two hour per day schedule for each group; 41% of resource teachers made this two hour schedule their preferred choice, compared with 25% of regular teachers. Very little support was given to scheduling options that provided for less than daily resource sessions. For example, no respondent preferred a two hour session once per week, and fewer than 5% favored a schedule of one hour sessions three times per week. Apparently, less than daily service was seen as a source of disruption to schedules, routines, and services for both the children and the regular and resource teachers.

4. SERVICES

With such limited support for part time scheduling, there was little wonder that only two teachers saw itinerant resource service as desirable. Because of this limited preference for itinerant service (one resource teacher serving more than one school), question 11 asked about the problems associated with itinerant service. The two responses most often mentioned were that all schools present enough problems to warrant a full time resource teacher, and that valuable teaching time is lost in travel. The problems of not feeling part of a school's faculty and of needing to transport material from place to place were seen as only slight obstacles posed by itinerant service.

Question 12 asked teachers how they would prefer to implement a mainstream program through the use of resource personnel. Both groups of teachers preferred letting resource teachers work on a one to one basis with regular teachers, without administrative restrictions; 80% and 54% of regular and resource teachers, respectively, voiced this option as their first priority. Because of these high percentages, the second choice—allowing the school staff to work out their own problems regarding mainstreaming—received considerably less support.

The final question concerned factors related to categorical and noncategorical service. The responses to this question give evidence that resource teachers (46%) and regular teachers (60%) favored noncategorical services. It appears that teachers in general recognized that noncategorical services reduced the harmful effects of labels. Regardless of a categorical or noncategorical orientation, both groups of teachers expressed confidence that the major teaching consideration is individualization, with 75% of regular teachers and 59% of resource teachers voicing a first priority for the statement, "Teachers who individualize can teach a variety of students with varying problems." This response indicates that teachers were most concerned about the direct delivery aspects of instruction and less concerned about structural and labeling issues. It also reconfirms the strong request for demonstrations on individualized instruction during inservice sessions. However, the ability to individualize and to reach more children with a wide range of skill differences would certainly facilitate a noncategorical resource approach.

Discussion

A report of the National Advisory Committee on the Handicapped (1976) indicated that the crucial issue in special education today is one of attitude. This present study hoped to accentuate this point by acknowledging the preferences of a group of regular and resource teachers who had demonstrated a positive attitude toward mainstreaming exceptional children. A number of major points and implications can be derived from this study.

The important role played by individualized instruction in helping to realize the goals of mainstreaming handicapped children into regular classrooms was acknowledged. In fact, demonstrations on how to individualize instruction was the number one inservice and teaching priority of both regular and resource teachers. These results reconfirm the continuing commitment of teachers to meet the individual needs of children (Frankel, 1974) and warrant periodic inservice sessions and demonstrations on this subject. Techniques on how to organize the learning environment, deliver efficient instruction, coordinate classroom activities, and deal simultaneously with a number of children and their accompanying problems are a few noteworthy topics for inservice sessions. As important as group inservice training is, however, it should also be stressed that one to one interaction between resource teachers and regular teachers concerning a child can be one of the most effective and rewarding forms of continuous inservice training.

Teachers were unanimous in their preference for a given case load size and amount of direct and indirect teaching. An overwhelming preference for 20 children served directly and 10 children served through teacher consultation was interpreted to mean two things. First, both groups of teachers preferred resource teachers to provide instruction to the child. There was a recognition that regular and resource teacher consultation should occur, but that it should not replace direct service or even approximate the amount of time given to direct service. Secondly, 30 children being served by the resource teacher appeared to be an equitable number as perceived by both the regular and resource teachers. This also has meaning in relationship to hiring practices, since an overwhelming percentage of teachers preferred setting a maximum case load size and hiring based on a case load formula.

A preference for regular and predictable activity was also noted within the study. This applied to classroom teachers in particular, as shown by their desire for regularly scheduled intervals between inservice sessions and by their quest to know what should be taught to handicapped children and who should teach it. Their resource counterparts expressed the need for regularly scheduled cooperative planning with classroom teachers. However, planning time appeared to be one of those necessary yet reluctantly supported activities, as shown by the low percentage of responses favoring any form of joint planning effort.

Teachers also preferred regularity in providing services to students, seeing daily instruction as vital and less than daily service as both disruptive and inefficient. It is interesting that accompanying research (Jenkins & Mayhall, 1977) found daily resource services to be superior to nondaily service for handicapped students in both reading and mathematics. The implications are obvious.

In order to enhance joint planning between regular and resource teachers, use of the curriculum program of regular classrooms was strongly supported. The resource teacher working with regular curriculum programs, showing how to modify them and explaining the difficulties faced by mainstreamed children under routine classroom circumstances, conveys an appreciation of classroom programing and is consistent with other professional literature (Christoplos, 1973).

In summary, this study examined the opinions and preferences of those closest to the actual mainstream situation—teachers themselves. It should be noted, however, that the specific outcomes of this study are indigenous to Tennessee. Whether similar findings would generalize to other geographical areas throughout the country remains to be seen. For this reason, the authors strongly recommend that a similar research methodology be used by school systems to evaluate their own teachers' preferences. In doing this, it is hoped that school systems will be responsive to the preferences of their teachers in serving the needs of exceptional children.

References

Brenton, M. Mainstreaming the handicapped. *Today's Education*, 1974, *63*, 22–25.

Christoplos, F. Keeping exceptional children in regular classrooms. *Exceptional Children*, 1973, *39*, 569–572.

Cruickshank, W. M. The false hope of integration. *The Slow Learning Child*, 1974, *21*, 67–83.

Frankel, J. Special educators speak out on their needs for resource products and services. *Exceptional Children*, 1974, *41*, 187–189.

Gickling, E. E., & Theobald, J. T. Mainstreaming: Affect or effect. *The Journal of Special Education*, 1975, *9*, 317–328.

Harris, W. J., & Mahar, C. Problems in implementing resource programs in rural schools. *Exceptional Children*, 1975, *42*, 95–99.

Hewett, F. M., Artuso, A. A., & Taylor, F. D. The Madison Plan really swings. *Today's Education*, 1970, *59* (8), 14–17.

Jenkins, J. R., & Mayhall, W. F. Development and evaluation of a resource teacher program. *Exceptional Children*, 1976, *43*, 21–29.

Jenkins, J. R., & Mayhall, W. F. Scheduling daily or less-than-daily instruction: Implications for resource programs. *Journal of Learning Disabilities*, 1977, *10* (3), 159–163.

Martin, E. W. Some thoughts on mainstreaming. *Exceptional Children*, 1974, *41*, 150–153.

National Advisory Committee on the Handicapped. *The unfinished revolution, education for the handicapped*. Washington DC: US Government Printing Office, 1976.

Payne, R., & Murray, C. Principals' attitudes toward integration of the handicapped. *Exceptional Children*, 1974, *41*, 123–125.

Developing Resource Rooms for the Handicapped

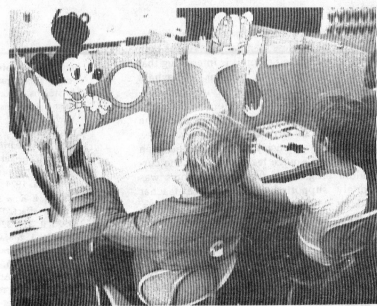

BRUNO J. D'ALONZO
ROSEMARIE L. D'ALONZO
AUGUST J. MAUSER

The full impact of Public Law 94-142 is currently being witnessed and felt not only by special educators but also by teachers and administrators in regular education. As attempts to comply with the "least restrictive environment" components of this federal mandate, a variety of educational and social environments are sure to be designed, implemented, and evaluated for handicapped students.

For the mildly handicapped student, regardless of whether the student exhibits a learning, social-behavioral, or physical disability, the resource room option is a viable alternative. Of course, this administrative arrangement, as with any other educational environment, must be appropriately staffed, operated, and supervised if the students' needs for a specialized education are to be achieved. Numerous writers including Deno (1970), Lerner (1976), Reger (1973), Sabatino (1972), Wiederholt (1974) and more recently Wiederholt, Hammill, and Brown (1978) cited the importance of the resource room concept and environment as the most promising alternative to segregated special class placement or regular class inclusion without supportive services.

VARIATIONS AND VALUES OF THE RESOURCE ROOM

Variations and models of the resource room concept have been described by Hammill and Bartel (1975), Sabatino and Mauser (1978), Wiederholt (1974), and Wiederholt, Hammill and Brown (1978). Five different types have been cited as being in use in the schools of today:

1. The *categorical,* which focuses on one primary type of handicap.
2. The *cross categorical,* where clusters of two or more categories of children are grouped.
3. The *noncategorical,* where students with mild or severe learning and behavior handicaps are serviced with the possible inclusion of nonhandicapped students.

4 The *specific skills* resource room where a specific curriculum area of deficit (i.e., reading, mathematics, etc.) is targeted and served.

5 The *itinerant resource room,* which is a mobile nonstationary resource environment that travels to the geographic area when and where the specialized education services are needed.

Wiederholt, Hammill, and Brown (1978, p. 10-11) succinctly stated the values associated with the resource room concept:

1. Students can benefit from specific resource support while remaining integrated with their friends and age-mates in the school.

2. The resource teacher has an opportunity to help more children than does a full-time special class teacher. This is especially true when the resource teacher provides indirect services to children with mild or moderate problems by consulting extensively with their teachers.

3. Resource programs are less expensive to operate than special self-contained classes.

4. Because young children with mild, though developing, problems can be accommodated, later severe disorders may be prevented.

5. Flexible scheduling means that remediation can be applied entirely in the classrooms by the regular teacher with some resource support or in another room by the resource program personnel when necessary; also, the schedule can be quickly altered to meet the children's changing situations and needs.

6. Since the resource program will absorb most of the handicapped children in the schools, the self-contained special education classes will increasingly become instructional settings for truly and relatively severely handicapped students, the children for whom the classes were originally developed.

7. Because of the resource teacher's broad experience with many children exhibiting different educational and behavioral problems, he/she may in time become an in-house consultant to the school.

8. Because the noncategorical approach avoids labeling and segregation, it minimizes the stigma that might be associated with receiving special help.

9. Since many elementary schools are large enough to accommodate one or more noncategorical resource teachers, most students can receive help in their neighborhood school; thus, the necessity of busing handicapped children across the town or country to a school that houses an appropriately labeled class or resource program is eliminated or at least reduced.

10. Because placement in the resource program is an individual school matter involving the principal, the teachers, and the parents, no appreciable time lapse need occur between the teacher's referral and the initiation of special services for the child.

11. In the noncategorical alternative, medical and psychological work-ups are done only at the school's specific request rather than on a generalized screening-for-placement basis; thus, the school psychologist is freed to do the work that he/she was trained to do instead of being relegated to the role of psychometrist.

Wiederholt (1974) succinctly described the resource room as "any instructional setting which a child enters for services for specific periods of time on a regularly scheduled basis." The major difference between the resource room and the traditional self

FIGURE 1. The Physical Structure of a Resource Room

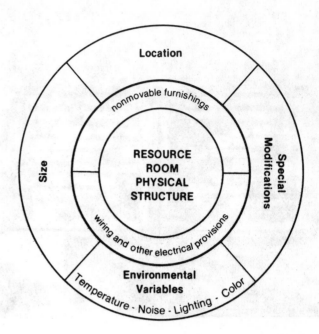

contained special class is that the student attends the resource room on a part time basis and remains for at least a portion of the day in his or her regular class. The authors believe that a resource room combined with the regular classroom is the optimum arrangement for mildly handicapped students. It is assumed that the resource room and the teachers of these students are well prepared and systematically monitored. It is also assumed that the students will be given assistance and support while they are included in the regular classroom.

School personnel should view the resource room as an alternative, not a panacea, to the debate of regular versus special class placement. Recent contributions to the literature regarding mainstreaming handicapped pupils also supported the credo that no single program is "best" for all pupils and that we must function as pupil advocates and not program advocates (Keogh & Levitt, 1976). Carroll (1974) noted the importance of relating appropriate environment and learner characteristics to an ecological point of reference and ecosystem structure. This point of view offers positive, direct, and practical suggestions and questions related to the variables that are important in the selection and design of any type of educational setting.

CONSIDERATION IN DESIGNING THE RESOURCE ROOM
Personnel

The personnel involved in the instruction of the pupils are the most important variables in the resource room program. The resource teacher and supportive ancillary personnel (e.g., aides and paraprofessionals) will generally be assigned to work with approximately 20 students on a regular basis, depending on the specific needs of the pupils. The personnel are involved in diagnostic based instruction of a compensatory or remedial nature. They meet with individual and small groups of students. The resource teacher func-

4. SERVICES

tions as a consultant and resource person to other teachers as well as parents. Additional responsibilities may include test administration. The resource room teacher may also serve as an ombudsman and crisis teacher. Materials development, preparation, and ordering are also vested responsibilities of the resource room teacher. Keeping confidential records, attending staffings, inservicing regular staff and ancillary personnel definitely require the resource teacher to be a true "superteacher."

Physical Structure

Location

Because of the heterogeneity of behavioral characteristics that the students possess, the resource room should be located away from halls and corridors with heavy traffic. The resource room should, however, be accessible in more than one way to give the students and staff a choice of entry and exit. The resource room facility should be located near ancillary services, conference rooms, and the media center. There should be easy access to washroom facilities, drinking fountains, and, if the school code allows, for older students, a smoking area.

Size

Reger (1973) suggested that the size of a resource room be the same as that of a regular classroom. A minimum resource area would be no less than half the size of a regular classroom. Included or adjacent to the area should be a conference room and office/storage area.

Special Modification

A "time out" area for disruptive students and learning stations or centers with specific materials should be part of the room arrangement and design. Carrels or booths should also be included to serve those students working individually or in need of a more confined, less distracting environment. Portable walls and partitions can also be used for variable sectioning purposes. For resource room students with physical disabilities that require crutches, wheelchairs, or other means for mobility, other conveniences will be needed. If the resource room is located above or below ground level, elevators must be available.

Additional Environmental Variables

Although documented research on the influence of temperature, noise, lighting, and room color on the behavior of mildly handicapped children is minimal (Bartholomew, Mauser, & Miller, (1976), consideration of these environmental variables is essential in the planning and design of the resource room.

Temperature. Total air conditioning, including an electronic air filtering system, is necessary for producing an optimum learning environment that will be free from allergens that might produce negative behavior. The controls for such a system must not be located within the classroom or easily accessible to the students. These systems must operate with a minimal noise level to insure that distraction is not fostered.

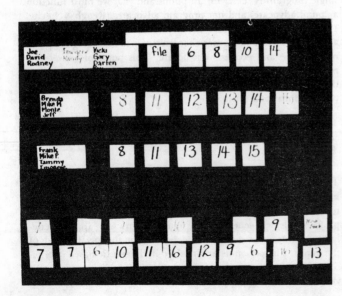

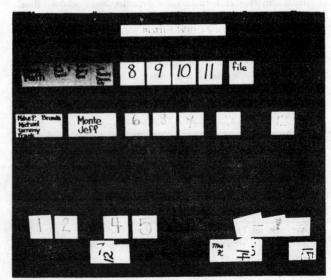

Noise. Fassler and Bryant (1971) cited the importance of noise reduction. The surrounding walls should be thoroughly soundproofed and carpeting and acoustical ceiling tiles should be used. Draperies should be mounted adjacent to each window outlet. If a central office sound system is located in the resource room it should be modulated to a comfortable level to prevent "startle" types of behavior.

Lighting. Optimum lighting must be available for all work areas in the resource room. Glare and reflection should be minimized. Windows should be located above eye level to reduce distraction from outside environmental stimuli. The selection of specific types of lighting sources should be examined thoroughly since research linking fluorescent lighting with hyperactivity is presently emerging. A less stimulating source of candle power might be considered.

Wiring and Other Electrical Provisions. Since many types of electrical equipment might be used simultaneously in the room, the wiring system must be heavy duty. The multitude of audiovisual equipment — tape recorders, teaching machines, record players, overhead projectors, films, and filmstrips — all require an efficient electrical system and numerous outlets. These, of course, are in addition to items generally found in a classroom such as a telephone, alarm system, PA system, intercom, and clocks which also require electrical power.

Nonmovable Furnishings. Seven foot bulletin boards and chalkboards should be mounted on the walls of the resource room. Depending on the age and size of the students and if a student is in a wheelchair, the accessibility of the chalkboard in terms of distance from the floor must be considered. Steel bookcases and space for storing equipment and materials not in use should be built into the walls of the resource room.

Room Color. Common sense supports the notion that extremely bright reds, greens, blues, or yellows would not have the resulting calming effect of pale shades of blue, green, yellow, and beige. Bartholomew, Mauser and Miller (1976) cited the negative influence of color in the behavior of handicapped children. Of course, whatever colors are chosen, it should be insured that the composition of the paint used does not radiate a toxic effect that promotes hyperactivity and misbehavior of the students assigned to the resource room.

FIGURE 2. Classroom Design of a Resource Room in Popular Grove, Illinois

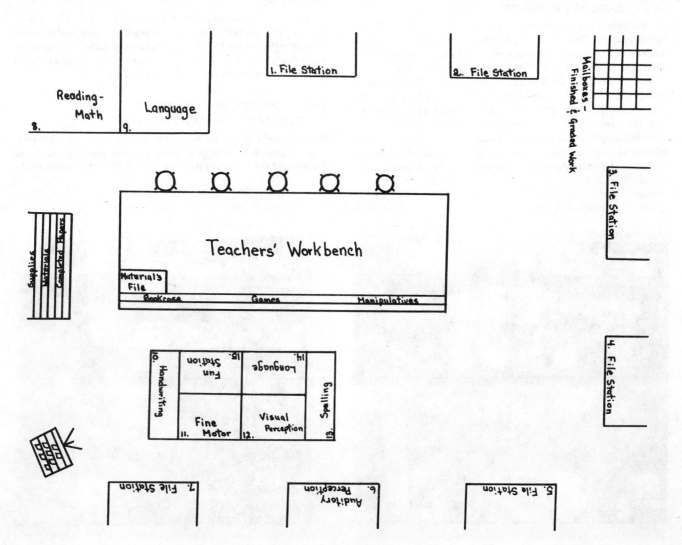

4. SERVICES

A PILOT STUDY OF EXISTING FACILITIES

A pilot study of 35 randomly selected resource programs (D'Alonzo & Mauser, 1976) revealed the following data related to the previously discussed variables.

Less than half (17) of the resource rooms were half as small as regular classrooms.

Over half (19) of the resource rooms were not located away from heavy traffic.

The majority (30) did not have alternative exit and entry points.

Over half (19) were not located near a media center.

The majority (27) did not have work facilities, toilets, and drinking fountains in the room.

The majority (27) did not have a "time out" room.

Carrels or booths were present in the majority (22) of rooms.

Over half (19) were located on ground level.

Additional information indicated that over half (18) had air-conditioning and four had electronic filtering systems, the majority (32) had total room carpeting, the majority indicated adequate lighting with the fluorescent type being the most common, and over half (19) had windows at eye level. An interesting finding showed that nine rooms had no windows at all.

AN EXEMPLARY RESOURCE ROOM

An exemplary resource room is located in Poplar Grove, Illinois (see Figure 2). This classroom, for 20 to 25 students, is designed to encourage working independently and to meet the individual needs and interests of each student assigned to this facility.

The emphasis is on learning-working independently and in group situations. The students receive individual help from the teacher as well as taking the responsibility of working independently at the various "file" stations set up around the classroom.

This resource room has been arranged as a workshop. In the central area of the room is the teacher's work bench. This is a 3 foot by 7 foot table surrounded with carpenter's benches and arranged with teacher made materials, games, manipulatives, a materials file, and various daily task sheets. This "station" provides a large area for three to four students and the teacher to work individually or in small group instruction.

Sixteen stations (work areas) around the room provide activities for auditory perception, visual perception, haptic perception, reading, language, math, writing, and spelling. Six of these stations are called *file stations* (individual work desks) which allow the students to work independently on activities, task sheets, or workbook activities that are placed in their cumulative files. Daily records are kept on what the student has accomplished, what he or she needs to complete, and how many points were earned for that particular day's activities. Also included in the organizational plan is a "fun" station, where the student has a choice of a variety of activities. This station is for those students who earn the privilege of using it.

Scheduling the students into the various stations is managed easily by preparing a pocket chart that shows which students are to be working at what station at a designated time. The numbers on the pocket chart cards correspond to the numbered work areas (stations). The students rotate to the various stations at 10 to 15 minute intervals per station.

The morning activities concentrate on reading and related skills. The afternoon is reserved for math activities and related computational skills.

The 20 to 25 students arrive in groups of 7 or 8 for 1 hour work periods. The resource room serves students from kindergarten through eighth grade for 1 hour work periods. Grade level does not determine where and when a student works; the important factor is the commonality of each child's program needs.

THE RESOURCE ROOM MISSION: FLEXIBILITY AND ADAPTABILITY

Since the field of special education is in a period of transition, inquiry, and often indecision, resource room planning should be flexible and readily adaptable to future change. All aspects of the

resource room design should take into consideration the unique physical, cognitive, and affective needs in order to meet the varying needs of students assigned to the resource room. The resource room design is modeled to serve students on the basis of specific need(s) rather than on the basis of previously assigned label(s). The major goal is movement from the resource room assignment and gradual diminishment of support to independent function in the regular classroom, and ultimately, complete societal independence.

EVALUATION: THE TRUE MEASURE OF EFFECTIVENESS OF THE RESOURCE ROOM PLAN AND OPERATION

Carroll (1974) offered timely questions related to the analysis of (a) facilities, (b) resources, and (c) personnel. The authors of this article see a direct relationship between each variable and the effectiveness and change in pupil behavior.

Facility Analysis

According to Carroll (1974), the following questions should be answered about the facility (adapted with permission of author and publisher):

1. Are facilities available to provide for large and small group interaction within the classroom? Yes _____ No _____

2. Are individual study areas available (i.e., portable bookshelves or bulletin boards that can be used to divide the areas?) Yes _____ No _____

3. Are learning carrels available (i.e., portable desk top carrels)? Yes _____ No _____

4. Are activity centers available (i.e., communication centers, science centers, etc.)? Yes _____ No _____

5. Are book corners readily accessible to students? Yes _____ No _____

6. Does the student have his or her own desk or cupboard where he or she can store personal material? Yes _____ No _____

7. Are there facilities available in the room or in the school for crisis intervention (i.e., a time out room)? Yes _____ No _____

8. Are there large areas available in the building or outside that can be used for play activities, drama presentations, etc.? Yes _____ No _____

9. Is there an area around the building that can be used for exploration? Yes _____ No _____

10. Are small rooms available within the building for subdividing the class into subunits? Yes _____ No _____

Personnel Analysis

1. What is the ratio of students to teachers? _____

2. What personnel are available to help in the personalizing approach (i.e., within the classroom)? _____
   a. Community volunteers or senior citizens groups? Yes _____ No _____
   b. Peers within the classroom for additional teaching? For example, intrapeer tutoring or older students to help younger students? Yes _____ No _____
   c. Paid aides? Yes _____ No _____
   d. College interns in preservice educational programs? Yes _____ No _____

3. Interested parent groups? Yes _____ No _____

Resource Analysis

1. Building Resources
   What resources are available to the classroom teacher?
   a. Health resources — nurses, school physicians? Yes _____ No _____ (specify)
   b. Psychological resources — psychologists, consulting psychiatrists, social workers? Yes _____ No _____ (specify)
   c. Parent involvement? Yes _____ No _____
   d. Instructional resource materials? Yes _____ No _____
   e. Resource room? Yes _____ No _____
   f. Human resources available within the building — reading specialist, counselor, etc.? Yes _____ No _____ (specify)

2. District Resources? Yes _____ No _____ (specify)

3. Community Resources? Yes _____ No _____ (specify)

4. State Resources? Yes _____ No _____ (specify)

5. National Resources? Yes _____ No _____ (specify)

Final Comment

The previous questions and statements regarding components of the resource room plan must be considered as guidelines and not as absolutes. Each will be subject to a variety of interpretations and will ultimately effect the resource room facilities' operational procedures. It is conceivable that each school district will have a different idea and conceptual framework regarding its program. Each building principal, who is responsible for all teachers and facilities with the school building, will add an additional series of modifications and personal wrinkles based on his or her individual perception of the program.

It is hoped that the ideas and strategies presented will be adaptable to a variety of school systems. The successful implementation of the ideas presented must keep in sharp focus the aspect of quality, comprehensiveness, and ultimate practicality and realism in providing efficient educational alternatives for the identified and yet to be identified exceptional children.

REFERENCES

Bartholomew, R., Mauser, A., & Miller, S. The effects of color on the behavior of handicapped children. Unpublished McDonald Foundation Report, Northern Illinois University, DeKalb, 1976.

Carroll, A.W. The classroom as an ecosystem. Focus on Exceptional Children, 1974, 4, 1-12.

D'Alonzo, B.J., & Mauser, A.J. A survey of selected resource rooms in the State of Illinois. Unpublished report, Northern Illinois University, DeKalb, 1976.

Deno, E. Special education of developmental capital. Exceptional Children, 1970, 37, 229-237.

Fassler, J., & Bryant, N.D. Disturbed children under reduced auditory input: A pilot study. Exceptional Children, 1971, 38, 197-204.

Hammill, D., & Bartel, N. Teaching children with learning and behavior problems. Boston: Allyn & Bacon, 1975.

Keogh, B., & Levitt, M. Special education in the mainstream: A confrontation of limitations? Focus on Exceptional Children, 1976, 8(1), 1-11.

Lerner, J. Children with learning disabilities. New York: Houghton Mifflin, 1976.

Reger, R. What is a resource room? Journal of Learning Disabilities, 1973, 6, 611-614.

Sabatino, D. Resource rooms: The renaissance in special education. Journal of Special Education, 1972, 6 (4), 335-347.

Sabatino, D., & Mauser, A. Intervention strategies for specialized secondary education. Boston: Allyn & Bacon, 1977, p. 206-207.

Wiederholt, J.L. Resource rooms for the mildly handicapped. Focus on Exceptional Children, 1974, 5, 1-10.

Wiederholt, J.L., Hammill, D., & Brown, V. The resource teacher: A guide to effective practices. Boston: Allyn & Bacon, 1978.

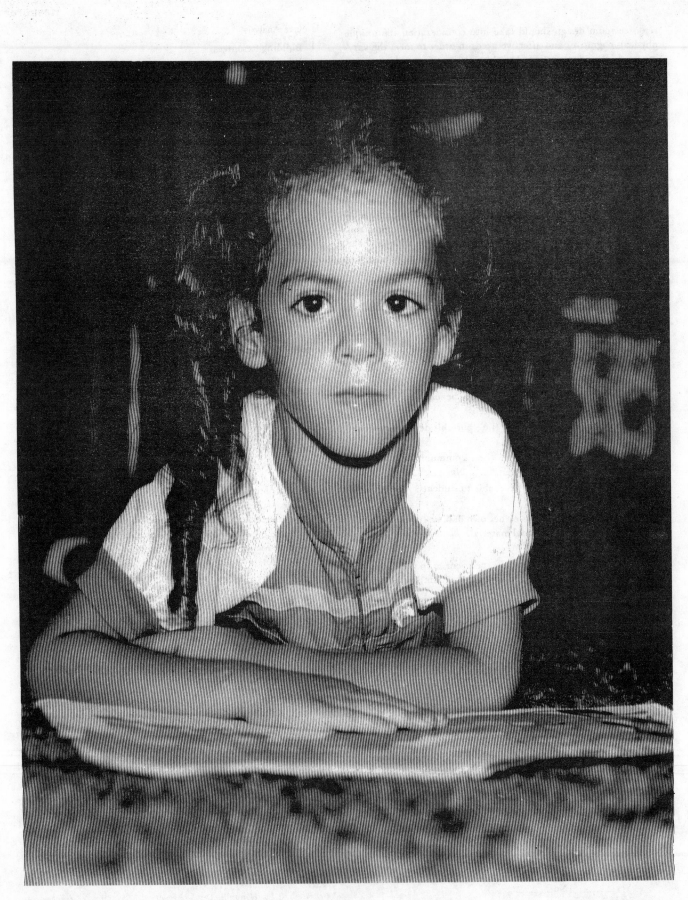

photo: David Carofano

FUTURE TRENDS

As has been mentioned before in this book, the learning disabilities field is a rather new phenomenon to the educational system. This does not mean that learning disabled children did not exist years ago; it does mean that this population has now begun to receive special services, however. The emphasis has been to insure learning disabilities programs in all schools. With the advent of P.L. 94-142 and other legislation this desire has become closer to a reality in many school districts.

At this point in time the professionals concerned with the education of learning disabled individuals must begin to address other issues. These issues may go beyond just the services learning disabled youngsters will receive in the elementary schools. Wallace and McLoughlin in their major text on learning disabilities states that support for the learner is broader than the schools and that a learner's needs encompass many areas including vocational-career requirements. The field must also address itself to the

fact that support for the learning disabled population may span the total period of a child's life. This could include preschool and post-school settings.

Pertinent literature in this chapter focuses on some of the future issues the learning disabilities area must address. Among these concerns are career education, vocational and occupational involvement, counseling parents of learning disabled children, the overemphasis of academic achievement in the schools, the learning disabled youth and juvenile delinquency, the provision of secondary programs for the disabled learner, new approaches to remediation theory, and teacher re-education.

If all learning disabled citizens are to function at an optimal level it is obvious that the competencies of personnel in this field must be enriched and broadened. While this might not be done by formal training, it may happen by close cooperation with people in ancillary service areas.

Essentials of Special Education For Regular Educators

Colleen S. Blakenship
and
M. Stephen Lilly

The mainstreaming movement has resulted in the need to re-evaluate and restructure special education teacher education programs. The former practice of training special education graduates to assume the role of teachers in self-contained special classrooms for the "mildy handicapped" is outmoded. The practice of integrating "mildy handicapped" students into regular education programs, and the emphasis upon non-categorical teacher training, demands a very different sort of teacher preparation program.

In the last ten years, an increasing number of special educators have spoken of a cooperative relationship between special and regular education, with regular educators assuming a greater responsibility for the education of students with learning and behavior problems, assisted by special educators who can function in a supportive and consultive role (Lilly, 1975; McKenzie, Egner, Perelman, Schneider, & Garvin, 1970; Reynolds, 1975). The need to prepare both regular and special educators to assume these new roles is of paramount importance if mainstreaming is to result in quality educational experiences for children.

The focus of this article will be on the preparation of regular educators to teach children with mild learning and behavior problems. The issues to be addressed include: the present level of training offered regular educators, the need to provide regular educators with pre- and inservice training in special education, and considerations in planning preservice programs. A preservice program for undergraduate education majors will be presented, and delivery systems for providing inservice training to regular educators will be discussed. Finally, conclusions will be drawn concerning pre- and inservice training for regular educators.

Present Level of Training

One of the first concerns expressed by many special educators relative to mainstreaming is, "Are regular classroom teachers equal to the task of educating the mildly handicapped?" (Brooks & Bransford, 1971, p. 259). The consensus has been that few regular educators have received training which would

Reprinted from *Teaching Education and Special Education* by Colleen S. Blankenship and M. Stephen Lilly by permission of The Council for Exceptional Children. Copyright ©1977 by The Council for Exceptional Children, 1920 Association Drive, Reston, Virginia 22091.

equip them to teach children with mild learning and behavior problems (Brooks & Bransford, Gearheart & Weishahn, 1976). It can be expected that, at most, regular educators may have listened to one introductory lecture on exceptional children.

The certification requirements for teachers and other educational personnel are only now beginning to include coursework in special education. At this time, only five states require regular classroom teachers to take even one course in special education. While this is a step in the right direction, there is a danger that this practice may delude us into thinking that one course will somehow be sufficient. The question is not one of the number of courses which should be required, but rather one of content of the courses to be offered. Of the states passing new certification requirements, only the legislation from Missouri specifies that the course should include information on teaching techniques. None of the remaining four states requiring a course in special education has set any restrictions on the type of course to be taken. In those states, a teacher could satisfy the certification requirement by enrolling in a single survey course on exceptional children. While we might expect teachers enrolling in such a course to increase their knowledge of handicapping conditions, it is unrealistic to expect that a survey course would contain the more practical and skill-oriented information which would be of assistance to teachers in regular classrooms.

It is safe to assume that the present level of training afforded regular educators is not equal to the demands which will be placed upon them in instructing children with mild learning and behavior problems. It is incumbent upon special education teacher education institutions to work cooperatively with general educators to assure that all regular teachers will receive sufficient training in teaching children with mild learning and behavior problems.

Need for Preservice and Inservice Training

In the past ten years an increasing number of "mildy handicapped" students have been returned or allowed to remain in the mainstream of education. The continued emphasis which will be placed upon special education in the regular classroom is evident in the passage of PL 94-142, which requires placement of children in the least restrictive environment. For the majority of children with mild learning and behavior problems, the least restrictive environment will be a regular classroom.

The need to provide preservice and inservice education to regular classroom teachers has a wide base of support. The training of regular educators has been identified as an area of concern by the Bureau of Education for the Handicapped. BEH funding, which was nonexistent in 1974-1975, has increased to over 3 million dollars for preservice education of regular educators. Similarily, funding for inservice training over the last three years has increased from 1 1/2 million to over 4 million dollars (Comptroller General, 1976).

Numerous special educators have voiced support for training regular educators, as have state, local, and university special education administrators (Comptroller General, 1976). As Gearheart & Weishahn (1976) aptly pointed out, "The question is no longer one of 'should all teachers learn how to deal with handicapped children?' but rather, 'what should they learn?' " (p. vi).

Planning Preservice Programs

There are a few difficulties which must be overcome if we are to provide regular educators with preservice training in special education. First among them is the characteristic separation which exists among departments within colleges of education. In recent years, some special educators have come to realize that they share common interests with their colleagues in curriculum and instruction, particularly in the areas of remedial reading and arithmetic.

Several benefits could be derived from a closer association between regular and special education teacher educators at the college level, among them the opportunity to engage in cooperative research. One area which needs to be explored concerns the applicability of applied behavior analysis techniques in regular classroom settings. As Lovitt (1975) pointed out, logistics research concerning the application of measurement techniques to children in regular classrooms has been a neglected area of study. The results of research in this area could be of assistance in selecting and modifying the measurement skills to be included in preservice courses for regular educators.

It will take more than common interests, however, to get departments to work together. The impetus for change would most likely arise within departments of special education. What is needed is an organizational structure which encourages discussion and development of cooperative teacher education programs.

A second difficulty which may hamper the development of preservice programs concerns the manner in which training in special education can be incorporated into on-going teacher preparation programs. There are at least two solutions to this problem. The first would be to make the completion of a course(s) in special education a college requirement for regular educators. This approach has a number of pitfalls. First, it suggests little control over the training to be offered. Unless the course(s) are specified, students would be free to choose from among special education courses, some of which may be knowledge-based rather than skill-oriented. Second, if regular educators enroll in methods courses designed to prepare resource teachers, the course may not focus on the skills which are directly relevant to the regular classroom situation. Third, the requirement of a single course denies departments of special education the opportunity to systematically develop model training programs for regular educators.

A second option would be to offer a minor, or an area of concentration, in special education to regular educators; a minor which does not result in special education certification. This approach has much to recommend it. First, it implies a cooperative effort between different departments within a college of education. Second, it does not entail adding additional coursework to the regular education teacher preparation program. Third, it allows a greater degree of direction on the part of special educators over the training to be provided. Fourth, it encourages the development of courses which are specifically designed for regular educators and tailored to the demands of the regular classroom.

If training in special education is offered on an elective basis, then it stands to reason that some regular educators will receive appropriate training while others will not. There seems to be a trade off between the need to train all regular educators and offering comprehensive programs to a limited number of persons. In the initial stages of developing training experiences for regular educators, we would be wise to err on the side of quality training for a few, rather than mediocre training for the masses.

The second option for providing preservice training to regular educators was seen as the most attractive possibility by the Department of Special Education at the University of Illinois. Planning was begun in 1975 by the Department of Special Education in cooperation with the Department of Elementary and Early Childhood Education to develop an undergraduate program to provide future classroom teachers with the necessary skills to deal with children with mild learning and behavior problems in the regular classroom. The decision to offer preservice training to regular educators, the decreased demand for teachers in self-contained classrooms for the "mildy handicapped", and the increased demand for resource teachers, led to a restructuring of programs offered by the Department of Special Education.

At the time planning was initiated to develop the undergraduate area of concentration in special education, a decision was made to discontinue admittance to the undergraduate EMH program. At the present time, two on-going programs dealing with the education of children with mild learning and behavior problems are offered through the Department of Special Education. One is the Resource/Consulting Teacher program, a master's level program preparing experienced teachers to assume special education resource teaching positions; and the other is the Specialized Instruction (SI) program for undergraduate elementary and early childhood education majors. The SI program is described in the following section.

Specialized Instruction Program

The intent of the SI program at the University of Illinois is to provide regular educators with the necessary skills to deal with children with mild learning and behavior problems in the regular classroom. Program development was based on the following assumptions: graduates are expected to seek regular teaching positions in grades K-9 and it is anticipated that supportive help from a special educator, analagous to a Resource/Consulting Teacher, will be available.

Several parameters served to define the nature of the program. First, the emphasis was to be on a functional approach to behavior problems. Second, a list of hypothesized job skills were to form the basis for establishing performance objectives to be attained by students in the SI program. Third, practicum experience was to be provided to allow for the application of learned skills in a regular classroom setting.

Due to the desire to provide an intensive and well supervised practicum experience, enrollment was limited to approximately 20 undergraduate education majors. The students were selected on the following basis: sophomore standing, cummulative GPA of 3.5 (5 point scale), elementary or early childhood education major, and expressed interest in the SI program. Although enthusiasm was not included among the selection criteria, it has proved to be an unexpected bonus.

Students in the SI program begin their coursework in special education during Spring Semester of their sophomore year. The first course deals with trends and issues in special education. During the students' junior year, they enroll in one special education course per semester; the first focusing on assessment and remediation of social behaviors and the second dealing with assessment and remediation of academic behaviors. The practicum experience, which occurs during the senior year, is arranged so that half of the students enroll during the Fall Semester and the other half during the Spring Semester.

The SI program was conceptualized around the role that a regular classroom teacher would assume in education children with mild learning and behavior problems. Essentially, the role requires the teacher to act as a team member, a student and program advocate, an instructional planner and implementer, and a behavioral manager. Mastery of a set of skills is implied in each of the aforementioned functions ascribed to a classroom teacher. Each of these functions will now be addressed accompanied by a description of the major skills to be mastered.

Team member. The intent of the SI program is to prepare regular educators to assume a major responsibility in educating children with mild learning and behavior problems. It is not anticipated that they will be able to function as program planners and implementers without the supportive help of special educators, nor is it intended that they should. Rather, it is expected that regular educators will function as team members in planning and implementing educational programs for exceptional children.

The emphasis on involving regular educators in program planning is evident in the federal regulations for PL 94-142, which require the presence of a child's regular or special teacher, or both, at the placement and planning conference. It stands to reason that due to the number of students with learning and behavior problems who will be placed in regular classrooms, a significant number of regular educators will be involved in jointly planning and carrying out individualized education programs. Therefore, regular classroom teachers need to acquire those skills which will allow them to function as members of an educational team.

Some of the skills which are stressed in the SI program include: 1) identifying needed supportive services and making appropriate referrals, 2) participating in placement and planning conferences, 3) working cooperatively with other team members, and 4) communicating progress to a child's parents and to other team members. Students in the SI program are given the opportunity to act as team members via role playing exercises which are incorporated into their coursework. During the practicum experience, SI students meet with the parents of at least one child with whom they have been working, to discuss the child's progress.

Student and program advocate. A regular classroom teacher is in a rather unique position to advocate placement in the least restrictive environment. His/her very presence at a placement or planning conference for a child can signify a willingness to integrate the student into the mainstream of education. Who is in a better position to know the demands which will be placed upon a handicapped child than the teacher of the regular class in which the child will be placed? Based on the child's present level of performance and the demands of the setting, the regular educator is in a good position to request the provision of an appropriate level of special education services to allow the child to function in the regular classroom.

In order to serve as an advocate, SI students must have a knowledge of the literature pertaining to least restrictive placement, legislation, litigation, and the services of professional organizations. SI students are given the opportunity to demonstrate their advocacy skills via simulation exercises which are part of their coursework.

Instructional planner and implementer. As an instructional planner, a teacher must be able to accurately assess a student's present levels of educational performance. In all cases, a teacher will find it necessary to go beyond the results of standardized tests in order to precisely identify a student's strengths and weaknesses. Knowledge of and the ability to use criterion-referenced tests and curriculum-based assessment devices should be of great assistance to teachers in planning instructional programs. One of the major goals of assessment should be to identify skills in need of remediation and to describe them in measurable terms. Based on a child's performance during assesment, the teacher will need to sequence the skills which, when mastered, will result in the amelioration of identified academic deficits. Attention must also be given to the selection of instructional materials. A teacher must be prepared to adapt materials when possible and to create instructional materials when none exist.

Once a teacher has identified a starting place for instruction, it is necessary to select an instrutional technique which can then be systematically applied. A thorough knowledge of a variety of instructional techniques and their uses will be needed if teachers are to select appropriate interventions. In order to precisely identify academic deficits and to determine the effectiveness of corrective techniques, a teacher must be familiar with measurement techniques and become proficient in their use.

The specific skills which students in the SI program are expected to master include the ability to: 1) conduct criterion-referenced and curriculum-based assessments, 2) describe instructional problems in behavioral terms, 3) construct and use task analyses, 4) write instructional objectives, 5) sequence instructional objectives, 6) generate and select teaching techniques, 7) observe and chart academic data, 8) make data-based decisions, and 9) adapt/create instructional materials. Students demonstrate their knowledge of these skills by completing a number of projects in their courses, and by planning and implementing instructional programs for children during the practicum experience.

Behavioral manager. A teacher can be expected to encounter a number of behavior problems with which he/she will have to deal in order to provide a proper learning environment. Being able to reduce the occurrence of socially inappropriate behaviors and to increase the occurrence of appropriate ones are critical skills for a teacher to possess.

An aspect of significant concern is improving the behavior of "mildy handicapped" children to the extent that they are able to successfully interact with their non-handicapped peers. A teacher is seen as being in a pivotal position as the facilitator of interaction to increase the social acceptance of "mildy handicapped" students by their classmates.

It is a wise teacher who can make use of natrual reinforcers in the classroom, arrange group contingencies, and use self-management techniques to improve the behavior of students. The teacher who can effectively employ behavioral management techniques will be in a good position to structure the learning experiences of students and assure success in the regular classroom for students experiencing problems.

In order to increase the ability of SI students to deal with social behavior problems, they are expected to be able to: 1) use a variety of observation techniques, 2) identify problem behaviors in measurable terms, 3) record and chart social behaviors, 4) select appropriate intervention techniques, 5) make use of behavioral management techniques, and 6) make data-based decisions. Coursework offers the opportunity for SI students to complete a number of projects requiring the application of behavioral techniques to classroom behavior problems. During the practicum experience, the students design and implement strategies for improving a child's study and social behaviors.

It should be stressed that the SI program confers no new teaching certificate. It does provide, however, an opportunity for regular educators to take a substantial block of coursework in special education and to gain experience in teaching children with mild learning and behavior problems in the regular classroom setting. It is anticipated that due to the nature of the program, graduates will have a distinct hiring advantage as they seek positions as regular classroom teachers. In order to help assure that this occurs, each graduate of the SI program will have a special set of materials included in his/her placement credentials describing the SI program and assessing the student's performance in the program.

Inservice Training

Recently, Ed Martin, Deputy Commissioner of Bureau of Handicapped, U. S. O. E., commented that "efforts to provide training and experience for regular classroom teachers are not keeping pace with the efforts to mainstream" (1976, p. 6). While this is not excusable, it is certainly understandable considering the number of regular educators (approximately 1.8 million) who require inservice training in special education.

If inservice training of regular educators is to be effective, it must overcome at least two obstacles. The first deals with teachers' attitudes and the second concerns the mystique which has surrounded special education. It is not so difficult to understand the reticence felt by some regular educators, such as those questioned by Hall & Findley (1971), concerning their willingness to teach low achieving pupils. Nor is it difficult to understand why some regular educators feel they cannot teach "mildy handicapped" youngsters without the aid of special equipment (Shotel, Iano, & McGettigan, 1972). These teachers have simply accepted the mystique which surrounds special education and which has been fostered by maintaining self-contained classrooms, thereby implying that regular classroom teachers were not capable of teaching children with mild learning and behavior problems.

Several special educators have placed a great deal of stress on changing teachers' attitudes (Brooks & Bransford, 1971; Shotel et al., 1972) and some researchers have been successful in bringing about desirable attitude changes (Brooks & Bransford, Glass & Meckler, 1972). An undue emphasis upon changing attitudes to the neglect of providing teachers with the skills necessary to teach problem students should not be encouraged. Changing attitudes is a tricky business; sometimes attitude shifts are accompanied by concomitant changes in behavior and sometimes not. A more direct approach is to focus on improving the skills of classroom teachers. It seems unlikely that a teacher could maintain a "poor attitude" toward a child if he/she possessed the skills to individualize instruction and to demonstrate that the child was making prograss as the result of his/her teaching efforts.

The skills approach to inservice training has the support of a number of school district administrators, who when asked for suggestions concerning inservice training responded that it should be "practical and specific", include "both observing special educators and working with the handicapped," and provide "follow-up" to assist participants in their regular classes (Comptroller General, 1976, p. 11).

If everyone agrees that inservice training of regular educators is necessary, the question then becomes, "How is inservice to be provided?" There are at least three options: 1) onsite training conducted by special education personnel who are employees of the school district, 2) onsite instruction provided by specialists under contract as consultants to the school district, and 3) stipends for short-term study at colleges or universities. When school district administrators were asked to indicate their preference of the above mentioned options, they rated onsite training by contracted specialists as the most desirable and stipends for short-term campus study as the least desirable alternative (Comptroller General, 1976). The preferences of school district administrators seem to suggest a rather cautious view concerning the capabilities of school district special education personnel to conduct inservice training. This may be due to the fact that insufficient numbers of special educators have been trained to serve in a role analagous to that of a Resource/Consulting teacher. If sufficient numbers of special educators were trained in that capacity, it would seem logical that they would be in the best position to provide the kind of "practical" information and "follow-up" which school district administrators indicated they desired for inservice training. In recognition of this reality, trainees in the master's level Resource/Consulting Teacher program at the University of Illinois are taught to plan and implement inservice workshops as a part of their preparation for that role in the public schools.

Conclusion

Based on the discussion thus far, the following recommendations concerning pre-and inservice training of regular educators seem warranted:

1. A single survey course in special education is not sufficient to prepare regular educators to assume the responsibility of educating children with mild learning and behavior problems. What is needed is a program which stresses skills and includes practicum experience in a regular classroom setting. While the clear implication of this statement is that training of regular educators will be a task of greater duration than many special educators would like, the alternative is likely to be mass training, almost sure to result in sparcity and mediocrity of application.

2. Training of regular educators should focus on increasing direct teaching skills, on the assumption that successful experiences in teaching children will result in positive attitudes toward the children being taught. If programs are initiated which focus on change of attitudes of regular educators, assessment of concomitant changes in teacher behavior should be an integral part of such endeavors.

3. Departments of special education, elementary education, secondary education, vocational-technical education, etc. should engage in cooperative planning to develop quality preservice programs in special education for regular education students.

4. College and University Departments of Special Education should consider reallocation of scarce financial and human resources from undergraduate preparation of special educators for self-contained teaching situations to training of regular educators to deal constructively with learning and behavior problems in the regular classroom. This is not to say that continued preparation of special educators is not needed, as is implied in the Comptroller General's report (1976) on the federal role in special education teacher preparation. Rather, it is suggested that the majority of special education teacher training should be done at the master's level, and an increasing amount of our capability for undergraduate education should be focused on regular educators.

5. Inservice training should be skill-oriented and be conducted onsite, preferably by special educators who work in the schools as Resource/Consulting teachers and who can provide follow-up assistance to regular educators.

As mentioned earlier, the question is no longer whether regular educators should be trained to deal with learning and behavior problems in the classroom, but rather, how such training should be provided. It is the opinion of these authors that the monumental task of providing such training to regular educators must be approached with patience, and with constant attention to quality as well as quantity of effort. We must remain constantly aware of ill-advised and often ineffective efforts to prepare large numbers of special educators during the 1950's and early 1960's, and insist that new undertakings be systematically planned and executed. Undoubtedly, the need for training of regular educators will outstrip our capability to deliver such training in the forseeable future, for the change process in education is political in nature and does not follow a logical, developmental pattern. Even if change in education tends to be chaotic, however, we must be systematic in our response to it. The current demand for special education training for regular educators offers a unique opportunity for improving the educational experience of countless children, and our response to the challenge must be nothing short of the best we have to offer.

Mainstreaming and Teacher Re-education: A Rationale for Reform

Norman A. Sprinthall[1]

University of Minnesota

ABSTRACT. *After reviewing studies that examine the impact of schooling upon the cognitive and emotional development of pupils, the author calls for a comprehensive reform in teacher education. Before children can be mainstreamed effectively, the mainstream must be de-polluted. The need for such change is now and includes broad implications for pre-service teacher-education programs.*

In 1882, William James concluded one of his famous talks with teachers with an optimistic review of the state of education and the future of teachers. He noted,

> There is perhaps no more promising feature than the fermentation which for a dozen years or more has been going on among teachers. In whatever sphere of education their functions may lie, there is to be seen among them a really inspiring amount of searching of the heart about the highest concerns of their profession. . . . The outward organization of education which we have in the United States is perhaps, on the whole, the best organization that exists in any country. The state school systems give a diversity and flexibility, and opportunity for experiment and keeness of competition. . . . All these things, I say, are most happy features of our scholastic life, and from them the most sanguine auguries may be drawn. (James, 1958, pp. 21-22)

Yet today, in 1984 minus six and counting, what do we see of the happy organic relation between children and teaching and the curriculum? Also, what do we see of the optimistic predictors of future success?

Few positive indices can be found for the current state of education. Instead of sanguine auguries, we see harbingers of gloom and doom, such as zero-growth budgeting superseded by retrenchment, declining enrollments, and the diminution of innovation. Also, there is increasing community concern about the management of the schools and growing public criticism of curriculum content. It seems that in the 1970s the general problem of effective schooling for all children appears almost insol-

---

[1]Professor, Department of Psychoeducational Studies; Coordinator, Dean's Grant Project, 1975-78.

Reprinted from *Teacher Education: Renegotiating Roles for Mainstreaming* by Norman A. Sprinthall.

vabie. Many critics would claim that the educators of the 1970s have lost their way. Cynical comments suggest that educators today are similar to pasengers scrambling for deck chairs on the next voyage of the Titanic.

J.A. March at Stanford underscored the significance of our response to the present crisis. He warned us (March, 1975) that some of our responses may be totally inadequate: For example, some educators tend simply to retreat and agree with Christopher Jencks that the over-all process of schooling is meaningless; research studies often have shown that school effects accumulate, at best, to zero. The life of the educator in retreat becomes simply a series of numerous minor events with minor obligations that have no point or consequence. Educators may be living out lives of quiet desperation, to use Thoreau's phrase.

A second possibility is that we will turn inward and retire from the struggle or, perhaps, move toward self-aggrandizement. We may become excessively concerned with our own careers and positions and the petty indulgences of personal pleasure (March, 1975). In one sense, March has echoed F. Scott Fitzgerald's observation of the 1930s as a period for creative artists when all the wars were fought, all the gods were dead, and all faith was shaken. From this observation we might draw an analogy for the 1970s: All that is left for educators is to watch out for themselves, protect their positions through seniority, and hold survival as a primary goal.

The third possibility suggested by March is that we face the harsh reality that American education has not delivered in accordance with its promise. We are, metaphorically at least, a light year away from effective school programs that will promote the intellectual and emotional growth of all pupils. Thus, the problem is substantial. In the 1970s, the New Frontier no longer exists, the Great Society has disappeared, and the New Federalism also has vanished. These massive programs either have faded from memory or whimpered into extinction. In 1963, John F. Kennedy pointed out that one-third of the nation was ill-clothed, ill-housed, and inadequately educated; in 1977, it seems that we have made little progress toward reducing these proportions, especially in the last category — education.

If we look at the harsh reality of schooling, what do we find? What is life like in regular classrooms? What is the quality of learning environments in mainstream education? It is important, obviously, to examine most carefully these questions. As we work assiduously to admit previously excluded children to mainstream education, do we need also to work as assiduously to change what it is they are entering?

Although I do not wish to perform yet another educational autopsy on the effects of schooling, I want to present a few brief comments on the current reality in order to buttress the rationale that the need for over-all school reform is pressing and will not disappear. Also, it is my view that mainstreaming and school reform are closely linked, like the two sides of the same coin.

Three general areas of schooling are reviewed in the rest of this paper: The first two are the effect of schools on the intellectual and psychological development of children, and the third is the teaching process itself, as commonly practiced in most classrooms.

Impact of Schooling on Intellectual Development

A national study, Project Talent (Flanagan, 1973), has provided us with valuable insights to the eternal question of schooling: "Do students master academic content?" Flanagan's findings do very little to brighten our day. He found, for example, that in the English curriculum, less than

65% of high school students could understand Robert Louis Stevenson's novel, *Treasure Island*, hardly the most intellectual of readings. Less than 36% could understand Rudyard Kipling and only 8% could understand Jane Austen. These studies were done on a massive scale over the decade 1960-1970. Most depressing is the fact that he found very little change in these percentages over the 10-year span.

Scriven (1972) examined the effect of social studies education and found that over two-thirds of the high school pupils in this country could not produce a reasoned argument on the pros and cons of democracy as a form of government. He also found that almost 70% of high school students resolutely opposed every practical instance of free speech.

In a more recent study by Renner and his associates (1976), the results in biology and chemistry were equally distressing. The investigators found that 64% of the students studying biology were not capable of thinking at an abstract level, and 92% of the students in chemistry were similarly incapable of understanding academic content at the required abstract level.

These various findings mean that most pupils have not experienced the educational process in a manner that provides them with the ability to process the fundamental concepts of thought in those academic disciplines. To some degree, of course, this conclusion is not really surprising. Ralph Tyler produced a series of studies in the 1930s that clearly indicated that teaching academic content to pupils in the traditional basic sense was a hopeless enterprise. He found that pupils retained only 50% of the academic content of formal disciplines after one year, and less than 20% after two years. To make the point, he noted somewhat wryly that most students thought all banks paid 6% interest on savings accounts because that was the figure used in the math textbooks of the time for teaching compound interest computation (Tyler, 1933). Parenthetically, I would add that as the public demand increases for "basic education," we must remember that we already have gone that route. To return to the basics is clearly a non-event or an invitation to recycle the failure implicit in the content acquisition model for learning.

Impact of Schooling on Psychological Development

If we look at the impact of schooling upon all levels of psychological development we find a similar set of distressing findings. Studies by Ralph Ojemanin, Richard Suchman, James Coleman, Charles Silberman, and others have found that the longer pupils remain in school, the more evident are declines in positive self-concepts as learners, pupil autonomy and exploration, and intrinsic motivation (see summaries in Sprinthall & Sprinthall, 1977, Ch. 21). Silberman coined the term "the mindless school" to suggest, essentially, that too often we place students in learning environments in which what they learn is not understandable and why they are learning it is problematic, with a negative impact on overall development. Jackson's (1968) excellent account of life in classrooms indicates that all too often teachers are involved in traffic management rather than instruction. His observations have been cross-validated by such empirical studies as Gump (1975). Routine classroom management activity tends to emphasize socialization rather than the growth of psychological maturity in pupils.

Against criticisms of overgeneralization, it is fair to say, based on these studies, that the general curriculum in too many schools tends to be too narrow in focus and too pedantic in orientation, and to be based on content that assumes but does not promote either the psychological or intellectual development of pupils. Many pupils simply do not understand the purpose of schooling nor the material they are asked to learn. Instead, all too often, they have learned only to engage in an elaborate pretense or conspiracy of silence to repeat back what the teacher wants them to say.

The Content of the Teaching Process

What about the teaching process itself? Can we find evidence to provide us with some important information on the actual process employed in most classrooms in the country? In 1912, a series of studies was published that illustrated what has come to be known as the Flanders (1970) rule: 60-70% of the time in a classroom, the teacher is talking, and 60-70% of that teacher talk is in the form of short rote-like questions. Essentially, this process asks students to recite the textbook. The teachers in all subject matter asked such questions at the rate of four times per minute in the 1912 study. In the 1960s, another series of studies indicated that the ratios still held: Teachers were still doing between 60-70% of all talking in the classroom and two-thirds of the talk was in the form of direct questions requiring short rote answers. The only change was that the cycle was now down to three times per minute (see summaries in Sprinthall & Sprinthall, 1977, Ch. 2).

Goodlad and Klein (1974) studied a random selection of 156 elementary classrooms across the country and brought in the same results. The investigators noted,

> At all grade levels the teacher to child pattern of interaction overwhelmingly prevailed. This was one of the most monotonously recurring pieces of datum. The teacher asked questions and the children responded usually in a few words and phrases. It is fair to say that this form of interaction was the mode in all but 5% of the classrooms. (p. 51)

The bottom line on studies of teaching styles can be found in Brophy and Good (1974). They examined how teachers respond to pupils who were thought to be slow learners and observed that the teacher waited less time for such pupils to answer, did not follow up on incorrect answers, rewarded inappropriate behavior, and provided little positive feedback. The picture could hardly be more depressing.

This state of affairs might be summed up in a paraphrase of an analogy by Paul Tillich: Too often, teaching is throwing answers like stones at the heads of those who have not yet asked the question.

The State of the Art of Teacher Preparation

This is not to say that classroom teachers are the culprits in our depressing story. Whether we like it or not, they are the products of our pre-service and inservice education programs. If we look for a moment in that direction, we find even less to brighten our view today. A massive study by Joyce, Howey, and Yarger (1976) indicated that inservice teacher education is close to total disarray. The data were collected from more than 1,000 school personnel and community, congressional, and state department members, and a review of some 2000 volumes and 600 journal articles. The over-all findings indicate that inservice education is at best weak or impoverished and, on any scale, a relative failure.

The relative effectiveness of pre-service teacher-education programs is a long story in and of itself and need not be repeated here. Instead, I will say that both inservice and pre-service teacher education need a broader framework in order to become effective and to meet the increased demand for quality schooling. Teacher education cannot be simply a series of discrete skills that are divided by subject matter and divided again by teaching methods. We cannot simply add on a few new skills to either pre-service or inservice programs or graft on some bit of additional new content. Clearly, such changes will be too little and too late.

Before significant change can come about in the quality of education which pupils experience in classrooms, it is my view that we need to stimulate the personal and professional developmental levels of teachers. Teaching teachers a few human relations skills in brief "weekend" workshops leads to no change; the skills do not transfer to the classroom. Observational studies indicate that if one returns to a classroom three months after such an educational experience, one finds no evidence that the teacher ever went through the training (Rustad & Rogers, 1975). The reasons for such findings are obvious: Teaching is a highly complex activity. We cannot simply change one variable, such as learning one new skill, and expect it to be incorporated into the teacher's teaching style or to be generalized to over-all teaching performance. It is a myth to think that we can focus on one variable and change the general learning atmosphere in the classroom. We must simply work on a broader scale.

TEACHING AND THE CONCEPTUAL LEVELS OF TEACHERS

In our own Dean's Grant Project at the University of Minnesota, we have been working as a team[2] to develop a teacher-education program that will stimulate both the professional and personal levels of the teacher. Our work is based on some empirical studies conducted by Hunt and Sullivan (1974) at the Ontario Institute, and the theories of, for example, O.J. Harvey, Bruce Joyce, and Lawrence Kohlberg. These theorists have suggested, using somewhat different rhetoric, that humans who process experience at higher levels of developmental stages will be more adequate as classroom teachers. Hunt and Sullivan refer to the process as Conceptual Level (CL) and indicate that teachers at higher conceptual levels provide a more facilitating learning environment for their pupils. High conceptual level teachers exhibit a greater repertoire of teaching styles and are able to use more of the models of teaching, in the sense of Joyce and Weil (1972). Such teachers are more responsive to individual differences. They can employ children themselves as educational resources, are more empathic in their understanding and response to pupils' emotions, are capable of asking higher order questions in their classrooms to promote self-exploration, and are more indirect (in the Flanders system) in their approach to teaching (Hunt & Sullivan, 1974). The conclusion is that teachers at higher stages of development are more advanced as professionals. They can both think and do in the classroom at high levels of effectiveness. We are not talking simply about a higher level of intelligence; in fact, one of the great difficulties has been the common misperception of equating conceptual development with intelligence. The studies by Hunt and his colleagues do not imply that CL is synonymous with IQ; "conceptual level" refers to a much more complex function — the ability to process human experience at a more complex level in both thought and feeling.

What are the implications of conceptual level? If we accept the premise that teachers who process at higher stages are more adequate professional educators, what does this premise hold for the mainstream question? A recent volume by Reynolds and Birch (1977) on issues in mainstream education contains a chapter, "The Interface Between Regular and

[2]Other members of the team have included James Ysseldyke, Lois Erickson, and Stanley Deno, Department of Psychoeducational Studies, and Kenneth Howey, Department of Curriculum and Instruction.

5. FUTURE

Special Education," in which the authors suggest that for mainstream education to work, teachers will have to operate at complex levels of professional activity. The latter is broken down into a series of domains that includes how the teacher arranges the space in his/her classroom; what settings the teacher provides for teaching and learning activities; what materials the teacher uses; the classroom management techniques that are employed; the quality of the social environment; the rule system that the teacher follows; the content of the curriculum; the degree of structure; and the instructional method employed. In each domain, Reynolds and Birch have provided descriptive scales that detail the different levels of the teaching-learning interaction. If one examines the scales, in every instance it is clear that teachers will have to operate at a high level of professional activity to increase the accommodative capacity of their classrooms. That is, teachers must have at their fingertips a broad repertoire of teaching styles; they must be able to respond to individual differences, acknowledge the wide range of individual differences, and modify curriculum materials to provide a constructive educational match between learning activities and the levels of the learners. Examples of the Reynolds and Birch descriptive scales are given in Tables 1 and 2.

It is obvious from the scales that the more complex activities will provide for more adequate learning outcomes. If one examines these scales in relation to some of the earlier sections of this paper in which there were outlined the present inadequacies of schooling in terms of curriculum content and teaching styles, it is apparent that most classrooms in this country would have to be rated low, that is, at the first or second level of functioning.

The scales are serving as guidelines for our project. Because they have not yet been standardized, we cannot employ them directly, but we are able to use them as theoretical and behavioral descriptions of goals for teacher-education programs.

For the past two years, we have been finding out just how complex the issue of teacher education is.[3] We have found that we can make little change if we simply tag a new three-credit course (perhaps even named "Mainstream Education and You") to an already existing curriculum. That would be like dusting off the human relations curricular packages of the 1960s and replacing "black" and "Chicano" with "MR," "TMR," and "Multiply Handicapped." A few tinkering adjustments or cosmetic applications to the surface are not sufficient. Business as usual in teacher education will not do.

We see the current problem of mainstream education as providing all educators with the chance to rethink and synthesize how all teachers, both pre-service and inservice, can be trained to fulfill the mandates of least restrictive environment, individualized educational plans, and due process. Thus, we see the present as the chance for a major overhaul of the present curricular content and process of teacher education. Also, we view the present as the opportunity to deliberately try out new approaches that are designed to promote the over-all professional development of teachers. We need deliberate innovation.

Conclusion

Essentially, what I am pleading for is a new synthesis of theory and practice for pre-service as well as inservice education. This means that counseling and school psychology professors will need to expand their

---

[3]For an extended description of the project, see S.N. Oja & N.A. Sprinthall, *Character potential: A record of research* (in press).

Table 1

Learning Environment Scale[4]

Control of and Responsibility for Environment

1. Each individual class and the school is a rule-governed operation; with rules based almost totally on the teacher's "police" power and competencies.

2. Students share occasionally in discussion of how the school environment shall be managed. A degree of "consent of the governed" is achieved.

3. Formal arrangements are made for the regular involvement of students in governance — as in student government, student-management of classroom materials, weekly class meetings or the like.

4. Individual students and groups of students are given special training and responsibility for management of much of the school environment and processes. Included are technical matters such as running audio-visual machines, administering competency exams, orienting new students, and showing the school to visitors. In addition, training may be included in counseling skills (listening, reinforcing, etc.) and other aspects of interpersonal and group behavior.

5. Students share significantly in the governance (policy-making and administration) of their classes and school. Their obligations run to other students as well as to school officials; they are expected to help make the learning environment productive. They receive instruction, where necessary, to help them take responsibilities. The teacher shares in all of this as well, but gives particular attention to instruction for constructive initiatives and "autonomy" by students.

Table 2

Learning Environment Scale[5]

Social Environment

1. Students are expected to work essentially alone as far as instructional tasks are concerned. Student-student relationships tend to be non-sharing, even competitive. The teacher rewards individual performance and seems non-deliberate about group processes.

2. Students work mainly in isolation, but occasionally in small groups. The teacher praises and supports friendly interactions, but no systematic provision for education in group processes is provided. Evaluation tends to be individually oriented and to encourage competition.

3. Students work in small groups frequently and must share materials. All records are individual. Students are expected to learn to work with each other, but goals are nonspecific.

4. Students are clustered so that they can interact freely. Some group projects are assigned with considerable frequency. Group projects are evaluated informally, but grade records emphasize individual achievements. Social skills are valued.

5. The development of positive social skills and attitudes is one avowed objective of the teacher. Students are expected to interact and share with each other and to help one another. Sometimes they work on group projects, dividing up work. The teacher assists in group process and rewards effective group work. Students have every reason to be mutually helpful. Definite efforts are made to provide socially integrative experiences for exceptional students.

---

[4]Source: M.C. Reynolds & J.W. Birch, *Teaching Exceptional Children in All America's Schools*. Reston, Va.: Council for Exceptional Children, 1977, p. 142.

[5]Source: M.C. Reynolds & J.W. Birch, *Teaching Exceptional Children in All America's Schools*. Reston, Va.: Council for Exceptional Children, 1977, p. 139.

5. FUTURE

vision beyond individual counseling and isomorphic assessments; educational psychologists will need to drop some of their more esoteric and heuristic approaches to classroom learning; special educators will need to forget (at least) some of their excessive fascination with their own disciplines. As a somewhat cynical friend of mine once remarked, "English educators need to realize that a pupil's world doesn't begin and end between Beowulf and James Joyce, nor Social Studies education between the Tigris and Euphrates and Yalta."

All of us will be required to give up some of our academic autonomy. The goal, however, can be attractive. An interdisciplinary and cross-professional program for pre-service and inservice education is a major and remarkable opportunity. The serious and virtually unmistakable implication for the mainstream movement is that such a chance is at hand.

We will need to develop the ideas and practices but, most of all, we will need men and women of vision and leadership. As I view the current educational framework, I would say that the responsibility for training such teachers is ours.

References

Brophy, J., & Good, T. *Teacher-student relationships: Causes and consequences.* New York: Holt, Rinehart, and Winston, 1974.

Flanagan, J. Education: How and for what. *American Psychologist,* July 1973, 551-56.

Flanders, N. *Analyzing teacher behavior.* Reading, Mass.: Addison-Wesley, 1970.

Goodlad, J., & Klein, F.K. *Looking behind the classroom door.* Worthington, Ohio: Charles Jones, 1974.

Gump, P.V. Education as an environmental enterprise. In R.A. Weinberg & F.H. Wood (Eds.), *Observation of pupils and teacher in mainstream and special education settings: Alternative strategies.* Reston, Va.: Council for Exceptional Children, 1975, 109-22.

Hunt, D., & Sullivan, E. *Between psychology and education.* New York: Dryden, 1974.

Jackson, P. *Life in classrooms.* New York: Holt, Rinehart, & Winston, 1968.

James, W. *Talks to teachers on psychology and to students on some of life's ideals.* New York: Norton, 1958.

Joyce, B., Howey, K., & Yarger, S. *Issues to face.* Report #1, Inservice teacher education. Palo Alto: Education Research and Development Center, 1976.

Joyce, B., & Weil, M. *Models of teaching.* Englewood, N. J.: Prentice Hall, 1972.

March, J.A. Education and the pursuit of optimism. *Texas Tech Journal of Education,* 1975, **2**(1), 5-18.

Reynolds, M.C., & Birch, J.W. *Teaching exceptional children in all America's schools.* Reston, Va.: Council for Exceptional Children, 1977.

Rustad, K., & Rogers, C. Promoting psychological growth in a high school class. *Counselor Education and Supervision,* 1975, **14**(4), 277-85.

Scriven, M. Education for survival. In D.E. Purpel & M. Belanger (Eds.), *Curriculum and the cultural revolution.* Berkeley: McCutchan, 1972, 166-204.

Sprinthall, R.C., & Sprinthall, N.A. *Educational psychology: A developmental approach* (2nd ed.). Reading, Mass.: Addison-Wesley, 1977.

Tyler, R. Permanence of learning. *Journal of Higher Education,* 1933, **4**, 203-04.

THE RIGHT NOT TO READ

Russell D. Snyder, M.D.

From the Departments of Pediatrics and Neurology, University of New Mexico Medical Center, Albuquerque

ABSTRACT. Skill in reading is desirable. However, the importance of reading may be overemphasized in schools. Reading skills are determined relatively and not absolutely. Thus, relatively poor readers will persist. Schools cannot eradicate individual differences. Biological makeup and societal pressures are the important factors in determining reading skill. Present methods of reading remediation are of questionable efficacy and are traumatic to some children. Time with its associated normal development succeeds in remediating the majority of children with dyslexia. Most poor readers eventually attain reading levels that enable them to comprehend the types of printed materials commonly encountered. If a child finds reading difficult or distasteful, that child should be encouraged to read but should have the right not to be forced to read. *Pediatrics* 63:791–794, 1979, *dyslexia, reading, learning disability, remedial reading, school failure.*

A high level of reading proficiency is considered an important aspect of public education. Parents, schools, and government agencies become concerned over any apparent shortcomings in the teaching or learning of reading, a concern reflected in the national Right To Read program. The existence of reading problems and their eradication have become major issues.

DEFINITION

No precise definition of childhood dyslexia or reading disability exists. The typical dyslexic child is a boy of normal intelligence, motivated to learn, with no major sensory deficit and no socioeconomic or cultural disadvantage. Dyslexia is often equated with learning disability. However, learning disabilities may occur in areas other than reading. Problems in acquiring skill in mathematics, music, or even physical education do not receive the intense attention that is directed toward reading disability.

The assumption that the child with dyslexia is a nonreader constitutes a common error. In the majority of cases, the child with dyslexia is a poor reader but has at least a modicum of skill in the interpretation of the visual symbols of language.

NORMALITY

Developmental variations are readily accepted in early life. A normal child may begin walking independently between 11 and 14 months of age. Meaningful speech may begin between 10 and 14 months of age. There is a corresponding normal range for the onset of the ability to read, extending from about 3 to 14 years of age, depending on nervous system maturation and perhaps other factors.[1] However, many school systems rigidly demand that the development of reading skills begin at approximately the same age for all children.[2] The failure to accept variation in the age of onset of reading skill leads to unnecessary teacher and parent anxiety and unnecessary pressure on the student. Reading skills do not correlate well with chronologic age.

Test scores for reading ability fall roughly on a normal distribution (Gaussian) curve slightly skewed to the left.[3] Dyslexic children will be on the lower end of this distribution curve. Nothing can modify the statistical fact that the reading curve will have a lower end. Improving reading skills merely shifts the curve up the scale or modifies its shape, but does not abolish its lower end. Reading skills are measured relatively and not absolutely. Thus, the problem of the relatively poor reader persists. If a race is run, someone will inevitably finish last.

In the hypothetical "average school," 50% of the students will read at or below grade level

5. FUTURE

when grade level is defined as the class median. This statistical fact is generally not recognized. Educators and parents tend to view below-average performance as unsatisfactory. A student performing below average in a classroom should not necessarily be considered an adverse reflection on either the parent or the teacher.

ANATOMIC BASIS

The anatomic basis of acquired adult dyslexia was described by Dejerine[1] in 1892. He described a 68-year-old man in whom dyslexia and right hemianopsia developed after a cerebrovascular accident. An infarct was found in the left occipital region with involvement of the splenium of the corpus callosum. Neither the sudden onset nor the associated hemianopsia are characteristic of the usual child with reading disability. At present, there is uncertainty regarding the pathologic substrate for childhood dyslexia. Possibly two groups exist. Children in the first group are rare and constitute the "hard-core" childhood dyslexia. This group may have identifiable brain lesions, does not respond appreciably to remediation, and has deficits that persist into adult life. The second group is much more common and may simply represent slow CNS maturation, in some cases on a familial basis. Children in the second group do not have an identifiable brain lesion and improve with time and remediation or both. Thus, in most cases "childhood dyslexia" is not a disease in the usual sense. Providing a medical or neurologic diagnostic label does not necessarily imply the need for a specific diagnostic or therapeutic approach.[5] It appears unlikely that further refinements of the neurologic examination will advance the understanding of childhood dyslexia or other learning disorders.[6,7]

EARLY IDENTIFICATION

A pervasive notion exists that the reading problem could be obviated by identifying poor readers earlier in their school careers and subjecting them to special training programs. This notion exists in spite of the lack of evidence for effective means of early identification.[8] Kindergartens and even prekindergartens are now attempting to identify potential problem readers. If the young poor readers include a substantial number with maturational delay, they will improve in time with or without special reading programs. Any program directed toward such a group will be assured of reasonably good results. There is no evidence that the proportion of students with reading problems in later grades is significantly reduced by early remedial programs,[8] and the

involved children may be unnecessarily traumatized by the experience.

Perhaps delay in the introduction of reading into the school curriculum would have more benefit than early introduction. Early childhood may not be the optimal age for introduction of the academic content traditionally required. Reading instruction generally begins with the onset of formal schooling, usually at age 5. Progress in reading becomes the major factor in judging success in school. The evidence that delay in the onset of reading instruction would prove deleterious is extremely thin.[9]

IMPORTANCE OF READING

The language arts include reading, writing, speaking, and listening. In everyday activities for the majority of adults, speaking and listening may well be the more important skills. Reading may not be the principal method by which a child acquires information.[9] Neither intelligence nor income has been clearly related to literacy. Although we decry high school seniors who have attained only a "seventh-grade reading level," that level is actually more than adequate for most reading activities and for most jobs, even professions.[10] Many newspapers in this country are written at the fourth- or fifth-grade reading level. A poor reader develops strategies to help cope with the reading problem and utilizes alternative methods to acquire information. Nevertheless, reading receives the bulk of the time in elementary education. Even mathematic problems become based on an understanding of the printed word.

To the child, school appears to be primarily concerned with right answers; teachers and books are seen as the major reservoirs of the right answers.[11] Our society has a pervasive belief in the truth of the printed word. Although schools continue to emphasize the importance of books and reading, the United States is not a nation of bibliophiles.[12] "Print is not dead; it is just an old technology, no longer very exciting."[13] Technology now offers effective alternative methods of communication, a fact frequently overlooked by schools.

REMEDIAL READING

Remedial reading programs are based on the hypothesis that reading deficits are correctable, but that the deficits will not improve spontaneously or fully in the ordinary school program. Remedial reading programs can produce a slight increase in the reading level and can be of immense help in selected situations. Remedial reading instruction can make poor readers into passable readers, but it will not make poor readers into good readers. The improvement in reading ability gained through such programs generally washes out with time, and the child returns to his previous learning curve.[14-16] This should not be at all surprising, as intensive training programs for many other skills have similar outcomes.

A number of factors assure some degree of success in most remedial reading programs: (1) early identification leads to the inclusion of children with maturation delays who will ultimately do well under any circumstances; (2) an expectation of success in a well-presented program may evoke at least a temporary increase in effort and acceleration of the learning curve; (3) inexact definitions of reading problems and pressures to identify large numbers of poor readers will lead to the inclusion of a substantial number of normal children from the lower end of the normal distribution curve who have at least a reasonable learning capacity and therefore a potential for improvement; (4) evaluation immediately after an intense training program will show improvement to the greatest advantage; (5) the financial incentives for successful programs encourage the most optimistic interpretation of the data regarding results of treatment; and (6) a more favorable teacher-student ratio is beneficial to most students.

Eye-movement exercises and perceptual motor training are currently popular methods of remediation. The evidence of benefit from these therapies is tenuous.[17-19] If a corrective program is to be employed, the educational strategy should be directed to the skill that is to be learned.[20]

The use of oral-aural rather than written communications is a frequently overlooked form of remediation. Is it intrinsically incorrect to learn from audiovisuals or even from actual experience? Why should a student be forced to take written notes or written examinations when a recorder or a direct personal dialog might be used equally well? For many students with severe reading deficits, the oral-aural route is the major alternative route for education.

Remedial reading programs may be emotionally damaging to a child. These programs focus not on the child's strengths and accomplishments but on his failure. With our present methods of remediation, a child with dyslexia can very rapidly become a child receiving special attention to reading during school, remedial instruction after school, and special tutoring from his parents at night. A large percentage of the child's waking day can be occupied by the very thing he cannot do and often finds distasteful. Childhood can thus be marred by systematic humiliation. Any interest the child may have in the reading process can be abolished.

Constant emphasis on the child's area of failure may also set in motion the self-fulfilling prophecy. According to this process, children viewed as capable perform well while those considered not capable do, in fact, perform poorly.[21]

The reading-disabled child may be criticized for not working at his maximum potential. Few of us, however, work at maximum potential for any length of time. Pressures for such constant high-level performance may have adverse effects.

The perpetuation of the intense emphasis on childhood dyslexia is to some degree financially guaranteed. Remedial reading teachers may receive higher salaries than regular classroom teachers. School districts may receive additional appropriations for children identified as learning disabled. Some optometrists, psychologists, and physicians have profited from association with the area of reading problems. A large and influential industry is involved in the manufacture of reading tests and special reading programs.

Reading is a skill similar to all other skills in that ability is determined by biological makeup and societal pressures and modified only minimally by education or training.

RECOMMENDATIONS

Perhaps our educational system could consider a decrease in the emphasis on the attainment of skill in the interpretation of the printed word. For many children, this skill is elusive at best. A recognition that reading ability is related in part to the degree of neurologic maturation is in order. Reading ability may correlate better with neurologic maturation than with educational technique or chronological age.

In our technological society, alternatives to reading exist. The oral-aural approach is one such alternative. Educational television and movies are also alternatives. Other methods for the teaching of reading should be tried, such as the sequential phonetic, gestalt, and kinesthetic approach.

Children need to be encouraged to read, but perhaps not with the intensity presently occurring in many schools. Also, the timing of the introduction of reading materials into the school curriculum should be reevaluated.

SUMMARY

Reading ability is an important but not irreplaceable skill. Most poor readers eventually attain reading levels that enable them to comprehend the types of printed materials commonly encountered. A tolerance should be developed for those who are not efficient in the reading process or who do not like to read. Schools should not make reading the sole, and perhaps not even the predominant, route for learning. If a child finds reading difficult or distasteful, that child should have the right not to be forced to read.

However, all children should be encouraged to read. They should be helped when appropriate. For those children who have difficulty with the visual symbols of language, allowances can be made to permit maturation and alternative methods of learning can be used and even encouraged.

REFERENCES

1. Jennings W, Nathan J: Research data supporting educational change, in Kohl HR (ed): *On Teaching.* New York, Schocken Books, 1976, pp 167-181.
2. Downing J: How society creates reading disability. *Elem School J* 77:274, 1977.
3. Yule W, Rutter M, Berger M, et al: Over- and under-achievement in reading: Distribution in the general population. *Br J Educ Psychol* 44:1, 1974.
4. Dejerine J: Contribution à l'étude anatompathologique et clinique des différentes variétés de cecite verbale. *C R Soc Biol* 1892, 9s, iv, pt 2, 61.
5. Kinsbourne M: School problems and their causes. *Pediatrics* 54:253, 1974.
6. Barlow CF: "Soft signs" in children with learning disorders. *Am J Dis Child* 128:605, 1974.
7. Erickson MT: Reading disability in relation to performance on neurological tests for minimal brain dysfunction. *Dev Med Child Neurol* 19:768, 1977.
8. Alberman E: The early prediction of learning disorders. *Dev Med Child Neurol* 15:202, 1973.
9. Rohwer W: Prime time for education: Early childhood or adolescence? *Harvard Educ Rev* 41:316, 1971.
10. Postman N, Weingartner C: The reading problem, in *The School Book.* New York, Delacorte Press, 1973, pp 82-93.
11. Glasser W: *Schools Without Failure.* New York, Harper & Row Publishers, 1969, p 37.
12. Peterson T: The literate nonreader, the library, and the publisher, in Jennison PS, Sheridan RN (eds): *The Future of General Adult Books and Readings in America.* Chicago, American Library Association, 1970, pp 90-126.
13. Postman N: The politics of reading. *Harvard Educ Rev* 40:244, 1970.
14. Silberberg NE, Silberberg MC: Myths in remedial education. *J Learn Disabil* 2:209, 1969.
15. Weinberg WA, Penick EC, Hammerman M, et al: An evaluation of a summer remedial reading program. *Am J Dis Child* 122:494, 1971.
16. Silberberg NE, Iversen IA, Goins JT: Which remedial reading method works best? *J Learn Disabil* 6:18, 1973.
17. The eye and learning disabilities: Joint organizational statement. *Pediatrics* 49:454, 1972.
18. Gardiner P: The eye and learning disability. *Dev Med Child Neurol* 16:95, 1974.
19. Vellutino FR, Steger BM, Moyer SC, et al: Has the perceptual deficit hypothesis led us astray? *J Learn Disabil* 10:375, 1977.
20. MacKeith R: Do disorders of perception occur? *Dev Med Child Neurol* 19:821, 1977.
21. Rosenthal R, Jacobson LF: Teaching expectations for the disadvantaged. *Sci Am* 218:19, April 1968.

BEH FINAL REGULATIONS FOR LEARNING DISABILITIES: IMPLICATIONS FOR THE SECONDARY SCHOOL

Libby Goodman and Marianne Price

The final regulations for learning disabilities under PL 94-142 were published in December, 1977. As school districts have attempted to comply with these regulations, questions have been raised regarding their impact on assessment and instructional planning for learning disabled populations. So far, most of the literature on the LD regulations has focused on the preschool- and elementary-aged child. Goodman and Price, however, have analyzed the regulations as they relate to the evaluation of specific learning disabilities and to instructional planning for LD adolescents. This article raises several concerns on behalf of the learning disabled adolescent about the application of the regulations within secondary school settings. — D.D.D.

Definition problems and the closely alligned issue of specific criteria have plagued the field of learning disabilities for many years. Definitions abound (Mercer, Forgnone, & Wolking, 1976) and schemes for the operationalization of various definitions have appeared in the literature (Chalfant & King, 1976; Grill, 1977; Bateman, 1965). However, competing definitions of learning disabilities along with varying estimates of the number of learning disabled students (figures ranging from 1 to 40% can be found in the literature) have exposed the field of learning disabilities to considerable criticism. The conceptual validity of learning disabilities as a separate identifiable category of exceptionality has been challenged (Lane, 1976), and as a result the professional credibility of learning disabilities specialists has been undermined.

In the midst of lingering confusion over the issues of definition and criteria and the concomitant interprofessional confrontation,

Congress, in drafting the legislation for PL 94-142, included the learning disabled as a discernible category of the handicapped school-age population, and consequently directed BEH to promulgate criteria for the identification of specific learning disabilities. Until specific identifying procedures were developed, the legislation restricted learning disabilities to 2% of the 12% total incidence figure.

PL 94-142 resolved the question of definition in favor of the familiar and widely used

LIBBY GOODMAN, Ed.D., is Director of Special Education for Administrative Services, Div. of Special Education, Philadelphia, PA.

MARIANNE PRICE, Ed.D., is Coordinator, Learning Disabilities Program, Montgomery County Intermediate Unit, Montgomery, PA.

5. FUTURE

NACHC definition, which was retained in toto. The shortcomings of this definition have previously been discussed and need not be repeated here (Myers & Hammill, 1976). For the service provider, any definition is second in importance to specific procedures which will be used to identify members of the target population, i.e., the criteria used to identify learning disabled from nonhandicapped students and, to distinguish learning disabilities from other types of handicapping conditions. Therefore, our attention is drawn to the specific procedure contained in the final regulations for learning disabilities which were published in the December 29, 1977 issue of the Federal Register and became law forty-five days thereafter.

Though some discussion of them has appeared in the professional literature (Senf, 1978; Danielson & Bauer, 1978), the utility of the "procedures" is unknown at this time. It is noteworthy, however, that these discussions included reference to preschool and school-age children but almost totally excluded any reference to the impact of the new regulation on the secondary school-age learning disabled population. Surely, the new procedures will impact on educational programming for the learning disabled at all levels and consequently discussion is needed of the implications of the BEH final regulations for the evaluation of specific learning disabilities in secondary school students.

ADDITIONAL REQUIREMENTS

Because the field of learning disabilities, as we know it today, began as a movement for young children, it is not surprising to find that the new regulations embody a decided elementary bias consistent with the needs of young handicapped children. However, in light of the growing awareness of the existence of a significant population of older learning disabled youth (Goodman & Mann, 1976), this is very disconcerting. Neither the definition nor the added procedures make

any distinction between the primary- and secondary-aged student. We assume, therefore, that absence of any reference distinguishing elementary- and secondary-level students means that the regulations are to be applied equally across all school levels. In this article, the final regulations for evaluation of specific learning disabilities will be reviewed and critiqued for their applicability to the learning disabled student in the secondary school.

Team Members

The first of the new procedures concerns the addition of members to the multidisciplinary team which bears responsibility for evaluation, diagnosis, and program recommendation. The regulations call for the inclusion of qualified teaching personnel and a diagnostician as part of the multidisciplinary team. The inclusion of a "person qualified to conduct individual educational diagnostic examination of children" is most significant as it emphasizes the desirability of an individualized and prescriptive diagnostic process. This diagnostic approach can be subsumed under the broader heading of clinical or diagnostic teaching, a teaching approach which has equal applicability for students of all ages. The implicit endorsement of this methodology in the regulations will pose no problem for secondary programs. If anything, it underscores the need for a highly individualized and diagnostically oriented approach to evaluation and programming in our secondary schools. Exemplary instructional methods such as these need not be restricted to the elementary school.

Discrepancy Requirement

The second of the additional procedures concerns the criteria to be used to establish the existence of a specific learning disability. According to the regulations, a specific learning disability exists if "the child does not achieve commensurate with his or her age and ability levels in one or more of the following areas - oral expression, listening comprehension, written expression, basic reading skill, reading comprehension, mathematics calculation, or mathematics reasoning". This criterion consists of two parts: a discrepancy statement and specified performance areas, which will be discussed separately below.

Discrepancy statement. The requirement that there be a discrepancy between achievement and age and ability is but one form of the discrepancy model applied to the identification of learning disabilities. That underachievement in the face of ability is a hallmark of learning disabilities is beyond dispute. However, unless age and ability are on a par (e.g., IQ = 100), we must choose one or the other, i.e., age or ability, as the yardstick against which to measure achievement. Age and ability are not interchangeable and the implications of their use need to be given careful consideration.

When the student's ability level falls below chronological age, ability is a better indicator of performance expectancy than MA. However, when MA is higher than CA, MA does not necessarily yield a more accurate estimate of performance levels. Ability, for example, as represented by MA, does not guarantee that the student has had exposure to material at a higher grade level(s) or that he/she has been instructed on the specific tasks, skills, or content material at a level commensurate with expectancy extrapolated from ability estimates. If we indiscriminately use ability in this manner, we may find ourselves in the awkward position of suggesting that a student is disabled when the main reason for his/her less-than-anticipated achievement may be that the student is not a vicarious learner. Other instances could be cited, but we believe the point is made.

Rather than precluding the use of the discrepancy model, the difficulties cited above in reference to the use of MA or CA as stan-

dards against which to compare achievement indicate that an alternative to either of these variables needs to be considered. In place of CA or MA we suggest that a grade placement criterion be used as the standard against which to measure achievement. For the secondary school population, the recommended grade placement criterion is full sixth-grade proficiency in basic skills subjects. The arguments in favor of this standard are that: (1) this level of performance indicates that the student is functionally literate (Robinson, 1963), i.e., has successfully mastered the basic skill subjects of the elementary grades to the point that these skills are likely to be retained and to be used in life situations; (2) the student has attained a level of proficiency which enables him/her to function within the range of performance variability that is likely to be found among the student body at large in a typical comprehensive secondary school; (3) the standard is eminently practical because it facilitates communication among teachers and between parents and teachers; and (4) substitution of actual grade placement for MA or IQ estimates in the discrepancy model reduces the error factor.[1]

Another issue inherent in the use of the discrepancy model involves the degree of disparity between achievement and, in our scheme, grade placement (at time of testing). As a rule of thumb, a disparity of two or more years between measured achievement and grade placement at time of achievement testing can be considered significant for secondary school pupils. Therefore, the suggested discrepancy criterion is that the student's performance in basic skills (i.e., reading, math, language arts) be two or more years below placement *and* fall below the seventh-grade level. To be sure, seventh-grade level skills will not place a student at the top of the class. Nevertheless, they will place him/her in the academic ball park.

An additional benefit of the use of a functional performance standard is that it clearly emphasizes the remedial focus of the secondary learning disabilities program. Placement in the program is hereby restricted to those students whose functional skills fall below the seventh-grade level while consigning to regular education all students who have successfully passed beyond the acquisition of basic skills and are ready to apply basic skills to content subjects. For special education teaching personnel, it delimits the scope of their instructional responsibilities to reasonable proportions. Thus, the primary role of the special education teacher is to be a remediator of basic skill deficiencies in the learning disabled while regular educators retain their responsibility for instruction of content subjects.

In effect, the discrepancy model advocated here utilizing achievement and a grade equivalent standard contrasts achievement with a functional, curriculum-based standard. The model presumes that students of "average or above average ability," given adequate instructional opportunity, can be expected to master curricular material to which they have been exposed and that, on the threshold of the secondary school, they will be able to demonstrate proficiency in the basic skills subjects of the elementary-school program.

Specified performance areas. The second part of the discrepancy requirement specifies the performance areas which are vulnerable to learning disability. While the emphasis placed upon basic skill acquisition is welcomed (as it is consistent with an advocacy of a remedial programmatic focus), the relevance must be questioned of two of the specified performance areas for the secondary school youth: oral language and listening comprehension.

A student of average intellectual ability who is nonverbal (rather than inclined to be nonverbal) would be a rare find in the second-

ary school setting. Severe language delay or deficiencies are so detrimental to normal growth and development patterns that they are readily identified in the young child and remedial efforts begun at an early age. Persistence of severe disfluency or lack of language development would probably have resulted in the placement of such a child outside a regular program, very likely in one for children termed "aphasic" or "hearing impaired", if impaired hearing is the underlying problem. Subtle disabilities in language functioning may go undetected for a long time. However, by the time a student has progressed to the secondary school, he/she is well beyond the age at which children acquire a language facility, and it is most likely that the student has acquired a language facility, albeit defective, which is functional for him/her. There is, in any event, considerable controversy as to the amenability of language development training and, certainly, the issue is even more problematic for the older student. At this point in time, we have neither the research nor sufficient pragmatic experience to know to what extent language can be adequately assessed or trained in an older student population.

An additional precaution to which educators must be sensitive is the presence of regional or dialectical speech patterns which may deviate markedly from standard English forms. A growing tolerance for language differences suggests that oral language patterns must be respected and regarded as "different," not "deviant". On the other hand, language skills which are required for written forms of communication are seen as distinct from oral language skills. These functions are subsumed under the area of "written expression" and the assessment of language arts and written communications skills would be most appropriate with secondary populations.

Listening comprehension is a skill widely associated with "readiness" in young children. It is a developmental construct which has relevance for young children but with little, if any, carry-over to the older student. The secondary student whose listening skills, i.e., ability to comprehend auditory stimulation, are so defective that he/she is unable to function would very likely have been identified at an early age. Beyond a minimal threshold, discrimination of auditory stimulation may be more a matter of taste and attention than ability or inability, i.e., a student may choose not to listen. The concept of listening comprehension which is so familiar in learning disabilities for primary children has little relevance for the secondary-aged learning disabled population.

It should be emphasized that specification of the seven performance areas does not dismiss the question of "disorder in one or more of the basic psychological processes." The BEH evaluative procedures are mute on this point and provide no direction for the evaluation of process disorders. It would appear that the problematic process issue is being skirted once again. Yet, without attention to the process component of the definition, we are left with merely an underachievement model. However, underachievement alone is an insufficient substantiation of the diagnosis of learning disability even though it constitutes one criterion for the identification of the learning disabled individual. The identification of process disorders becomes increasingly important at the secondary level as the proportion of "underachievers" to the total school population increases with the transition from the elementary to the secondary school. Despite the difficulties, the assessment of process disorders must be part of the evaluation procedure for learning disabled adolescents (for specific recommendations regarding tests and procedures, the reader is referred to Goodman and Mann's (1976) discussion of assessment of process disorders in secondary-aged students). Clearly the relationship between process disorders and specific learning disabilities warrants further investigation.

Observation

The BEH regulations also require that "at least one team member other than the child's regular teacher shall observe the child's academic performance in the regular classroom setting." The regulations further state that observations of the student who is non-attending, e.g., preschooler or out-of-school, be done "in an environment appropriate for a child of that age"

Observation of the secondary school student in the regular classroom setting may be particularly awkward. First, the observer must decide in which of the many classes attended daily by the student to conduct the observation, i.e., does he/she want to see the student at his/her worst or at his/her best? While little children may respond positively to the added adult presence, the older student may resent the intrusion and feel embarassed before his/her peers. If the student chooses not to participate or perform (which may be the typical behavior pattern), the observer may only note the presence of a passive or withdrawing behavior. Should the teacher then focus on the student and attempt to elicit class participation in order to give the outsider something to observe? The results could be most awkward. At any rate, what is observed may well be behavioral disability rather than the specific functional learning disability. Classroom observation will not take the place of direct testing or examination of work samples for identification of the manifestation of the disability.

The diagnostician may find, as we did, that a private interview with the student is much more revealing. Teenage students are often very perceptive about their abilities and disabilities and quite candid in their percep-

5. FUTURE

tions of themselves relative to their classmates. Though the perception may be distorted, e.g., college aspirations from a student with third-grade reading proficiency, they are generally truthful and provide invaluable information on which to base placement and programming recommendations. Interviews with all the student's teachers offer valuable insights into the interactive patterns which exist in the classroom. Recognizing that teacher attitudes, no less than student abilities, contribute to success and failure in the classroom, it is most revealing to contrast students' perceptions of themselves, their perceptions of teachers, and the teachers' perceptions of the students.

Written Report

The regulations require that the team prepare a written report of the results of the evaluation to provide a substantiation for the diagnosis of specific learning disability. Each team member is required to sign the report to indicate that it represents his/her conclusion or, if a disagreement exists, to write and submit a separate statement.

Because the requirement has been included only for the evaluation of specific learning disabilities and no other exceptionalities embraced by PL 94-142, we believe it is discriminatory regardless of the age of the students. It adds a considerable burden to the diagnostic evaluative function of the multidisciplinary team and may discourage legitimate disagreement within the team and/or the diagnosis of learning disabilities. While this requirement is a given, what is to be done with the written report? If there is dissent, how is it to be resolved? For example, does the majority rule? The requirement is so onerous and difficult that we must question whether or not it truly strengthens the diagnostic processes involved in the identification of children with specific learning disabilities.

SUMMARY

While the BEH final regulations for the evaluation of specific learning disabilities provide much needed guidance for program development and operation, their application poses problems for secondary school programs. Examination of the regulations reveals no differentiation between elementary- and secondary-aged students even though we know that much more than age separates the primary- and secondary-school student. For example, social and cognitive differences as well as programmatic and organizational differences between the school structures argue for differentiation in evaluative procedures. Thus, the secondary school educator should carefully consider the implementation of the final regulations.

We believe that the procedures/regulations provide a framework for evaluation of the learning disabled which does not prevent adaptation or flexibility as may be needed for the adolescent or young adult. Adaptations include use of grade placement standard rather than estimates of ability or achievement expectancies to be used in the determination of performance deficiencies. Additions relate to the inclusion of an interview procedure in addition to or in place of a classroom observation, and assessment of process disorders. Finally, the purpose of the "written report" must be questioned since it is required only for identification of learning disabilities and for no other handicaps.

It would appear that there is a need to monitor the application of the new regulations to all students, but most certainly to the older learning disabled student. We would hope that BEH will solicit feedback from the field on the application of the new regulations and that there will be an opportunity for a second look at the applicability and utility of the regulations for secondary learning disabled youth.

Learning Disabilities and Juvenile Delinquency

Peter W. Zinkus, Ph.D., Marvin I. Gottlieb, M.D., Ph.D.

Failure to Recognize the Impact of Academic Underachievement, on Fanmily and Peer Relationships and on the Developing Self-Concept of the Individual May Result Ultimately as Disturbed Adolescent Behaviors and Juvenile Delinquency

JUVENILE delinquency represents a form of adolescent maladaptive behavior, arising out of a complex of socioeconomic, psychologic, neurologic and emotional disturbances. Academic underachievement has been implicated as a significant factor contributing to juvenile delinquency during the past decade.[1-3] Earlier it had been believed that the delinquent child failed to develop adequate academic skills because of his rebellion against school and other social institutions. More recently it has been suggested that perhaps the lack of academic success and the resulting frustrations were contributing factors to the development of juvenile delinquency.[4,5] The poor educational development of the youthful offender is usually not the result of impaired intellectual ability[6,7] though recent evidence does suggest that developmental dyslexia, dysgraphia, auditory and visual perceptual disturbances and impaired language development are frequently found in delinquent populations.[8-10]

Subtle neurologic abnormalities are often observed in children with learning disabilities.[11,12] Similarly, many children with antisocial behavior have electroencephalographic abnormalities, neurologic "soft signs" and perceptual deficits.[13,14] Although the neurologic deficits are not grossly apparent, they do seem to have a profound effect on learning and social adaptation.[15] In addition to learning deficits, the characteristic behavioral disturbances associated with "Minimal Brain Dysfunction" also appear to interfere with the social adaptation of the learning-disabled child, placing him at high risk for conflict with society.[16] Furthermore, in the learning-disabled child, difficulties with self-concept frequently develop as a consequence of the academic underachievement.

The studies here described were designed to survey the prevalence, characteristics and significance of learning disabilities in a population of adolescent delinquents. Comprehensive psychologic, educational and personality evaluations were carried out with a

From the Department of Pediatrics, University of Tennessee, Center For The Health Sciences, Memphis, Tennessee. GRS Grant R07-3230-78 (UTCHS).

Correspondence to: Dr. Peter W. Zinkus, Clinic For Exceptional Children, University of Tennessee Center For The Health Sciences, 800 Madison Avenue, Memphis, TN 38163.

5. FUTURE

group of institutionalized youthful offenders in order to assess their intellectual functioning, perceptual skills, and academic achievement in reading, spelling and arithmetic. Their self-concept and self-esteem were evaluated by personality inventories. Epidemiologic statistics identify the prevalence of perceptual disorders in the normal population at approximately 10 per cent.[17,18]

The Population Studied

The subjects were 44 male delinquents between the ages of 13 to 18 years (mean age: 15.9 years), who were committed by Juvenile Court to a residential treatment program. Placement in this program was based on the subject's rehabilitation potential as assessed by Juvenile Court staff, independent of considerations of the present study. The presence of learning disabilities was *not* part of the admission criteria to the residential treatment program. Assignment of youthful offenders to the study series was done randomly.

Twenty four of the subjects (54 per cent) were white; twenty (46 per cent) were black. All had histories of multiple legal offenses, ranging from habitual disobedience and vandalism to more serious felony convictions. The average number of appearances in Juvenile Court for the group was 7.8. Analysis of social data indicated that most of these young men had come from a lower middle income background. Based upon previous screenings, all subjects were judged to have normal vision and hearing. From the original pool of forty-six subjects, two subjects were later removed from the study series, since they failed to demonstrate adequate motivation or full cooperation during the examinations. The final population for the survey then consisted of forty-four subjects.

Methods and Procedures

General intelligence in subjects under 17 years of age was measured with the Wechsler Intelligence Scale for Children-Revised (WISC-R); in those over 17 years of age, with the Wechsler Adult Intelligence Scale (WAIS). Auditory and visual perceptual skills were assessed by analyzing the pattern of verbal and nonverbal subtest performances on the WISC-R and WAIS. Particular emphasis was focused on auditory sequential memory, visual-spatial orientation and visual-motor coordination, as these are common deficit areas in perceptually handicapped children.[19,20] The Rhodes Scatter Profile procedure[21] was utilized to further assess those perceptual deficits which were statistically significant at the .05 level. The Bender-Gestalt Visual-Motor Test was employed to evaluate visual-perceptual and visual-motor deficits. Scoring of this test, by the Koppitz method,[22] enabled the assignment of a test age to the subject's performance. Deficits in visual perception result in a test age lower than a subject's chronologic age.

Reading, spelling and arithmetic skill levels were determined with the Wide Range Achievement Test.[23] The grade levels obtained for each of these academic skills were compared with the subject's actual grade placement and also an expected achievement level (EAL) which is derived from the subject's age and I.Q. The expected achievement level was obtained from normative data on the general population.[23] The normative group for expected achievement levels included all socioeconomic levels; this makes its usage appropriate for comparison purposes in this survey.

A lateral dominance examination to determine hand, foot and eye preference employed standard test procedures familiar to most clinicians.[24]

Measures of self-concept were obtained from the Tennessee Self-Concept Scale[25] which was routinely administered by the staff at the residential center. Additional impressions of self-esteem and self-confidence were obtained by clinical interviews.

Observations Made

The initial data analysis defined the intellectual ability of the juvenile delinquent group as a whole. As indicated in Table 1, the mean I.Q. scores were within the average range (90–109) for overall intelligence (Full Scale I.Q.). Verbal (Verbal I.Q.) and nonverbal (Performance I.Q.) intelligence scores were also within the average range. Individual scores

TABLE 1. *Results of Intelligence Testing on Forty-four Delinquent Subjects (Mean I.Q. Values for the Normal Population = 100, S.D. = 15)*

	Mean	S.D.*	Range of Scores
Full Scale I.Q.	91.8	14.6	127 to 73
Verbal I.Q.	91.6	13.9	123 to 70
Performance I.Q.	92.9	14.8	130 to 77

* Standard Deviation.

ranged widely in all three areas of intellectual competence. Due to the variability of the scores, a cut-off point of minus one standard deviation (I.Q. = 85) below the mean for the normal population was chosen to define the lower limits of average intelligence. Seventy-five per cent (N = 33) of the subjects obtained Full Scale I.Q.'s at or above this cut-off point. Furthermore, of the 25 per cent (N = 11) of the subjects with Full Scale I.Q.'s below the cut-off point, 54 per cent (N = 6) had either a Verbal I.Q. or Performance I.Q. above 85. Therefore, of the delinquent subjects, 88 per cent had evidence of intellectual ability or potential at or above the average range.

The past academic performance for each member of the delinquent group was reviewed. Of the subjects, 43 per cent had not been required to repeat grades in school; 36 per cent had repeated *one* grade and 21 per cent had repeated *two* grades. Of those who repeated grades, 35 per cent repeated during the first three grades, 20 per cent during the 4th through 6th, and 45 per cent from the 7th through 12th. Whereas 57 per cent of the subjects repeated one or more grades, only 18 per cent had access to special education programs in elementary school. Thus, even though most of these delinquent individuals evidenced average or above average intelligence, deficient overall academic performance was common.

Achievement levels in reading, spelling and arithmetic were evaluated. Examinations in each of these academic areas were given and the obtained grade level scores subtracted from the subject's actual grade placement. As a group, these individuals were significantly below grade level in all three academic areas (Table 2). The scores ranged widely, but only a few of the delinquents performed above their actual grade level placement.

TABLE 2. *Achievement Testing Discrepancies from Grade Level (GL) on the Wide Range Achievement Test*

| | | | Percentage of Subjects | |
	Mean	Range	Above Grade Level	Below Grade Level
Reading	−3.40	+1.6 to −7.7	11%	89%
Spelling	−4.39	+1.1 to −8.8	2%	98%
Arithmetic	−4.61	+1.6 to −8.0	2%	98%

Deviations from grade placement can be misleading due to variations in intellectual ability. Therefore, reading, spelling and

arithmetic test performances were compared with expected achievement levels (EAL) based upon age and intellectual ability calculated for each subject. The results (Table 3) indicate that academic skills were performed at or above their expected level in only a few.

The relationships between reading level on the WRAT and Full Scale I.Q. were analyzed. The correlation coefficient for the two variables was −.063, indicating no significant relationships between reading level and general intelligence.

Perceptual skills were evaluated from performances in the WISC-R subtests (Table 4). Only 21 per cent had intact visual and auditory perceptual abilities. 60 per cent had significant deficits in auditory sequential memory and 55 per cent had significant difficulty with visual-motor coordination. Almost half (46 per cent) of those with perceptual disturbances were categorized as having mixed auditory and visual processing disturbances involving auditory sequential memory and visual-motor coordination.

Performances with the Bender-Gestalt

TABLE 3. *Achievement Testing Discrepancies from Expected Achievement Level (EAL) on the Wide Range Achievement Test*

| | | | Percentage of Subjects | |
	Mean	Range	Above EAL	Below EAL
Reading	−2.84	+2.5 to −7.7	4%	96%
Spelling	−3.82	−0.3 to −8.0	0%	100%
Arithmetic	−4.49	+0.7 to −8.4	2%	98%

TABLE 4. *Percentages of 44 Juvenile Offenders with Specific Deficit Patterns*

	Total Group (N = 44)	Deficit Group (N = 35)
No Deficit	21%	—
Auditory Sequential Memory	60%	76%
Visual-Motor Coordination	55%	70%
Visual-Spatial Orientation	18%	23%
Auditory SEQ Memory + Visual-Motor Coordination	35%	46%

Visual-Motor Test further established the degree of deficit in visual perceptual skills. Utilizing the Koppitz scoring method,[22] 37 per cent of the subjects were judged to have visual-motor and visual-perceptual skills which were

5. FUTURE

age equivalent. Another 27 per cent had mild visual-motor and visual-perceptual deficits (less than 2 years below chronologic age), and 36 per cent were judged to be moderately to severly abnormal in these areas (greater than 2 years below chronologic age).

The influence of visual and auditory processing deficits on reading, spelling and arithmetic skills was analyzed. Delinquent subjects with intact perceptual skills were compared with three deficit groups: (1) pure visual-perceptual (2) pure auditory-perceptual and (3) multiple auditory and visual perceptual deficits. As indicated in Table 5, the visual-perceptual deficit group did not differ significantly from subjects with intact perceptual skills on any of the measures utilized (p > .05). The auditory-perceptual deficit group was significantly deficient (p < .05) in reading and arithmetic. The most significant (p < .05) deficiencies in reading, spelling and arithmetic were observed in subjects with multiple auditory and visual-perceptual deficits. The significance of these findings lies in the fact that the severity of perceptual dysfunction, rather than delinquency *per se*, appeared to be the primary factor in the observed academic deficiencies.

While the significance of mixed cerebral dominance is widely debated, this phenomenon has been associated with perceptual deficits[26,27] and has also been reported to occur with increased frequency in delinquent populations.[28] Each of the subjects in this study was tested for eye, hand and foot dominance. 64 per cent (N = 28) had mixed cerebral dominance and 36 per cent had (N = 16) unilateral dominance. Of those with mixed dominance, 89.2 per cent (N = 25) had mixed eye-hand dominance, and 10.8 per cent (N = 3) consistently showed unilateral eye-hand dominance but contralateral foot preference.

Self-concept (self-esteem, self-confidence, feelings of worth) was evaluated from personality tests. As a group, juvenile delinquents scored at the 8th percentile with measures of overall self-concept, as compared with distribution of values for children of the same age and intelligence. The results indicate that those in the delinquent group were significantly deficient in self-confidence and generally saw themselves as undesirable.

Discussion

These observations suggest several important considerations for pediatricians and other health care professionals. If the associations between impaired learning, academic underachievement and subsequent behavioral and emotional complications are valid, early detection becomes critical. As the first professional to deal with a child during early development, the pediatrician is in a unique position to recognize a learning disability and to initiate treatment. Such early detection and therapeutic intervention may help to forestall the later development of behavior disorders such as juvenile delinquency. Yet nearly all of the reports on the long term sequelae of learning disorders appear in educational and psychologic journals, not in the pediatric literature.

The relatively high incidence of severe aca-

TABLE 5. *Deviations from Expected Achievement Levels in Various Deficit Groups*

	Reading	Spelling	Arithmetic
No Deficit Group (N = 9)	−1.23	−1.64	−2.21
Pure Visual-Perceptual (N = 7)	−1.28	−2.38	−2.13
Pure Auditory Perceptual (N = 8)	−2.75*	−2.10	−2.92*
Multiple Visual and Auditory Perceptual (N = 20)	−4.40*	−5.46*	−5.63*

* Significantly different from no deficit group at .05 level of significance.

demic underachievement, auditory and visual-perceptual disturbances and associated damage to self-image appear to carry a significant potential for antisocial behavior. Understanding these effects of learning disabilities on subsequent social adaptation may be an extremely important key in helping to prevent juvenile delinquency.

The youthful offenders in this series, despite average intellectual capacity, presented profiles in the various tests which are characteristic of many learning-disabled children. Most had significant visual and auditory perceptual deficits, so often associated with academic failure. Poor performance with the Bender-Gestalt by many of the subjects further supported the presence of visual-perceptual or visual-motor deficits.

The significance of the high incidence of mixed eye-hand dominance in the test subjects is somewhat puzzling but seems to support the need for investigation of the neurologic integrity of delinquent subjects. Mixed dominance has been correlated with reading deficits, such as dyslexia[28] but the mixed cerebral dominance, as it relates to abnormal brain function, still remains an enigma. Additional neurologic studies with delinquent populations may provide needed answers.

The implications are readily apparent. Perceptual disturbances, academic underachievement and poor self-esteem may represent a vicious cycle which, in combination with other psychosocial and organic factors, can contribute to the behavioral maladaptation of the juvenile delinquent. The child does not leave his learning disability behind when he leaves the classroom. Social learning of values and norms may also be impaired, as evidenced by the delinquent's difficulty in profiting from past experiences.

During the past decade, the traditional scope of the pediatrician's intervention in health care delivery has been modified dramatically. Major successes in preventing and controlling infections, competencies in managing acute problems and advances in neonatology have altered roles and responsibilities. Chronic handicapping disorders, problems of exceptionality, family psychodynamics and other issues of psychoeducational and social significance are the new challenges for pediatricians. Possibly the single most challenging problem is the appreciation of learning disabilities and their effects on psychosocial maturation. As the first professional to assess development and behavior, the early detection of these disorders is particularly a unique responsibility for the physician.

Professionals serving the total health needs of children are obligated to consider new entities: visual and auditory perceptual deficits, dyslexia, minimal brain dysfunction and other less specific learning disabilities. If problems of this nature are to be suspected, the physician must expand the "routine" examination to include developmental and behavioral evaluations. Inventories such as the Denver Developmental Screening Test for preschoolers, and achievement tests and evaluation of perceptual skills for school-age children can be performed by other professionals and incorporated into the pediatrician's assessment. The norms of development extend beyond growth grids and the traditional gross motor, fine motor and language skills. Evaluations of perceptual development, receptive and expressive language, reading skills and more sophisticated cognitive levels are to be considered. Recognition of a deviant development, regardless of a child's age, should prompt a referral to professionals with specialized skills such as a psychologist, speech pathologist or special educator.

Recapitulation

Child health care professionals must be alert to the early recognition of academic and behavior problems. Learning-disabled children with perceptual deficits are at high risk for incurring educational and social disabilities.[29,30] When such disability is undiagnosed and untreated, the risk and complications may become exaggerated during adolescence.[31] The combination of learning difficulties, perceptual disturbances, poor self-concept and behavioral reactions represent a challenge to pediatricians, teachers, parents and all other child health care professionals. Failure to recognize the impact of academic underachievement on family and peer relationships and on the developing self-concept of the individual may result ultimately as disturbed adolescent behaviors and juvenile delinquency. The dictum of "the earlier the diagnosis, the better the prognosis" is particularly applicable here.

References

1. Kratoville, B. L., Ed.: Youth in Trouble. San Rafael, Calif., Academic Therapy Publications, 1974.
2. Monroe, M.: Children Who Cannot Read. Chicago, University of Chicago Press, 1932.
3. Fendrick, P., and Bond, G. L.: Delinquency and reading. J. Genet. Psychol. **48:** 236, 1936.
4. Kvaraceus, W.: Delinquency: A by-product of the schools? School and Soc. **59:** 350, 1944.
5. Jacobson, F.: Learning disabilities and juvenile delinquency: A demonstrated relationship. In: Handbook of Learning Disabilities: A Prognosis for the Child, the Adolescent, the Adult, New Jersey Association for Children with Learning Disabilities, R. Weber, Ed. Englewood, N.J., Prentice-Hall, 1973.
6. Kessler, J.: The Psychopathology of Childhood. Englewood, N.J. Prentice-Hall, 1966.
7. Woodward, M.: The role of low intelligence in delinquency. Br. J. Delinquency **5:** 281, 1955.
8. Weinschenk, C.: The significance of diagnosis and treatment of congenital dyslexia and dysgraphia in the prevention of juvenile delinquency. World Med. J. **14:** 54, 1967.
9. Tarnapol, L.: Delinquency in minimal brain dysfunction. J. Learn. Disabil. **3:** 200, 1970.
10. Critchley, E. M. R.: Reading retardation, dyslexia and delinquency. Br. J. Psychiatry **115:** 1537, 1968.
11. Clements, S.: Minimal Brain Dysfunction in Children. NINDB Monograph No. 3, Washington, D.C.: U.S. Government Printing Office, 1966.
12. Myklebust, H., Ed.: Progress in Learning Disabilities, vol. 2. New York, Grune and Stratton, 1971.
13. Wikler, A., Dixon, J., and Parker, J.: Brain function in problem children and controls: Psychometric, neurological and electroencephalographic comparisons. Am. J. Psychiatry **127:** 94, 1970.
14. Denhoff, E.: Bridges to burn and build. Develop. Med. Child. Neurol. **7:** 3, 1965.
15. Keldgord, R.: Brain damage and delinquency: A

question and a challenge. Acad. Ther. Q. **4**: 93, 1968.

16. Williams, J.: Learning disabilities: A multifaceted health problem. J. School Health **46**: 515, 1976.

17. Walzer, S., and Richmond, B. R.: The epidemiology of learning disorders. Pediatr. Clin. North Am. **20**: 549, 1973.

18. Lerner, J., Ed.: Children with Learning Disabilities. New York, Houghton Mifflin Co., 1971.

19. Rampp, D. L., and Plummer, B. A.: Auditory Processing Dysfunctions and Impaired Learning, Learning Disabilities: An Audio Journal for Continuing Education, Vol. 1, No. 7., New York, Grune and Stratton, Inc. July 1977.

20. Chalfant, J. D., and Scheffelin, M. A.: Central Processing Dysfunctions in Children: A Review of Research. National Institute of Neurological Diseases and Blindness, Monograph no. 9, Bethesda, Maryland, US Dept. HEW, 1969.

21. Rhodes, F.: Rhodes WISC Scatter Profile. San Diego, Educational and Industrial Testing Service, 1969.

22. Koppitz, E. M.: The Bender-Gestalt Test for Young Children. New York, Grune and Stratton, 1964.

23. Jastak, J., and Jastak, S.: The Wide Range Achievement Test. Wilmington, Guidance Associates, 1965.

24. Eames, T. H.: Frequency of cerebral lateral dominance variations among school children of premature and full-term birth. J. Pediatr. **51**: 300, 1957.

25. Fitts, W. H.: Manual for the Tennessee Self-Concept Scale. Nashville, Counselor Recordings and Tests, 1964.

26. Orton, S. T.: Reading, Writing and Speech Problems in Children. New York, W. W. Norton Co., 1937.

27. Satz, P.: Cerebral dominance and reading disability: An old problem revisited. *In*: The Neuropsychology of Learning Disorders, R. Knights and D. Bakker, Eds. Baltimore, University Park Press, 1976.

28. Critchley, M.: Developmental Dyslexia. Springfield, Charles C Thomas, 1964.

29. Wender, P. H.: Minimal Brain Dysfunction in Children. New York, Wiley, 1971.

30. Olson, M. E.: Minimal cerebral dysfunction: The child referred for school-related problems. Pediatric Ann. **4**: 69, 1975.

31. Mauser, A. J.: Learning disabilities and delinquent youth. *In*: Youth in Trouble, E. E. Kratoville, Ed. San Rafael, Calif. Academic Therapy Publications, 1975, pp. 91–102.

LEARNING DISABILITIES CHICKLIST: Warning signals of physical conditions which may or may not be interfering with your child's achievement in academic or social areas. If you answer "Yes" to at least 10 (or 20%) of the questions, it may be that your child has a learning disability.

Grade 1-8

1. Does your child have difficulty understanding what he/she reads?
2. Does your child avoid sports or activities that involve catching and throwing a ball?
3. Is your child very afraid of heights? (i.e. won't climb on the jungle jim; doesn't like to be picked up)
4. Is your child extremely daring?
5. Does your child's running seem uncoordinated or sloppy?
6. Does your child get lost frequently?
7. Is your child easily distractible?
8. Does your child confuse right from left?
9. Does your child use one hand for some things and the other hand for other things?
10. Is your child always up and down from the table during meals?
11. Is your child a discipline problem?
12. Does your child go up or down stairs one step at a time?
13. Does your child seem very bright and articulate when in conversation but cannot seem to understand what he/she reads?
14. Is your child the class clown?
15. Is your child not working up to his/her potential?
16. Does your child seem to "tune-out" at times?
17. Is your child unusually forgetful?
18. Does your child find it necessary to touch everything he/she sees?
19. Does your child frequently walk into things or trip?
20. Is there inconsistency in your child's performance? (one day performs a task well, the next day can't)
21. Does your child have a short attention span?
22. Does your child move his/her lips while reading or follow the line with his/her fingers?
23. Does your child get frequent headaches?
24. Is your child ever purposely destructive?
25. Does your child frustrate easily?
26. Is your child unusually sensitive to light, noise, touch, or certain clothing material?
27. Was your child a late walker?
28. Was your child a prolonged tip-toe walker?
29. Was your child's speech late or abnormal?
30. Is your child a bed-wetter?
31. Does your child have uncontrollable rage reactions?
32. Does your child complain of seeing things bigger or smaller than they are?
33. Is your child unable to keep up with the other children's activity levels?
34. Does your child have a poor appetite?
35. Does your child have a history of allergies?
36. Is your child irritable before and/or shortly after meals?
37. Does your child crave sweets?
38. Has your child experienced excessive weight loss or gain?
39. Does your child frequently go out of the lines when coloring?
40. Did your child have trouble learning how to tie and/or button and/or lace?
41. Was your child colicky?
42. Was your child an unusually cranky baby?
43. Was your child an unusually passive baby?
44. Is your child a bully?
45. Is your child always picked on by his peers?
46. Is your child a loner?
47. Does your child seek out older or younger playmates?
48. Does your child's walking or running seem clumsy or disjointed?
49. When your child reads out loud, does he/she get mixed up or lose his/her place?

50. Does your child not complete his/her homework assignments?

High School

1. Does your child avoid sports or activities that involve catching or throwing a ball? Or did he/she?
2. Does your child's walking or running seem uncoordinated or sloppy?
3. Is your child easily distractible?
4. Does your child confuse left from right?
5. Is/was your child always up and down from the table during meals?
6. Is your child a discipline problem?
7. Does your child seem very bright and articulate when in conversation but cannot seem to understand what he/she reads?
8. Is your child the class clown?
9. Is your child below grade level or not working to his/her potential?
10. Is your child unusually forgetful?
11. Does your child frequently walk into things or trip?
12. Is there inconsistency in your child's performance?
13. Does your child have a short attention span?
14. Does your child move his/her lips while reading or follow the lines with his/her fingers?
15. Does your child get frequent headaches?
16. Does your child frustrate easily?
17. Does your child have difficulty keeping rhythm while dancing or clapping?
18. Was you child a late walker?
19. Was your child a prolonged tip-toe walker?
20. Was your child's speech late or abnormal?
21. Does your child complain that words blur or move on the page?
22. Is your child always tired?
23. Does your child have a poor appetite?
24. Does your child have a history of anemia of any type?
25. Is your child irritable before and/or shortly after meals?
26. Does your child exhibit excessive thirst?
27. Does your child crave sweets?
28. Has your child experienced excessive weight gain or loss?
29. Did your child have trouble learning how to tie and/or button and/or lace?
30. Was your child colicky?
31. Was your child an unusually cranky baby?
32. Does your child do everything to excess?
33. Does/did your child have poor bowel or bladder control?
34. Is your child a bully?
35. Is your child always picked on by his/her peers?
36. Is your child a loner?
37. Does your child seek out older or younger playmates?
38. When your child reads out loud, does he/she get mixed up or lose his/her place?
39. Is your child ever purposely destructive?
40. Does your child complete his/her homework assignments on time?
41. Is your child often truant from school?
42. Does it seem your child never pays attention to you?
43. Is your child unable to modulate his/her voice?
44. Does your child keep his/her head close to the paper or tilt it back and forth when reading or writing?
45. Does your child always seem to have a cold?
46. Does your child get frequent stomach aches?
47. Does your child seem to "tune-out" at times?
48. Does your child have uncontrollable rage reactions?
49. Does your child have a history of allergies?
50. Was your child an unusually passive baby?

Appendix: Agencies and Services for Exceptional Children

Alexander Graham Bell Association for the Deaf
3417 Volta Place, N.W.
Washington, D.C. 20007

Allergy Foundation of America
801 Second Avenue
New York, New York 10017

American Academy for Cerebral Palsy
1255 New Hampshire Avenue, N.W.
Washington, D.C. 20036

American Academy of Child Psychiatry
1800 R Street, N.W.
Washington, D.C. 20009

American Academy of Pediatrics
1801 Hinman Avenue
Evanston, Illinois 60204

American Alliance for Health, Physical Education
and Recreation
1201 16th Street, N.W.
Washington, D.C. 20036

American Association for the Education of the
Severely and Profoundly Handicapped
P.O. Box 15287
Seattle, Washington 98115

American Association for Gifted Children
15 Gramercy Park
New York, New York 10003

American Association of Psychiatric Services
for Children
250 West 57th Street
New York, New York 10019

American Association of Special Educators
107-20 125th Street
Richmond Hill, New York 11419

American Association of Workers for the Blind, Inc.
Suite 637
1151 K Street, N.W.
Washington, D.C. 20005

American Association of University Affiliated
Programs for the Developmentally Disabled
1100 17th Street. N.W.
Washington, D.C. 20036

American Association on Mental Deficiency
5201 Connecticut Avenue, N.W.
Washington, D.C. 20015

American Bar Association
Commission on the Mentally Disabled
1800 M Street, N.W.
Washington, D.C. 20036

American Civil Liberties Union
85 Fifth Avenue
New York, New York 10011

American Coalition for Citizens with Disabilities
1346 Connecticut Avenue, N.W.
Washington, D.C. 20036

American Diabetes Association
18 E. 48th Street
New York, New York 10017

American Foundation for the Blind
15 West 16th Street
New York, New York 10011

American Genetic Association
1028 Connecticut Avenue, N.W.
Washington, D.C. 20036

American Medical Association
535 North Dearborn Street
Chicago, Illinois 60610

American Occupational Therapy Foundation
6000 Executive Boulevard
Rockville, Maryland 20852

American Physical Therapy Association
1156 15th Street, N.W.
Washington, D.C. 20005

American Psychological Association
1200 17th Street, N.W.
Washington, D.C. 20036

American Psychiatric Association
1700 18th Street, N.W.
Washington, D.C. 20009

American Schizophrenia Association
Huxley Institute
1114 First Avenue
New York, New York 10021

American Speech and Hearing Association
9030 Old Georgetown Road
Bethesda, Maryland 20014

Arthritis Foundation
1212 Avenue of the Americas
New York, New York 10036

Association for the Aid of Crippled Children
345 E. 46th Street
New York, New York 10017

Association for Children with Learning Disabilities
5225 Grace Street
Pittsburgh, Pennsylvania 15236

Association for Education of the Visually
Handicapped
1604 Spruce Street
Philadelphia, Pennsylvania 19103

Bureau of the Education of the Handicapped
400 Maryland Avenue, S.W.
Washington, D.C. 20202

Center for Law and Social Policy
1751 N Street, N.W.
Washington, D.C. 2009

Child Study Center
Yale University
333 Cedar Street
New Haven, Connecticut 06520

Child Welfare League of America
67 Irving Place
New York, New York 10003

Children's Bureau
Administration for Children, Youth and Families
P.O. Box 1182
Washington, D.C. 20013

Children's Defense Fund
1763 R Street, N.W.
Washington, D.C. 20009

Children's Foundation
1028 Connecticut Avenue, N.W.
Suite 1112
Washington, D.C. 20036

Closer Look: National Information Center for
the Handicapped
Box 1492
Washington, D.C. 20013

Council for Exceptional Children
1920 Association Drive
Retson, Virginia 22091

Council of National Organizations for Children
and Youth
1910 K Street, N.W.
Washington, D.C. 20005

Day Care and Child Development Council of
America
1401 K Street, N.W.
Washington, D.C. 20085

Down's Syndrome Congress
1709 Frederick Street
Cumberland, Maryland 21502

Education Commission of the States
Handicapped Children's Education Project
300 Lincoln Tower
1860 Lincoln Street
Denver, Colorado 80203

Epilepsy Foundation of America
1828 L Street, N.W.
Washington, D.C. 20036

Goodwill Industries of America
9200 Wisconsin Avenue
Washington, D.C. 20014

International Association of Parents of the Deaf
814 Thayer Avenue
Silver Spring, Maryland 20910

International League of Societies for the Mentally
Handicapped
rue Forestiere 12
B-1050
Brussels, Belgium

International Society for Rehabilitation of
the Disabled
219 East 44th Street
New York, New York 10017

Joseph P. Kennedy, Jr. Foundation
1701 K Street, N.W.
Suite 205
Washington, D.C. 20006

Library of Congress, Division for the Blind and
Physically Handicapped
Washington, D.C. 20542

Mental Health Law Project
1751 N Street, N.W.
Washington, D.C. 20036

Muscular Dystophy Associations of America
810 7th Avenue
New York, New York 10019

National Society for Prevention of
Blindness,Inc.
79 Madison Avenue
New York, New York 10016

The National Association for Gifted Children
8080 Springvalley Drive
Cincinnati, Ohio 45236

National Association for Mental Health
1800 North Kent Street
Arlington, Virginia 22209

National Association for Music Therapy
P.O. Box 610
Lawrence, Kansas 66044

National Association for Retarded Citizens
2709 Avenue E East
Arlington, Texas 76011

National Association of Coordinators of
State Programs for the Mentally Retarded
2001 Jefferson Davis Highway
Arlington, Virginia 22202

National Association of State Directors of
Special Education
1201 16th Street, N.W.
Washington, D.C. 20036

National Association of Private Residential
Facilities for the Mentally Retarded
6269 Leesburg Pike
Falls Church, Virginia 22044

National Association of Private Schools
for Exceptional Children
P.O. Box 928
Lake Wales, Florida 33853

National Association of Social Workers
2 Park Avenue
New York, New York 10016

National Ataxia Foundation
4225 Bolden Valley Road
Minneapolis, Minnesota 55422

National Center for Child Advocacy
U.S. Department of Health, Education and Welfare
Office of Child Development
P.O. Box 1182
Washington, D.C. 20013

National Center for Law and the Handicapped
1236 North Eddy Street
South Bend, Indiana 46617

National Center for Voluntary Action
1735 I Street, N.W.
Washington, D.C. 20006

National Center on Educational Media and
Materials for the Handicapped
Ohio State Unviersity
220 West 12th Avenue
Columbus, Ohio 43210

National Committee
Arts for the Handicapped
1701 K Street, N.W.
Suite 801
Washington, D.C. 20037

National Committee for Citizens in Education
410 Wilde Lake Village Green
Columbia, Maryland 21044

National Council of Community Mental Health
Centers
2233 Wisconsin Avenue, N.W.
Washington, D.C. 20007

National Council for the Gifted
700 Prospect Avenue
West Orange, New Jersey 07052

National Easter Seal Society for Crippled Children
and Adults
2023 West Ogden Avenue
Chicago, Illinois 60612

National Epilepsy League
116 South Michigan Avenue
Chicago, Illinois 60603

National Genetics Foundation
250 West 57th Street
New York, New York 10019

National Information and Referral Service for
Autistic and Autistic-like Persons
302 31st Street
Huntington, West Virginia 25702

National Institute on Mental Retardation
Kinsman NIMR Building
York University Campus
4700 Keele Street
Donsview (Toronoto)
Ontario, Canada M3J 1P3

National Paraplegia Foundation
333 North Michigan Avenue
Chicago, Illinois 60601

National Rehabilitation Association
1522 K Street, N.W.
Washington, D.C. 20005

National Society for Autistic Children
169 Tampa Avenue
Albany, New York 12208

National State Leadership Training Institute on
the Gifted and Talented
316 West Second Street (Suite PH-C)
Los Angeles, California 90012

National Tay-Sachs and Allied Diseases
Association, Room 1617
200 Park Avenue South
New York, New York 10003

Office of the Gifted
400 Maryland Avenue, S.W.
Washington, D.C. 20202

Orton Society
8415 Bellona Lane
Towson, Maryland 21204

Physical Education and Recreation
for the Handicapped: Information and
Research Utilization Center
1201 16th Street, N.W.
Washington, D.C. 20036

President's Committee on Employment
of the Handicapped
1111 20th Street, N.W.
Washington, D.C. 20010

President's Committee on Mental Retardation
Washington, D.C. 20201

Spina Bifida Association of America
P.O. Box G-1974
Elmhurst, Illinois 60126

Therapeutic Recreation Information Center
University of Oregon
1597 Agate Street
Eugene, Oregon 97403

United Cerebral Palsy Association
66 East 34th Street
New York, New York 10016

"Mainstream on Call"*
1-800-424-8089

*A toll free number for individuals to obtain
answers to questions about Federal legislation
concerning the handicapped.

INDEX

STAFF

Publisher   John Quirk

Director of Design   Donald Burns
Typesetting   Carol Carr

Cover Design   Donald Burns

COMMENTS PLEASE:

SPECIAL LEARNING CORPORATION

42 Boston Post Rd.

Guilford, Conn. 06437

SPECIAL LEARNING CORPORATION

COMMENTS PLEASE ! ! !

1. Where did you use this book?

2. In what course or workshop did you use this reader?

3. What articles did you find most interesting and useful?

4. Have you read any articles that we should consider including in this reader?

5. What other features would you like to see added?

6. Should the format be changed, what would you like to see changed?

7. In what other area would you like us to publish using this format?

8. Did you use this as a
( ) basic text?   ( ) in-service?
( ) supplement?   ( ) general information?

––––––––––––––––––––––––––––– Fold Here –––––––––––––––––––––––––––––

Are you a ( ) student ( ) instructor ( ) teacher ( ) parent

Your Name _____

School _____

School address _____

_____

Home Address _____

City _____ St. _____ Zip _____

Telephone Number _____

L/D II

☐ **ORDER PLACED ON REVERSE SIDE**